"John MacArthur cuts through the sentimentality that often accompanies so-called visits to heaven by taking us back to the Scriptures, the only reliable guide when investigating our eternal home. In the process, John teaches us much needed lessons in biblical discernment."

Erwin W. Lutzer, Senior Pastor, The Moody Church, Chicago, Illinois

The Glory of Heaven

The Glory of Heaven

The Truth about Heaven, Angels, and Eternal Life

Second Edition

With New Material Addressing the
Current Debate and Issues

John MacArthur

WHEATON, ILLINOIS

Unless otherwise indicated, Scripture quotations are from the ESV® Bible (*The Holy Bible, English Standard Version*®), copyright © 2001 by Crossway. 2011 Text Edition. Used by permission. All rights reserved.

Scripture quotations marked KJV or introduced as "King James Version" are from the *King James Version* of the Bible.

All emphases in Scripture quotations have been added by the author.

Hardcover ISBN: 978-1-4335-3868-1
PDF ISBN: 978-1-4335-3869-8
Mobipocket ISBN: 978-1-4335-3870-4
ePub ISBN: 978-1-4335-3871-1

Library of Congress Cataloging-in-Publication Data

MacArthur, John, 1939-
   The glory of heaven : the truth about heaven, angels, and
eternal life / John MacArthur.—Second Edition, with new
material addressing the current debate and issues.
      p. cm
   Includes bibliographical references and index.
   ISBN 978-1-4335-3868-1
   1. Heaven—Christianity. 2. Heaven—Biblical teaching.
3. Angels—Biblical teaching. I. Title.
BT846.2.M32   2013
236'.24—dc23   2012044097

Crossway is a publishing ministry of Good News Publishers.

LB		23	22	21	20	19	18	17	16	15	14	13
15	14	13	12	11	10	9	8	7	6	5	4	3	2	1

If in Christ we have hope in this life only,
we are of all people most to be pitied.

—*1 Corinthians 15:19*

My thanks to Phil Johnson, who has labored to meet deadlines as my editor for more than thirty years. But this book is dedicated to Phil's precious wife, Darlene, and their sons, Jeremiah, Jedidiah, and Jonathan, who have faithfully endured Phil's long days, late hours, and short attention span whenever those deadlines approach.

Contents

Introduction   13

1   Heavenly Hash   21

2   Heaven *Is* Real; Hallucinations Are Not   37

3   Delusions of Grandeur   51

4   This World Is Not My Home   63

5   What Heaven Will Be Like   83

6   New Jerusalem   103

7   What *We* Will Be Like in Heaven   129

8   The Heavenly Host   157

Appendix 1: Seduced by the Light   175

Appendix 2: The Boy Who Came Back from Heaven   199

Appendix 3: To Heaven and Back   209

General Index   215

Scripture Index   219

Introduction

According to a 2007 Gallup poll, 81 percent of adult Americans say they believe in heaven.[1] That's a significant increase from just ten years earlier, when a similar poll revealed that only 72 percent believed in heaven.[2] Nearly 80 percent of those questioned in the 2007 poll also said they believe they will be admitted to heaven when they die. In other words, a very large majority of people believe in heaven, and almost everyone who believes in heaven expects to go there in the afterlife.

But here's a stunning irony: While interest in heaven is rapidly rising, belief in God is steadily declining. During the same decade bookended by those two Gallup polls, atheism was gaining unprecedented popularity,[3] and record numbers of people now say they regard the Bible as nothing more than a book of fables and legends.[4]

It is no secret that several very powerful secularizing influences are currently at work in Western culture. The media, governments, the academic community, and the entertainment industry—all the primary shapers of society's values—have more or less banded together against the God of Scripture. They promote a materialistic worldview while relentlessly attacking historic Christian belief and biblical morality. The resulting cultural drift has been significant. As a matter of fact, belief in God declined by four percentage points in just six years' time between the start of the new millennium and that 2007 poll—

[1] Gallup poll, May 10–13, 2007.
[2] Gallup/Nathan Cummings Foundation and Fetzer Institute Poll, May 1997.
[3] Greg Paul, "Atheism on the Upswing in America," *The Washington Post*, September 20, 2011.
[4] Gallup poll, May 5–8, 2011. See also Jeffrey M. Jones, "In U.S., 3 in 10 Say They Take the Bible Literally," July 8, 2011 at http://www.gallup.com/poll/148427/say-bible-literally.aspx.

even though there was a sharp increase in the number of people who say they believe in heaven and expect to go there. As I write these words, none of those trends has shown any signs of losing steam.[5]

Incidentally, nearly a third of those questioned in Gallup's 2007 poll said they don't believe in hell or aren't sure about it. Roughly the same number say they doubt the existence of the devil.

Given the rising tides of militant atheism, postmodern skepticism, biblical illiteracy, self-love, and gross immorality, what are we to make of the current interest in heaven? One thing is clear: it does not signal any significant upsurge of interest in what *biblical* revelation teaches about heaven. On the contrary, the data actually seem to indicate that lots of people are simply making up whatever concept of heaven pleases them. The ideas about heaven that get the most press are mostly figments of the human imagination that bear little (if any) resemblance to that glorious realm of Christ's kingdom as it is described in God's Word.

We would of course expect New Age practitioners, cranks, and cultists to abandon the Bible in favor of their own dreams and fantasies. But this trend of inventing one's own personal concept of heaven seems to be an even bigger problem in the evangelical community than it is in the world at large. Evidence of this can be seen in several recent evangelical mega–best sellers.

One of the most talked-about books of 2011 was *Heaven Is for Real*, by Todd Burpo with Lynn Vincent.[6] The book recounts four-year-old Colton Burpo's vision of heaven (as told by his father to Ms. Vincent). Colton claims he visited heaven during surgery after a burst appendix nearly took his life. His stories of heaven are full of fanciful features and peculiar details that bear all the earmarks of a child's vivid imagination. There's nothing transcendent or even particularly enlightening about Colton's description of heaven. In fact, it is completely devoid of the breathtaking glory featured in every biblical description of the heavenly realm. That doesn't deter Todd Burpo from singling out selective phrases and proof texts from Scripture, citing them as if they authenticated his son's account.

---

[5] Those same trends are likewise seen in data from polls conducted in 2003 and 2011 by the Barna Research Group.
[6] *Heaven Is for Real: A Little Boy's Astounding Story of His Trip to Heaven and Back* (Nashville: Nelson, 2010).

An article in the *New York Times Magazine* chronicled the book's success:

> "Heaven Is for Real" was published in late 2010, became a word-of-mouth best seller and has spent 59 (nonconsecutive) weeks as the No. 1 nonfiction paperback on The New York Times's best-seller list. Recently the publisher, Thomas Nelson, spun off a children's picture book, now also a best seller, with illustrations verified by Colton. And sometime in 2014, courtesy of DeVon Franklin, vice president of production at Columbia Pictures, who considers his faith "a professional asset," a movie version should be released in theaters.[7]

Televangelist T. D. Jakes will coproduce the movie.

Another blockbuster book in the same genre is *To Heaven and Back*, by Mary C. Neal, MD.[8] Dr. Neal's account of heaven is no less jejune than Colton Burpo's, and it is even more doctrinally deviant. Released at the end of May 2012, this book reached the top of the *New York Times* best-seller list in its first month.

In chapter 2, we'll look a little more closely at the story told in *Heaven Is for Real*. Then in a series of appendixes we'll examine Neal's story and some other popular books in the same genre. But my point here is merely to note the disturbing ease with which imaginary tales like those gain traction and garner passionate followers among evangelical readers. These are not books any reputable evangelical publisher would have given a second glance to just twenty years ago. At the moment, however, Christian booksellers are publishing and selling more books filled with false visions of the afterlife than all the commentaries and Bible reference works combined.[9]

It may be quite fascinating to read these intricately detailed accounts of people who claim to have come back from heaven, but the hobby is as dangerous as it is seductive. Readers not only get a twisted,

---

[7] Maud Newton, "My Son Went to Heaven, and All I Got Was a No. 1 Best Seller," *New York Times Magazine*, April 27, 2012.

[8] Mary C. Neal, *To Heaven and Back: A Doctor's Extraordinary Account of Her Death, Heaven, Angels, and Life Again* (Colorado Springs: Waterbrook, 2012).

[9] According to statistics from the publisher, *Heaven Is for Real* sold more than 7 million copies within 18 months of its release (not counting more than a half million copies of the Children's Edition). *To Heaven and Back* is on track to exceed that. Don Piper's 2004 book *90 Minutes in Heaven* sold 4 million copies—a phenomenal success that no doubt opened the doors for these later projects. In summer 2012, while two of those books were still riding high on the *New York Times* list, *The KJV Standard Lesson Commentary* was the only biblical reference work that even made the top fifty on the Evangelical Christian Publishers Association's best-seller list.

unbiblical picture of heaven from these tall tales; they also imbibe a subjective, superstitious, shallow brand of spirituality. There is no reason to believe anyone who claims to have gone to heaven and returned (John 3:13; 1:18). Studying mystical accounts of supposed journeys into the afterlife yields nothing but confusion, contradiction, false hope, bad doctrine, and a host of similar evils.

Nevertheless, the current popularity of such books shows how hungry people are to hear about heaven. There is nothing inherently wrong with that, of course. In fact, it is a desire that can be harnessed for good, as long as we look to Scripture and let God's Word inform our knowledge and shape our hopes.

Indeed, it is right and beneficial for Christians to fix their hearts on heaven. Scripture repeatedly urges us to cultivate that perspective: "If then you have been raised with Christ, seek the things that are above, where Christ is, seated at the right hand of God. Set your minds on things that are above, not on things that are on earth" (Colossians 3:1–2). "We look not to the things that are seen but to the things that are unseen. For the things that are seen are transient, but the things that are unseen are eternal" (2 Corinthians 4:18). "Our citizenship is in heaven, and from it we await a Savior, the Lord Jesus Christ" (Philippians 3:20).

Such a perspective is the very essence of true faith, according to Hebrews 11. Those with authentic, biblical faith acknowledge that they are strangers and pilgrims on this earth (v. 13). They are seeking a heavenly homeland (v. 14). They "desire a better country, that is, a heavenly one. Therefore God is not ashamed to be called their God, for he has prepared for them a city" (v. 16). The "city" that verse refers to is the heavenly Jerusalem, an unimaginable place—the very capital of heaven. It will be the eternal abode of the redeemed. No wonder Christians are intrigued with the subject.

The truth is, practically everyone (including the hardened atheist) *thinks* of heaven, imagines what it might be like, and wishes to be there. God inscribed such a longing into the very soul of humanity. "He has put eternity into man's heart" (Ecclesiastes 3:11). The truth of that verse is evident, even in a secularized, skeptical society such as ours.

Almost half a century ago, theologian Wilbur Smith (then professor of biblical studies at Trinity Evangelical Divinity School) wrote an excellent book on heaven in which he lamented the decline of interest in heavenly things and a corresponding preoccupation with worldly things. It was the late 1960s. Decades of modernist rationalism had left mainline churches spiritually bankrupt. People of that generation were enjoying a level of material prosperity their parents and grandparents never dreamed of. The public and the media were obsessed with politics, sports, entertainment, and other earthly things—and perhaps less concerned about spiritual matters than any generation in history.

Wilbur Smith began by noting that "only two really significant volumes on Heaven have been published in the last quarter century."[10] His book's first chapter was titled, "The Repudiation of the Idea of Heaven in Modern Thought."[11] He cited some well-known shapers of modern philosophy, including Friedrich Nietzsche, who boasted that his philosophy had finally killed God, and Karl Marx, who declared that the proper role of philosophy is to abolish religion and establish the truth of *this world*. He also quoted Vladimir Lenin, who cited Marx's famous dictum "Religion is the opium of the people." Lenin then likewise labeled the hope of heaven "a spiritual intoxicant, in which the slaves of capital drown their humanity and blunt their desires for some sort of decent [earthly] existence."[12]

Smith then went on to demonstrate how most fields of modern thought are overtly hostile to the very concept of heaven. *Science*, for example, has no means to investigate anything beyond the natural realm. Unfortunately, many scientists draw the false corollary that the natural realm is all there is. *Philosophy*, says Smith, "never did have a place for Heaven." (He quotes philosopher Alfred North Whitehead, who wrote, "Can you imagine anything more appallingly idiotic than the Christian idea of heaven?"[13]) Worst of all, modern *theology*, influenced by liberalism and rationalism, also abandoned the concept of heaven, joining other branches of modern thought in labeling it "superstition, a myth, an outworn concept."[14]

Today intellectual Sadduceeism is even more virulent (and certainly

---

[10] Wilbur M. Smith, *The Biblical Doctrine of Heaven* (Chicago: Moody, 1968), 7.
[11] Ibid., 17.
[12] Ibid., 19.
[13] Ibid., 21.
[14] Ibid., 22.

more shrill) than when Smith made those observations. Worldliness and materialism have become the hallmarks of postmodern culture. And yet it is rather amazing that all those trends combined have not managed to quell the human longing for heaven's glory and faith's assurance. Although people have been told relentlessly by the intellectual elite that there is no spiritual reality, that they evolved out of some primordial slime, and that they have no future in eternity—*they know better*. God has indeed put eternity in our hearts. Heaven *is* real, and it is human nature to long to be there.

The heart of our study together in this book will be an in-depth look at what the Bible says about heaven. No matter what one thinks about or wishes to imagine about heaven, the reality is different and better by magnitudes. You simply cannot gain a better understanding of heaven than we are given in Scripture—especially not from someone else's dreams and near-death experiences. In the words of Charles Spurgeon,

> It's a little heaven below, to imagine sweet things. But never think that imagination can picture heaven. When it is most sublime, when it is freest from the dust of earth, when it is carried up by the greatest knowledge, and kept steady by the most extreme caution, imagination cannot picture heaven. "It hath not entered the heart of man, the things which God hath prepared for them that love him." Imagination is good, but not to picture to us heaven. Your imaginary heaven you will find by-and-by to be all a mistake; though you may have piled up fine castles, you will find them to be castles in the air, and they will vanish like thin clouds before the gale. For imagination cannot make a heaven. "Eye hath not seen, nor ear heard, neither hath it entered the heart of man to conceive" it.[15]

What God has revealed in Scripture is the only legitimate place to get a clear understanding of the heavenly kingdom. This is a point we will come back to repeatedly: the Bible is our *only* reliable source of information about heaven. I want to show you why it is misleading and dangerous to probe and dissect people's near-death experiences, as if they could give us some important truth about the afterlife that we are lacking from Scripture.

---

[15] Charles H. Spurgeon, *The New Park Street Pulpit*, 6 vols. (London: Passmore & Alabaster, 1856), 2:20-21.

I also want to show you what Scripture teaches about heaven, angels, and the afterlife. And together we will see that what the Bible says about these things is indeed *sufficient*—because we know Scripture furnishes us with everything we need to know to be equipped for every good work (2 Timothy 3:17). There's nothing any eyewitness testimony could reliably add to that.

As we study what Scripture teaches, you're going to see that God's written Word does in fact give us a remarkably full and clear picture of heaven and the spiritual realm—*but* there are still many questions the Bible leaves unanswered. We need to accept the boundaries God himself has put on what he has revealed. It is sheer folly to speculate where Scripture is silent. It is sinfully wrong to try to investigate spiritual mysteries using occult means. And it is seriously dangerous to listen to anyone who claims to know more about God, heaven, angels, or the afterlife than God himself has revealed to us in Scripture.

When Scripture commands us to fix our hearts on heavenly things, it is teaching us that our focus should be on Christ, and on the true heavenly glory—not that we should immerse ourselves in fantasies about the heavenly life. Colossians 3:2—"Set your minds on things that are above, not on things that are on earth"—is simply another way of phrasing the first and great commandment: "You shall love the Lord your God with all your heart and with all your soul and with all your mind and with all your strength" (Mark 12:30).

No matter how much they might obsess over what heaven is like, people who fill their heads with a lot of fantastic or delusional ideas from others' near-death experiences have *not* truly set their minds on things above. If the inerrant biblical truth God has given us is the only reliable knowledge about heaven we have access to (and it is), then that is what should grip our hearts and minds. That, I hope, is the single most important message you will get from this book.

Now let's see why the Bible's account of heaven is so much better than the dreams and speculations of the human mind.

1

Heavenly Hash

I know you have thought about heaven and imagined what it might be like. Everyone does. The hope of life hereafter is intrinsic to human thought. Together with our innate moral sense, our love of beauty, and our inclination to worship, our fascination with heaven sets humans apart from animals. All those characteristics stem from the fact that *we are spiritual creatures, made in the likeness of God*. That is the very thing that defines humanity itself and sets our race in a unique position above all the rest of creation (Genesis 1:26; 5:1; James 3:9). God himself "has put eternity into man's heart" (Ecclesiastes 3:11).

In other words, the atheistic assertion that the end of this life means the end of one's existence is contrary to human instinct. It is fundamentally inhuman—a denial of the human spirit.

Scripture expressly teaches that humanity was created with a native awareness of God. "What can be known about God is plain to them, because God has shown it to them" (Romans 1:19). A literal translation of the Greek text would be, "Something about God is clearly known within them." Humans have an intuitive sense of God's existence. We know something about his nature. God himself created us with that knowledge built in. And we sense our ultimate accountability to him.

To supplement that innate knowledge, God has put his glory on display for us in everything he has created. "His invisible attributes, namely, his eternal power and divine nature, have been clearly perceived, ever since the creation of the world, in the things that have been made" (Romans 1:20). That's why no matter where we look in the vast universe, we see manifestations of God's wisdom, power, and greatness. Look through the most powerful telescope toward the outer edges of the universe, and you will be overwhelmed by infinite grandeur beyond your comprehension. Look at a drop of pond water through the finest microscope and you will likewise see intricate wonders that declare the inexpressible majesty and inexhaustible skill of our Creator. Either perspective—and every point of view in between—plainly reminds us of what we already know in our hearts and consciences: we were made by an unimaginably glorious God, and his plan for us is infinitely more expansive than this short earthly life.

All the atheist propaganda in the world cannot (and never will) eliminate humanity's innate knowledge about God, silence the testimony of creation, muzzle the human conscience, stifle that sense of eternity in the human heart, or quell our longing for heaven.

That explains why every major religion and every significant culture in the history of the human race has had some notion of perfect paradise—nirvana, Elysium, Valhalla, Utopia, Shangri-La, or whatever. But it doesn't explain why everyone seems to imagine heaven a little differently. Even those who claim to have been to heaven disagree among themselves about what it is like. If God built eternity into the human heart, why do different people have such different ideas about heaven?

Paradise Lost

The answer to that question lies in the sad truth that we are fallen creatures, tainted with sin and guilt. Sin affects our thinking, our desires, our imagination, and most of all, our understanding of spiritual things. We cannot even reliably discern our own hearts: "The heart is deceitful above all things, and desperately sick; who can understand it?" (Jeremiah 17:9).

So while we intuitively sense the reality of heaven and are drawn to it, we also perceive our own fallenness and guilt. It is significant that the first thing Adam and Eve did after they ate the forbidden fruit was desperately try to cover their own nakedness and hide from God (Genesis 3:7–11). Their profound shame overwhelmed even their sense of God's wonder, so their instinct as fallen creatures was to try to evade God. By all that is rational and sensible, they ought to have been drawn to him, enthralled with his glory, and engulfed with love and delight in his presence. Indeed, they *were* all those things—until the moment they disobeyed. But sin radically and instantly changed everything, and they irrationally tried to hide from the very One whom they most needed, the one true God who alone deserved their love and devotion.

All of humanity has been engaged in the same futile exercise ever since. We're born with a sinful bent. We feel the shame of our guilt. We know we are undeserving of God's benevolence. We are innately aware of (and alarmed by) his almighty power and infinite wisdom—and those truths are permanently written across creation lest we forget. We know we would have no valid argument or defense against the righteous wrath of the Almighty if we were summoned to stand alone before him in a court of perfect justice. "No creature is hidden from his sight, but all are naked and exposed to the eyes of him to whom we must give account" (Hebrews 4:13). So fallen people inevitably try to suppress and twist what God has revealed to them (Romans 1:18).

The more people silence that innate knowledge of the Godhead, the more spiritually confused and wantonly sinful they will become. Romans 1:21–25 traces the descent of human depravity:

> Although they knew God, they did not honor him as God or give thanks to him, but they became futile in their thinking, and their foolish hearts were darkened. Claiming to be wise, they became fools, and exchanged the glory of the immortal God for images resembling mortal man and birds and animals and creeping things. Therefore God gave them up in the lusts of their hearts to impurity, to the dishonoring of their bodies among themselves, because they exchanged the truth about God for a lie and worshiped and served the creature rather than the Creator, who is blessed forever! Amen.

Don't miss the fact that when people deliberately suppress their knowledge of God and reject what he has revealed about himself, they do not normally deny the existence of God completely. Instead, they invent a god of their own who is more to their liking. The false worshiper realizes he cannot totally eliminate that inborn knowledge of God's existence without sacrificing some of his own humanity, so he opts instead to concoct a lesser god out of his own imagination, more suited to his personal tastes. Some crassly worship mere creatures (even "birds and animals and creeping things"). Others make idols of stone or venerate fictional characters from human mythologies. Most nowadays simply envision a personal deity that is little more than a reflection of themselves. They may pretend—and even convince themselves—that they are paying homage to the God of Scripture, but in reality they are worshiping self. All of these are sinful forms of creature worship. One is no better or more sophisticated than the other, and none of them is any better than rank atheism.

In fact, false religion quite often turns out to be a more grotesque and more emphatic denial of the one true God than staunch atheism—because of the way man-made religion systematically twists and reimagines every spiritual truth.

What people believe about the afterlife is particularly susceptible to the corruption of false religion. People who invent their own gods must likewise invent their own heaven. That has suddenly become a very fashionable pastime, even among people who claim to believe in the God of the Bible.

Castles in the Clouds

Several extremely imaginative accounts claiming to describe what heaven is like are currently riding high on the best-seller lists, and the pace of such publications seems to be increasing. Fanciful lore about people's mystical visits to heaven (or hell, in some cases) constitute a new and fairly large category in publishing today: travelogues for the afterlife. Tim Challies, prolific evangelical blogger and book-review specialist, refers to the new genre as "heaven tourism" and says this:

> Travelling to heaven and back is where it's at today. DON PIPER spent ninety minutes there and sold four million copies of his account. COLTON BURPO doesn't know how long he was there, but his travel diary has surpassed 6 million copies sold, with a kids' edition accounting for another half million. BILL WIESE obviously booked his trip on the wrong web site and found himself in hell, which did, well, hellish things to his sales figures. Still, *23 Minutes in Hell* sold better than if he had described a journey to, say, Detroit, and he even saw his book hit the bestseller lists for a few weeks. There have been others as well, and together they have established afterlife travel journals as a whole new

genre in Christian publishing—a genre that is selling like hotcakes,
or Amish fiction, for that.[1]

Actually, books like those have been a staple in secular publishing since
the 1970s. Evangelical booksellers have been somewhat slow to follow
the trend. But now they seem to be making up for it in high volume
and heavy sales.

"Medical" Researchers Begin Probing the Afterlife

The reading public's fascination with heavenly excursions and near-
death experiences really began in earnest shortly after the publication
of Dr. Elisabeth Kübler-Ross's 1969 book *On Death and Dying*.[2] Kübler-
Ross was a Swiss American psychiatrist who in the 1960s made a study
of terminally ill patients. She is famous for her theory that there are
five stages of grief.

Along with her ideas about grieving she also recounted tales from
several people who, it seemed, had literally been brought back from
the dead—mostly resuscitated by surgeons in operating rooms or by
paramedics at accident scenes. Many had fascinating tales to tell about
what they supposedly saw and experienced on the "other side."

Kübler-Ross decided to investigate further into the phenomenon
of near-death experiences, and she said the study altered her own
views of the afterlife. Before doing research for *On Death and Dying*,
she was a rationalistic skeptic, believing that only oblivion followed
death. She later wrote, "When I started this work, I must say, I was
neither very interested in life after death nor did I have any really
clear picture about the definition of death."[3] But hearing about people's near-death experiences made her a believer in the supernatural,
she said.

About five years after Kübler-Ross published that first best seller
on dying, another leading academic researcher specializing in near-
death experiences rose to prominence. Like Kübler-Ross, Raymond A.
Moody was a medical doctor with an interest in human psychology.

[1] Tim Challies, "Heaven Tourism," blogpost June 18, 2012, at http://www.challies.com/articles/heaven
-tourism.
[2] Elisabeth Kübler-Ross, *On Death and Dying* (New York: Simon & Schuster, 1969).
[3] Elisabeth Kübler-Ross, *On Life after Death* (Berkeley, CA: Celestial Arts, 1991), 40.

He was making a study on how people cope with the reality of death. Moody's first book on the subject was *Life after Life*,[4] and it became a huge best-seller shortly after its release in 1975.

Moody's book chronicled more than a hundred cases of people who were clinically dead but then revived. In his recounting of their stories, virtually all of Moody's subjects described some kind of positive, enlightening, comforting, or simply peaceful experience on the other side of death.

Suddenly, it seemed, much of the world was obsessed with back-from-the-dead testimonies. What might these near-death experiences in the hands of scientific researchers tell us about the afterlife? More and more people claiming to have experienced heavenly phenomena came forward to tell their stories. Raymond Moody followed the success of his first volume with a series of sequels over the next decade and a half: *Reflections on Life after Life*; *The Light Beyond*; *Coming Back*; and *Reunions: Visionary Encounters with Departed Loved Ones*.[5]

Sentimentalizing Human Mortality and Toying with Gnosticism

Such a sudden keen interest in life after death might sound like an encouraging trend. It started, after all, with two scholars who claimed impeccable academic and medical credentials, working independently of one another, ostensibly using scientific research methods. Kübler-Ross had studied psychiatry under some of Europe's most prestigious practitioners at the University of Zurich. She was teaching in the University of Chicago's medical school when she published her landmark work. The year after her first book was published, she lectured on human immortality at Harvard. Raymond Moody had earned one PhD in psychology from the University of Virginia and another from the University of West Georgia. He also earned his MD; he had worked as a forensic psychiatrist; and he taught medical students at major universities in Georgia and Nevada.

Had these esteemed doctors finally discovered the nexus of spirituality and science?

---

[4] Raymond A. Moody, *Life after Life* (New York: Mockingbird, 1975; and Bantam, 1976).
[5] Raymond A. Moody, *Reflections on Life after Life* (New York: Mockingbird, 1977); *The Light Beyond* (New York: Bantam, 1989); *Coming Back: A Psychiatrist Explores Past-Life Journeys* (New York: Bantam, 1990); *Reunions: Visionary Encounters with Departed Loved Ones* (New York: Villard, 1993).

Hardly. To begin with, neither Elisabeth Kübler-Ross nor Raymond Moody had any regard for the authority of Scripture; and as they delved more deeply into people's near-death experiences, both of these esteemed doctors eventually spurned science as well. They frivolously embraced medieval superstition instead. The ongoing influence of their writings actually signifies a serious setback for both faith and reason.

Accepting the reality of supernatural things is not the same as believing the truth. When an unbelieving mind rejects the authority of Scripture but embraces the reality of the supernatural realm, the result is always catastrophic.

Both Elisabeth Kübler-Ross and Raymond Moody became living illustrations of that principle. Both said they began their research on near-death experiences as scientific rationalists, convinced that there must be some perfectly reasonable natural explanation for the strange sensations reported by dying people. But both of them soon abandoned their agnostic materialism for something even worse.

Kübler-Ross gradually veered off into the world of New Age occultism. After publishing her study of others' near-death experiences, she reported that she herself had been through a rather remarkable out-of-body experience where she traveled at the speed of light. She began experimenting with séances to contact the dead. She became a leading voice in the New Age movement. At one point she joined a bizarre religious cult led by Jay Barham, a blatant charlatan who claimed to be able to make spirits materialize in order to have sex with the living.[6] Kübler-Ross's drift into the occult soon led to a divorce and the loss of her reputation in the scientific world. ("Some began to wonder about her mental health.")[7]

Kübler-Ross came to believe "that the physical body is only the house or the temple, or as we call it the cocoon, which we inhabit for a certain number of months or years until we make the transition called death. Then, at the time of death, we shed this cocoon and are once again as free as a butterfly."[8]

It wasn't long before the world's most famous secular authority on

---

[6] "The conversion of Kübler-Ross: From Thanatology to Séances and Sex," *Time*, November 12, 1979, 81.
[7] Christopher Reed, "Obituary: Elisabeth Kübler-Ross," *The Guardian*, August 30, 2004.
[8] Kübler-Ross, *On Life after Death*, 40.

death and dying actually began questioning the reality of death itself. Kübler-Ross finally concluded that "there was no death, there were only 'transitions' from one permeable boundary to another."[9] As she grew more outspoken and more eccentric with these New Age–style beliefs, academic and scientific critics began to point out that even her best-known early works were not really objective scientific or scholarly studies to begin with. They were simply anecdotal accounts told with copious amounts of credulity and speculation, carefully wrapped in clinical-sounding language to give the appearance of academic legitimacy. But as Kübler-Ross immersed herself more deeply into occult and New Age thought, her reputation in the academic and scientific worlds gradually diminished. She was partially paralyzed by repeated strokes in the mid-1990s and died in 2004 in an Arizona care facility.

Nevertheless, to this day the influence of her work—particularly her gullible fascination with near-death experiences—strongly permeates the popular Western perspective on death and the afterlife.

In an article reviewing the life and eccentricities of Ms. Kübler-Ross, a writer in *Slate* noted that her work sparked "a kind of cult-like reverence for the allegedly superior truth-telling wisdom of the dying. . . . It's a sentimentalizing of mortality that's become incorporated into popular culture and can be seen as the source of such death-obsessed dramas as *Touched by an Angel* and *Dead Like Me*."[10] That is quite an insightful observation. One of the great dangers of these back-from-the-dead testimonies is that readers tend to romanticize the experience and impute otherworldly wisdom to the person who is making the claims.

What I have just described is actually a gnostic way of thinking. *Gnosticism* was a sub-Christian heresy (a whole class of diverse cults, really) that rose to prominence the second century and competed with early Christianity for at least four centuries. Remnants of gnostic belief have survived and bred and resurfaced frequently ever since. The current fascination with near-death experiences is a classic example of gnostic thought that has been revived and retooled for the New Age.

The distinctive claim of every gnostic belief system is that true

---

[9] Ron Rosenbaum, "Dead Like Her: How Elisabeth Kübler-Ross Went around the Bend," *Slate*, September 23, 2004.
[10] Ibid.

enlightenment comes from some source beyond Scripture. Gnostics did not overtly deny Scripture, but they taught that the necessary key that unlocks the true meaning of the biblical texts is *gnosis* (the Greek word for "knowledge")—supernatural enlightenment that comes from a mystical experience. Gnostic enlightenment can be imparted to select people only by those who have had the mystical experience.

The belief that nearly dead or dying people are given special insight into the spiritual realm is a classic gnostic idea—a devilish doctrine. Thus it is no wonder that people who become obsessed with near-death experiences and back-from-the-dead testimonies are easily drawn into superstition, mysticism, and occultism.

Raymond Moody's forays into supernaturalism likewise took a sinister turn. It was clear from the start that Moody himself flatly rejected what the Bible teaches about the human soul after death, divine judgment, heaven, and hell. In that first breakout best seller, he wrote,

> Through all of my research . . . I have not heard a single reference to a heaven or a hell or anything like the customary picture to which we are exposed in this society. Indeed, many persons have stressed how unlike their experiences were to what they had been led to expect in the course of their religious training. One woman who "died" reported: "I had always heard that when you die, you see both heaven and hell, but I didn't see either one." . . . Furthermore, in quite a few instances reports have come from persons who had no religious beliefs or training at all prior to their experiences, and their descriptions do not seem to differ in content from people who had quite strong religious beliefs.[11]

Moreover, according to Moody, even those with strong religious beliefs usually "returned [from their near-death experiences] with a new model and a new understanding of the world beyond—a vision which features not unilateral judgment, but rather cooperative development towards the ultimate end of self-realization."[12]

In other words, Moody claimed his subjects' near-death experiences led them to reject the truth that "it is appointed for man to die once, and after that comes judgment" (Hebrews 9:27).

---

[11] Moody, *Life after Life*, 128–129.
[12] Ibid., 92.

Moody's findings were carefully skewed against almost everything the Bible teaches about heaven, hell, and the disposition of souls after death. But he was *especially* keen to eliminate anything that might hint at the reality of divine judgment. He deliberately highlighted features in his subjects' testimonies that contradicted the Bible's clear and frequent assertion that "we will all stand before the judgment seat of God" (Romans 14:10). According to Moody, people's experiences in the afterlife had opened their eyes to a different, more profound *gnosis:*

> In most cases, the reward-punishment model of the afterlife is abandoned and disavowed, even by many who had been accustomed to thinking in those terms. They found, much to their amazement, that even when their most apparently awful and sinful deeds were made manifest before the being of light, the being responded not with anger and rage, but rather only with understanding, and even with humor.[13]

Having repudiated what Scripture teaches, but faced with mounting empirical evidence that there is an unseen spiritual realm and human existence doesn't end at death, Moody was forced to seek unbiblical explanations. He too began to dabble with occultism. His later books reflect a haunting obsession with necromancy. One of them, for example, is titled *Elvis after Life: Unusual Psychic Experiences Surrounding the Death of a Superstar.*[14]

These days Raymond Moody is essentially a medium, though he still operates under the guise of a medical researcher. He employs all the classic techniques of parlor-room spiritualist soothsaying in his "therapy"—including peering into crystal balls and mirror-gazing as means of contacting the dead. He describes in detail how he built a *psychomanteum,* or apparition chamber, "a modernized version of the ones found in ancient Greece, with the same goal in mind, that of seeing apparitions of the dead."[15] It is a special room with a mirror, in which Moody claims to commune with the ghosts of the deceased. In that room, he says, "I conversed with my deceased grandmother, who

---

[13] Ibid.
[14] Raymond A. Moody, *Elvis after Life: Unusual Psychic Experiences Surrounding the Death of a Superstar* (Atlanta: Peachtree, 1987).
[15] Moody, *Reunions,* 65–66.

appeared to be just as real as anyone could be."[16] If he is telling the truth, he was communicating with demons.

Moody believes he has connected others with their dead loved ones in his apparition chamber. He tells, for example, how one woman "felt the presence of her aunt. Her visit to the psychomanteum and its aftermath have changed her mind about the paranormal. Where before she had doubts about an afterlife, she is now persuaded of a life beyond death."[17]

Seduced by the Light

By the start of the 1990s, curiosity about near-death experiences and travelers' tales of heaven had spilled out of the New Age movement, spiritism, and other overtly occult communities, and it was seeping into more mainstream religious circles. That trend accelerated after 1992, when *Embraced by the Light*, by Betty Eadie, was published.[18] Here was a simple laywoman's personal account of her own near-death experience, replete with powerful religious overtones, narrated like a Christian testimony.

According to Melvin Morse, MD,[19] who wrote the foreword, Eadie's book "is really a textbook of the near-death experience, written as a

---

[16] Ibid., xvii. Moody says that during her life this woman "was habitually cranky and negative" [20], but during this ghostly encounter she seemed very different:

> I quickly sensed that the woman who stood before me had been transformed in a very positive way. I felt warmth and love from her as she stood there and an empathy and compassion that surpassed my understanding. She was confidently humorous, with an air of quiet calm and joyfulness about her.
> The reason I had not recognized her at first was that she appeared much younger than she was when she died, in fact even younger than she had been when I was born. I don't remember having seen any photographs of her at the age she seemed to be during this encounter, but that is irrelevant here since it was not totally through her physical appearance that I recognized her. Rather, I knew this woman through her unmistakable presence and through the many memories we reviewed and discussed. In short this woman was my deceased grandmother. I would have known her anywhere (ibid.).

[17] Ibid., 101.
[18] Betty J. Eadie, *Embraced by the Light* (Detroit: Gold Leaf, 1992).
[19] In August 2012, Morse was arrested and charged with using waterboarding techniques on his eleven-year-old daughter. Police who investigated the case speculated that he may have been using simulated drowning to bring the girl to a near-death state. (His particular area of specialization involves the near-death experiences of children.)
Morse's ex-wife says he has overdosed on pills and alcohol multiple times. He admits to only one such incident but denies that it was a suicide attempt, calling it a "suicide gesture" instead.
Morse has appeared as an expert on near-death experiences on "Larry King Live" and "The Oprah Winfrey Show." He has written or coauthored at least four books on the subject ("Near-death Experiences Doctor May Have Been Experimenting by 'Waterboarding' Stepdaughter, Police Say," [Associated Press, August 15, 2012]).

simple and wonderful story that we can all understand."[20] The book soared quickly into the top position on the *New York Times* list and hovered there for 78 weeks, selling more than 13 million copies.

Ms. Eadie told a fantastic tale that begins in the hospital, where she says a partial hysterectomy left her on the very threshold of death. She claims that as her soul began to depart her body, she did not go directly to heaven but first experienced out-of-body travel to several earthly locations. Along the way she says she encountered angels—"guardian spirits who helped her to understand important things about her life and then to comprehend her relationship with her family. They assisted her transition into death."[21]

She says she was then taken through a dark tunnel before finally crossing over into the intense white light of heaven. She recounts her experience in remarkably vivid detail.

Embraced by the Light is strongly influenced by Mormon and New Age precepts (see appendix 1), but Betty Eadie's telling of the tale is expertly suffused with lots of evangelical clichés and biblical imagery—enough so that when it shot to the top of secular best-seller lists, it was welcomed and widely read in the evangelical community and quickly gained a sizable following there. Evangelical critics pointed out an abundance of antibiblical ideas, Mormon teachings, and serious theological flaws in Ms. Eadie's worldview,[22] but her book seemed to have far-reaching and long-lasting influence in the evangelical community anyway. It clearly helped whet an appetite for similar tales.

That craving for stories about heaven soon grew into a dangerous addiction.

Hooked on Heavenly Hallucinations

Booksellers love when their readers' interests become an obsession. Publishing houses are now churning out new accounts of mystical heavenly excursions practically every month. Titles in that category

---

[20] Melvin Morse, in Eadie, *Embraced by the Light*, xv.
[21] Ibid., xvi.
[22] The first edition of this book (*The Glory of Heaven* [Wheaton, IL: Crossway, 1996]) devoted much of the opening chapter to a critique of Eadie's teaching. Most of that material is preserved in appendix 1 of this edition. See also Douglas R. Groothuis, *Deceived by the Light* (Eugene, OR: Harvest House, 1995); and Richard Abanes, *Embraced by the Light and the Bible: Betty Eadie and Near-Death Experiences in the Light of Scripture* (Camp Hill, PA: Christian Publications, 1994).

are some of the hottest products in the publishing industry today—and the book-buying public is still clamoring for more.

What I find most intriguing (and disturbing) about the whole trend is the speed and subtlety with which it has invaded the church. Before 1995, no reputable Christian publisher would have seriously considered publishing any book about heaven that was based on a mystical experience someone had while clinically dead. But incredibly, the best-known, top-selling celestial travelogues today are practically all produced and aggressively marketed by major evangelical publishers.[23] They are written by authors who profess faith in Christ. They specifically target Bible-believing Christians. And all of them are teeming with false, flawed, and fanciful notions about heaven.

In fact, the features that tend to stand out in these tales are macabre phenomena and offbeat "revelations" that biblically minded believers have no business paying attention to. Communication between the living and the dead is of course a common feature in all these stories. People converse with their dead relatives and then return with family news from the other side. One woman claims she could taste, feel, and smell people in heaven merely by looking at them. An accident victim says the devil appeared to him visibly somewhere between the crash site and paradise, falsely accusing and taunting him. Another man describes celestial warehouses full of human appendages, which he says are miracles and healings waiting to be claimed. Still another says the necktie he was wearing during his visit to heaven retained the fragrance of paradise, so whenever he wants to be transported back there, he simply sniffs that tie.

This may sound ironic, but a fixation with worldly things is another common feature in tales such as these. Many heavenly travelers suggest that in heaven it's possible to observe earthly events as closely as one chooses. The favorite pastimes in heaven often have a strong terrestrial flavor, too. There are lawn games, picnics, sporting events, and various kinds of heavenly horseplay. Of course, most returnees from

---

[23] According to lists published by both Amazon.com and *The New York Times*, four of the top best-selling nonfiction works during the summer of 2012 were accounts of people who claimed to have been to heaven and back. All four were published by evangelical publishing houses: *Heaven Is for Real* (Nelson); *To Heaven and Back* (Waterbrook Multnomah); *The Boy Who Came Back from Heaven* (Tyndale); and *90 Minutes in Heaven* (Revell).

heaven report that the colors, sounds, smells, sights, and sensations they encountered in paradise are amazingly vivid. But when they actually describe the heavenly scene, the narrative always sounds terribly mundane by comparison to Ezekiel 1 or Revelation 4.

In most respects, the Christianized versions of these stories bear a troubling resemblance to their secular predecessors. The truly distinctive elements of their message have nothing to do with any biblical teaching about heaven and the afterlife. The authors of these stories don't seem particularly troubled by that. After all, they are claiming a superior understanding of the afterlife—gained not from Scripture but from visions, phantasms, out-of-body travel, and other occult means.

They don't always agree with one another in the key details, however. One heavenly visitor says languages aren't necessary in the after-life because everyone communicates telepathically; another says people in heaven speak an angelic language that sounds like music. One says people in heaven carry swords in order to keep the devil out; others say heaven is a place of perfect peace and calm, with no hint of any conflict whatsoever. One insists that there is a hole in heaven leading directly to hell. No bother that Jesus said emphatically that no one can ever pass from heaven to hell or vice versa (Luke 16:26).

All the best-selling stories in this genre contain whimsical quackery like that—some more, some less. But that is what they all seem to accentuate, thus trivializing the true glory of heaven.

There is no warrant anywhere in Scripture to treat the reveries of comatose or seriously injured people as if they had prophetic significance. In fact, Scripture warns us repeatedly not to take the claims of *any* prophet at face value. "Beloved, do not believe every spirit, but test the spirits to see whether they are from God, for many false prophets have gone out into the world" (1 John 4:1; cf. Deuteronomy 13:1–5; Jeremiah 29:8–9; Matthew 7:15–16; 24:4–5; 2 Peter 2:1).

Contemporary evangelicals simply have a too-low view of Scripture and a too-high regard for trendy things. Perhaps no demographic is more easily suggestible or more lemminglike. Accordingly, evangelical readers have become the largest market for and the most voracious consumers of stories told by people who claim to have gone to heaven and come back.

The torrent of those tales is not likely to diminish soon, and evangelical publishing houses are not about to stop publishing them. Given the relatively high number of multimillion best sellers in the genre, these books no doubt already constitute the single most financially lucrative nonfiction category in the history of evangelical publishing.

Nonfiction? That, of course, is the label under which publishers and booksellers like to categorize these books. It would require a degree of stoic forbearance that I do not possess to acknowledge that label without disclaiming it. But it is a fact that these heavenly guidebooks are invariably marketed as nonfiction rather than fantasy. (One of the current best sellers is sold with the words "A True Story" imprinted on the cover in bold type as large as the book's title.)

Sadly, undiscerning readers abound, and they take these stories altogether seriously. The stratospheric sales figures and far-reaching influence of these books ought to be a matter of serious concern for anyone who truly loves the Word of God.

In the chapter that follows, we will examine one of the best-known examples of the genre to see why.

2

Heaven *Is* Real;
Hallucinations Are Not

Far too much of the present interest in heaven, angels, and the afterlife stems from carnal curiosity. It is not a trend those of us who accept the authority of Scripture should encourage or celebrate. Any pursuit that diminishes people's reliance on the Bible is fraught with grave spiritual dangers—especially if it is something that leads gullible souls into superstition, gnosticism, occultism, New Age philosophies, or any kind of spiritual confusion. Those are undeniably the roads most traveled by people who feed a morbid craving for detailed information about the afterlife by devouring stories of people who claim to have gone to the realm of the dead and returned.

Scripture *never* indulges that desire. In the Old Testament era, every attempt to communicate with the dead was deemed a sin on par with sacrificing infants to false gods (Deuteronomy 18:10–12). The Hebrew Scriptures say comparatively little about the disposition of souls after death, and the people of God were strictly forbidden to inquire further on their own. Necromancy was a major feature of Egyptian religion. It also dominated every religion known among the Canaanites. But under Moses's law it was a sin punishable by death (Leviticus 20:27).

The New Testament adds much to our understanding of heaven (and hell) but we are still not permitted to add our own subjective ideas and experience-based conclusions to what God has specifically revealed through his inerrant Word. Indeed, we are forbidden in *all* spiritual matters to go beyond what is written (1 Corinthians 4:6).

Lazarus of Bethany fell ill and died, and his body lay devoid of life and decaying in a tomb for four days before Jesus raised him (John 11:17). A whole chapter in John's Gospel is devoted to the story of how Jesus brought him back from the dead. But there's not a hint or a whisper anywhere in Scripture about what happened to Lazarus's soul in that four-day interim. The same thing is true of every person in Scripture who was ever brought back from the dead, beginning with the widow's son whom Elijah raised in 1 Kings 17:17–24 and culminating with Eutychus, who was healed by Paul in Acts 20:9–12. Not one biblical person ever gave any recorded account of his or her postmortem experience in the realm of departed souls.

The apostle Paul had an experience of heaven so real he wasn't sure whether he had been physically carried there or merely caught up in a vision. He mentions the experience only once—reluctantly—because false teachers were challenging his authority and this heavenly vision was a vital affirmation of his apostolic credentials. But he had kept completely silent about the whole affair until fourteen years after the fact. Even then, he framed his testimony as a third-person narrative: "I know a man in Christ who fourteen years ago was caught up to the third heaven—whether in the body or out of the body I do not know, God knows. And I know that this man was caught up into paradise" (2 Corinthians 12:2–3). Despite the third-person pronouns, this was clearly Paul's own experience, because he shifts into first person as soon as he starts talking about how God humbled him in the aftermath of that experience: "To keep me from becoming conceited because of the surpassing greatness of the revelations, a thorn was given me in the flesh, a messenger of Satan to harass me, to keep me from becoming conceited" (v. 7).

The typical contemporary evangelical response to an event like that would be to write (or have a ghostwriter produce) a sensational account. It would be filled with specific details of what heaven is like and what's currently happening there. A large publishing conglomerate would publish it, and once it was clearly established as a blockbuster, they would start working on sequels and movie rights.

But having mentioned the *fact* of his experience, the apostle Paul declines to give any details whatsoever. He merely says that he "heard things that cannot be told, which man may not utter" (2 Corinthians 12:4). He employs a Greek expression that means it is not lawful for any human to speak of the things he heard.

So Paul, who had been called to one of the most important apostolic roles in the early church, was forbidden to discuss what he saw and heard in paradise. The brief three-verse account he gives of his vision makes quite a stark contrast to all the currently popular volumes written by people who claim to have been to heaven and come back.

Why would it have been unlawful for Paul to describe what he heard in heaven? After all, Ezekiel, Isaiah, and the apostle John each had visions of the very throne room of heaven and wrote about what they saw and heard. Their accounts are even part of inspired Scripture.

That is precisely the point. Those in the Bible who wrote about seeing heaven were expressly commanded by God to do so and were carried along by the Spirit of God as they wrote (2 Peter 1:21). The relatively brief accounts they each gave are part of the God-breathed text. The Almighty himself had those men record that information for our benefit in the precise words that he chose. No extrabiblical account of heaven can legitimately make that claim.

Those who demand to know more than Scripture tells us are sinning: "The secret things belong to the Lord our God, but the things that are revealed belong to us and to our children forever" (Deuteronomy 29:29). The limits of our curiosity are thus established by the boundary of biblical revelation.

The typical Christian today seems oblivious to the principles established by Deuteronomy 29:29 and 1 Corinthians 4:6 ("that you may learn . . . not to go beyond what is written"). In fact, people seem to be looking for spiritual truth, messages from God, and insight into the spirit world everywhere *but* Scripture. Today's evangelicals have been indoctrinated by decades of charismatic influence to think God regularly bypasses his written Word in order to speak directly to any and every believer—as if extrabiblical revelation were a standard feature of ordinary Christian experience. Many therefore think charity requires them to receive claims of "fresh revelation" with a kind of pious gullibility. After all, who are we to question someone else's private word from God?

So when dozens of best-selling authors who profess to be Christians are suddenly claiming they have seen heaven and want to tell us what it's like, most of the Christian community is defenseless in the wake of the onslaught.

Where the Angels Sang to Me

Todd Burpo's astonishing multimillion best seller, *Heaven Is for Real*,[1] epitomizes the phenomenal success Christian authors and publishers have had with books about alleged visits to heaven. It also illustrates the danger of basing one's ideas about the afterlife on personal experience rather than Scripture alone.

Most of the familiar features of the genre are included in Burpo's story: conscious out-of-body travel; the ability to see things from an ethereal perspective; visions of angelic beings; sublime emotions; vivid lights and colors; and lots of unexpected but finely detailed trivia about heaven's look and feel. But *Heaven Is for Real* also includes dozens of biblical references throughout. The entire story is carefully clothed in familiar evangelical language and imagery.

A decade ago, Betty Eadie seemed to be trying hard to sound like an evangelical, but she failed. Todd Burpo has clearly succeeded in selling a near-death-experience story to evangelicals as if it were a legitimate source of knowledge about heaven. Droves of Christian readers have heartily embraced his book.

Burpo is the bivocational pastor of a quasi-Pentecostal Wesleyan church in a remote southwestern Nebraska farm community. He is culturally, if not doctrinally, evangelical—a fairly typical middle-American small-town pastor. In his own words, he is "one of those pastors who walks back and forth during the sermon. Not a holy-rolling, fire-and-brimstone guy by any stretch, but not a soft-spoken minister in vestments, performing liturgical readings either. I'm a storyteller, and to tell stories I need to move around some."[2]

So Burpo is comfortably familiar with evangelical culture and expectations. He says he believes in the authority of Scripture, and he at-

---

[1] Todd Burpo with Lynn Vincent, *Heaven Is for Real: A Little Boy's Astounding Story of His Trip to Heaven and Back* (Nashville: Nelson, 2010).
[2] Ibid., 10.

tempts to draw as many connections as possible between his story and what the Bible says about heaven, angels, and the spiritual realm. That's why so many of the details he gives are carefully set alongside biblical allusions and proof texts. In that respect at least, *Heaven Is for Real* certainly includes more references from the Bible than most in the genre.

What sets the book apart, however, is that it is based on the experience of a not-quite-four-year-old boy.[3] It is the story of Pastor Burpo's eldest son, Colton, who as a toddler nearly died from a burst appendix. Four months after the medical crisis, when Todd's wife, Sonja, asked little Colton if he remembered being in the hospital, he answered, "Yes, Mommy, I remember. . . . That's where the angels sang to me."[4]

Todd Burpo's response to that comment was breathless amazement. In fact, the level of awe and stupefaction he describes seems quite out of proportion to the significance of such a statement from a typical four-year-old. He writes, "Time froze. Sonja and I looked at each other, passing a silent message: *Did he just say what I think he said?*"[5] As Pastor Burpo himself recounts the story, he was easily, immediately, and utterly convinced that Colton had indeed had some kind of out-of-body experience:

> Colton said that he "went up out of" his body, that he had spoken with angels, and had sat in Jesus' lap. And the way we knew he wasn't making it up was that he was able to tell us what we were doing in another part of the hospital: "You were in a little room by yourself praying, and Mommy was in a different room and she was praying and talking on the phone."[6]

That same unhesitating credulity sets the tone for the entire book. Showing little understanding of how fertile the imagination of a barely four-year-old boy can be, Pastor Burpo embraced Colton's testimony with implicit faith. He instantly decided to subjugate his whole understanding of heaven to little Colton's instruction. "If he

---

[3] Most of the book's publicity indicates that Colton Burpo was four years old when he says he visited heaven. According to the timeline given in the book, however, he was born May 19, 1999, and the crisis that nearly took his life occurred March 5, 2003 (ibid., 155–158). That means he was only three years and nine months old at the time, making it all the more remarkable that his retelling of the experience years later is so detailed and specific.
[4] Ibid., xiii.
[5] Ibid., xiv.
[6] Ibid., 61.

had really seen Jesus and the angels, I wanted to become the student, not the teacher!"[7]

Well, It Was Just Incredible

Many of the things Todd Burpo interprets as irrefutable proof his son was given special revelation are clearly little more than standard Sunday school stories with a typical preschooler's slightly distorted slant. Pastor Burpo recounts this conversation that took place shortly after Colton began talking about heaven:

> "Did anything else happen?"
>
> He nodded, eyes bright. "Did you know that Jesus has a cousin? Jesus told me his cousin baptized him."
>
> "Yes, you're right," I said. "The Bible says Jesus' cousin's name is John." Mentally, I scolded myself: *Don't offer information. Just let him talk* . . .
>
> "I don't remember his name," Colton said happily, "but he was really nice."
>
> *John the Baptist is "nice"?!*
>
> Just as I was processing the implications of my son's statement—that he had *met* John the Baptist—Colton spied a plastic horse among his toys and held it up for me to look at. "Hey, Dad, did you know Jesus has a horse?"
>
> "A horse?"
>
> "Yeah, a rainbow horse. I got to pet him."[8]

Sonja Burpo was as quick as her husband to conclude that Colton had truly traveled to heaven and come back with powerful knowledge of what it is like. Here is Pastor Burpo's account of the conversation where he informed his wife that Colton had met John the Baptist. (She was attending a worship conference, so he excitedly phoned to tell her about the incident):

> I stood and bounded up the stairs, picked up the phone, and dialed Sonja's cell. She picked up and I could hear music and singing in the background. "Do you know what your son just said to me?!"
>
> "What?" she shouted over the noise.

---

[7] Ibid., 62.
[8] Ibid., 63.

"He told me he met John the Baptist!"

"*What?*"

I summarized the rest for her and could hear the amazement in her voice on the other end of the line.

She tried to press me for details, but the worship conference hall was too loud. Finally we had to give up. "Call me tonight after dinner, okay?" Sonja said. "I want to know everything!"[9]

Pastor Burpo seems to think Colton's perspective on John the Baptist and heavenly rainbow-horses is full of profound insight. In reality, precocious preschoolers make imaginative remarks that sound like authoritative-sounding observations all the time. Art Linkletter made a career of eliciting unintentionally witty commentary on profound matters from kids on live daily television.

Remember, Colton had lived his entire life in a pastor's home, overhearing conversations, listening to stories, and being exposed to teaching focused on biblical themes. At one point, Pastor Burpo acknowledges that he had read countless Bible stories from picture books to Colton.[10] And yet when Colton mentions in passing that "Jesus has markers" (meaning, evidently, the nail prints in his hands and feet), Todd Burpo's breathless response is, "*He saw this. He had to have.*"[11]

And thus the book continues. When Colton says something far-fetched, heterodox, or unbiblical, Todd Burpo finds a way to accept it as true just the same. At one point, for example, Colton says he was sitting in a little chair next to the Spirit of God. So Todd asks his son what the Holy Spirit looks like:

"Hmm," Colton replies. "That's kind of a hard one . . . he's kind of blue."[12]

Obviously, a remark like that begs for a follow-up question or some kind of explanation. *Blue?* Does Colton envision the Holy Spirit as Papa Smurf? Is he describing a bluish cloud of haze? "Blue"? What is he talking about?

At first, Todd seems to be pondering similar questions. ("I was

---

[9] Ibid., 64.
[10] Ibid., 66.
[11] Ibid., 65–67.
[12] Ibid., 103.

trying to picture that. . . .") But Colton immediately changes the subject, and no further explanation is ever given. The only hint we get
about what is in Colton's mind comes more than twenty pages later,
when he tells his father that Jesus "shoots down power" from heaven
while Todd Burpo is preaching. This time Todd presses for an explanation: "What's the power like?"

"It's the Holy Spirit."[13] Evidently Colton envisions the Holy Spirit
like the electrical discharge from a Tesla coil, and he pictures Jesus
with the ability to fire blue lightning bolts of power from his fingers
directly into preachers.

Todd Burpo is dumbfounded: "If there were comic-strip thought-
bubbles over people's heads, mine would've been filled with question
marks and exclamation points right then."[14] Clearly, however, Todd is
already a firm believer in Colton's vision of heaven. Recollecting that
he had always said a prayer for God's help every time he preached, he
writes, "To imagine God answering it by 'shooting down power' . . .
well, it was just incredible."[15]

Gnostic Enlightenment in the Hands of a Preschooler

Pastor Burpo evidently believes, based on Colton's testimony, that all
the inhabitants of heaven (except Jesus) have wings and halos;[16] that
what occupies their time is "homework";[17] and that Colton met and
conversed not only with a grandfather who died years before Colton
was born, but also with a sister who was never born because Colton's
mother suffered a miscarriage.[18]

Colton says his unborn sister appeared to him as a "little girl," and
his grandfather, who had died at age 61, looked like a 29-year-old.[19]
Colton himself evidently remained only three (going on four) during
his time in heaven. Although he says he had wings like everyone else,
he was evidently disappointed by how small his wings were.[20] He also

---

[13] Ibid., 126.
[14] Ibid.
[15] Ibid., 126.
[16] Ibid., 72–73. Colton says everyone in heaven flew—"Well, all except for Jesus. He was the only one in heaven who didn't have wings. Jesus just went up and down like an elevator."
[17] Ibid., 71.
[18] Ibid., 85–88, 94–95.
[19] Ibid., 96, 122–123.
[20] Ibid., 72.

says that everyone else in heaven had a sword, but he was denied one because he was too young. "Jesus wouldn't let me have one. He said I'd be too dangerous."[21]

The questions Todd Burpo asks his son betray a strange fixation on the physical appearance of things. Todd's peculiar inquiry about what the Holy Spirit "looks like" is by no means the only example of this. When four-year-old Colton first began to talk about seeing people in heaven, Todd immediately began pressing for visual descriptions. He writes, "All I could think to ask was: 'So what did the kids look like? What do people look like in heaven?'"[22] Later, when Colton informs his dad that he saw the devil in heaven, Pastor Burpo's first question was, "What did he look like?"[23]

And of course, Todd Burpo persistently asked his son questions about the physical appearance of Christ:

> When Colton saw Jesus in heaven, what did he look like? The reason for the frequency of this particular topic was that as a pastor, I wound up spending a lot of time at hospitals, in Christian bookstores, and at other churches—all places where there are lots of drawings and paintings of Christ. Often, Sonja and the kids were with me, so it became sort of a game. When we came across a picture of Jesus, we'd ask Colton, "What about this one? Is that what Jesus looks like?"
>
> Invariably, Colton would peer for a moment at the picture and shake his tiny head. "No, the hair's not right," he would say. Or, "The clothes aren't right."
>
> This would happen dozens of times over the next three years.[24]

In the end, Pastor Burpo says he saw a story on television about a twelve-year-old girl who claimed to have been in heaven and who had unusual skill as a painter. She had painted the image of a rugged blue-eyed man whom she said was Jesus. When Colton looked at the picture and pronounced it accurate, Todd says, "I finally felt that in Akiane's portrait, we'd seen the face of Jesus. Or at least a startling likeness."[25]

(Images of a blue-eyed Jesus can hardly be accurate. Blue eyes are

---

[21] Ibid., 133.
[22] Ibid., 72.
[23] Ibid., 134.
[24] Ibid., 93.
[25] Ibid., 145.

a recessive trait, not native to Semitic races. A Hellenized Jew in the first century with generations of intermarriage in his genetic background might have had blue eyes, but the genealogy of Jesus given in the New Testament would seem to rule out the possibility that he had blue eyes.)

Most of the details Todd Burpo recounts about Colton's near-death experience came to light months after Colton's release from the hospital, and even then the story did not spill forth unprompted in a coherent account. Fragments and anecdotes arose here and there over a long period of time—usually in response to tenacious parental questioning. Thus new details were unearthed from Colton's memory on a fairly regular basis for years. In every case, without fail, Pastor Burpo concludes that Colton's knowledge of the afterlife could not have been gained through any means other than firsthand experience, and therefore he is easily convinced his son's account of heaven is fully reliable, accurate, and authoritative.

In a pithy review of the book, Tim Challies observed this motif:

> Every one of Colton's experiences, or very nearly every one, follows a pattern. He tells his father some little detail. His father experiences a gasp or feels his heart skip a beat. "I could hardly breathe. My mind was reeling. My head was spinning." A Scripture verse comes to dad's mind that validates the experience. Colton gets bored and runs off. Repeat.[26]

A Faulty View of Faith

The inclusion of Bible references throughout *Heaven Is for Real* may convince superficial readers that Pastor Burpo has painstakingly compared his son's account to Scripture and judged it accurate on that basis. But to those who take the time to look up the citations and analyze them in context with any degree of discernment, it will be clear that Todd Burpo's facile method of proof-texting betrays a lack of any serious engagement with Scripture. He has failed to test everything carefully as we are instructed and encouraged to do (1 Thessalonians 5:21; Acts 17:11).

---

[26] Tim Challies, "Heaven Is For Real," blogpost March 28, 2011, at http://www.challies.com/book-reviews/heaven-is-for-real.

Amazingly, Todd Burpo himself admits that he rarely "tested Colton's memories against what the Bible says."[27] In the one instance where he mentions this, he declares on the thinnest possible evidence that Colton "passed [the biblical test] without batting an eye."

What was the biblical issue at stake on that occasion? Todd was asking his son if he had ever seen God's throne. He first needed to explain to the boy what a "throne" is. ("I picked up the Bible storybook and pointed . . .")

"Oh, yeah!" Colton replied. "I saw that a bunch of times!"

Todd, in keeping with the tone he maintains throughout the book, was utterly agog: "My heart sped up a little. Was I really going to get a glimpse into the throne room of heaven?"

Colton continued: "And do you know that Jesus sits right next to God? . . . Jesus' chair is right next to his Dad's!"[28]

Pastor Burpo's response again emphasizes his avid credulity (not to mention his cluelessness about what kind of images a four-year-old raised on illustrated Bible stories might have in his mind): "That blew me away. There's no way a four-year-old knows that. It was another one of those moments when I thought, *He had to have seen this.*"[29]

One of the most troubling aspects of *Heaven Is for Real* is the way Todd Burpo constantly insinuates that personal experiences—even the spectral memories of a three-year-old boy under anesthetics—are somehow more compelling than Scripture alone. "I had been a Christian since childhood and a pastor for half my life, so I believed that before. But now I *knew* it."[30] Colton's experiential exegesis of heaven has clearly made a far more profound impact on Todd (and has been more formative in his notion of the afterlife) than anything he had previously gleaned about heaven from his own study of Scripture.

That way of thinking is diametrically opposed to what the Bible says about faith, experience, and the authority of Scripture. In fact, the single most important defense Christians have against self-deception is a conviction that the written Word of God is more certain and more authoritative than *anyone's* experience. Scripture teaches this

---

[27] Burpo, *Heaven Is for Real*, 101.
[28] Ibid., 100.
[29] Ibid., 100–101.
[30] Ibid., 84.

explicitly and repeatedly. For example, writing about his experience on the Mount of Transfiguration—an undeniable miracle at which other eyewitnesses were present—the apostle Peter says, "We did not follow cleverly devised myths. . . . We ourselves heard this very voice borne from heaven" (2 Peter 1:16, 18). It was a stunning, unprecedented, up-close look at the glory of heaven—literally. Peter goes on to say, however, that the written Word of God is even more reliable than an experience of that caliber! "We have the prophetic word more fully confirmed, to which you will do well to pay attention" (v. 19).

Authentic faith "comes from hearing, and hearing through the word of Christ" (Romans 10:17)—not from mystical experiences; certainly not from blindly trusting a child's account of a mystical experience. That kind of naive conviction is not true faith at all; it has more in common with dangerous self-confidence.

Nevertheless, Pastor Burpo clearly believes that somehow, little Colton's experience has bolstered his family's faith in a way Scripture could never do. "I love the way my mom sums it up," Todd writes, and then he quotes his mother's words, which stand (except for a brief epilogue) as the book's closing sentence: "I accepted the idea of heaven before, but now I visualize it. Before, I'd heard, but now I know that someday I'm going to see."[31]

Where the Danger Chiefly Lies

I've given this prolonged critique of *Heaven Is for Real* not because it is the worst of the genre, but because of all the books in this category, it is the most likely to be read and deemed harmless by the typical evangelical. It is *not* harmless. It denigrates the authority and sufficiency of Scripture; it confounds faith with superstition; it subtly elevates human experience to a higher level than the Word of God; it purports to reveal things about God and the heavenly realm that are not taught in Scripture; and it repeatedly insinuates that the testimony of someone who has been mystically enlightened can be a more effective stimulant to faith than Scripture alone.

In the chapters that follow, I want to turn to the question of what

[31] Ibid., 150.

the Bible says about heaven. In a couple of appendixes, you'll find further critiques of some of the most popular and influential reports of near-death visits to heaven, including two mega-best-selling titles from evangelical publishers. All the authors of these stories—and evidently millions of readers as well—regard their testimonies as authoritative, reliable, and full of superior insights that can take readers to a higher level of understanding and enlightenment beyond what we can get from the Bible. In other words, all of these books take a similarly proto-gnostic stance on heaven and the afterlife. All of them are dangerous and misleading. That includes the ones that seem fairly benign as well as the ones that are clearly steeped in occult superstition. All of them stand as reminders to us that Scripture and Scripture alone is the only safe place for Christians to learn anything about the immortality of human souls, what happens to a person after death, what heaven is like, what awaits the unrighteous in hell, and what we can expect in the judgment to come.

That is the point I want to stress at the close of this chapter. It is the principle of *sola Scriptura*. That Latin expression means "Scripture alone." It is a kind of shorthand expression that signifies the authority and sufficiency of Scripture. It means that Scripture is the sole rule of faith and practice for Christians—so that no duty, no teaching, and no belief that lacks a biblical foundation is ever to be deemed binding on any Christian.

To state the same thing in different words: the principle of *sola Scriptura* starts and ends with a recognition of the Bible's superiority over every other source of knowledge, every truth claim, every religious tradition, and every supposed new revelation.

This principle was one of the fundamental pillars of biblical Christianity recovered by the early Reformers after it had fallen into neglect and denial. That happened because sound, biblical doctrine had been crowded out of mainstream church life by false teaching, medieval superstition, ecclesiastical corruption, and a host of problems all related to the visible church's failure to submit to the authority of Scripture. The current evangelical fascination with near-death experiences (and with other extrabiblical sources of alleged spiritual enlightenment) is pointing backward to the same kind of apostasy.

Clearly, if we believe Scripture is the Word of God, we must reject every anecdotal account that contradicts or goes beyond what Scripture teaches. We must also refuse to get caught up in every kind of speculation, every truth claim, and every supposed new revelation that detracts from or leads people away from simple reliance on the Word of God.

3

Delusions of Grandeur

The current best-selling heavenly travelogues all have one disturbing tendency in common: they manage to make the heavenly tourist seem heroic while making heaven itself sound somewhat mundane.

We live in a narcissistic culture, and it shows in these accounts of people who claim they've been to heaven. They sound as if they viewed paradise in a mirror, keeping themselves in the foreground. They say comparatively little about the glory of God, the very centerpiece of heaven. But all of them have a lot to say about how good *they* felt—how peaceful, how happy, how comforted they were; how they received privileges and accolades; how fun and enlightening their experience was; and how many things they think they now understand perfectly that could never be gleaned from Scripture alone. In short, they glorify self while barely noticing God's glory. They highlight everything but what's truly important about heaven.

What Stands Out Most in Heaven?

It is quite true that heaven is a place of perfect bliss—devoid of all sorrow and sin, full of exultation and enjoyment—a place where grace and peace reign totally unchallenged. Heaven is where every true treasure and every eternal reward is laid up for the redeemed. Anyone whose destiny is heaven will certainly experience more joy and honor there than the fallen mind is capable of comprehending—infinitely more than any fallen creature deserves. But if you actually saw heaven and lived to tell about it, those things are *not* what would capture your heart and imagination.

You would be preoccupied instead with the majesty and grace of the One whose glory fills the place.

Is no one truly awestruck by the glory of heaven anymore? Have we been so overexposed to Hollywood's special effects that the spectacle of Almighty God, high and lifted up, seems somehow less impressive than it was in Isaiah's time? Do we live in such a slick, sophisticated, high-tech age that the glory of heaven has begun to look a little pale by comparison?

I think not. For anyone who truly believes the biblical record, it is impossible to resist the conclusion that these modern testimonies—with their relentless self focus and the relatively scant attention they pay to the glory of God—*are simply untrue.* They are either figments of the human imagination (dreams, hallucinations, false memories, fantasies, and in the worst cases, deliberate lies), or else they are products of demonic deception.

We know this with absolute certainty, because Scripture definitively says that people do not go to heaven and come back: "Who has ascended to heaven and come down?" (Proverbs 30:4). Answer: *"No one has ascended into heaven except he who descended from heaven, the Son of Man"* (John 3:13). All the accounts of heaven in Scripture are visions, not journeys taken by dead people. And even visions of heaven are very, very rare in Scripture. You can count them all on one hand.

This much is absolutely clear: the stories that are being told and devoured in the evangelical community nowadays are nothing like the firsthand accounts of heaven we read in the Bible.

Whenever a prophet in Scripture was blessed with a heavenly vision, his focus was firmly fixed on God and the all-surpassing glory that surrounds God's throne. Scripture describes the scene in heaven as so magnificent that nothing in the universe—including the vast splendor of the universe itself—*nothing* could possibly shift any mere creature's attention away from God's glory. The magnificent angels who live in his presence *never* look away (Matthew 18:10).

Furthermore, in every instance in the Bible where a mere mortal has a heavenly vision, that person—if he mentions himself at all—is frightened, hyper-aware of his own insignificance, deeply conscious of his guilt and fallenness. Some of the greatest prophets in the Bible testified that when they saw heaven's glory they immediately felt ashamed, unworthy, and out of place.

Isaiah said, "Woe is me! For I am lost; for I am a man of unclean lips, and I dwell in the midst of a people of unclean lips" (Isaiah 6:5). The apostle John said, "When I saw him, I fell at his feet as though dead" (Revelation 1:17). Ezekiel likewise said, "I fell on my face" (Ezekiel 1:28).

Daniel was similarly brought low by a vision of Christ's preincarnate glory. Daniel said: "No strength was left in me. My radiant appearance was fearfully changed, and I retained no strength. Then . . . as I heard the sound of his words, I fell on my face" (Daniel 10:8–9). Daniel managed to raise himself, trembling, to his hands and knees. After a while he stood up, still trembling, and listened (vv. 10–11). Then when the voice finished speaking, Daniel said, "I turned my face toward the ground and was mute" (v. 15). When he finally recovered enough strength to speak, he could only do so with great pain: "By reason of the vision pains have come upon me, and I retain no strength. . . . No strength remains in me, and no breath is left in me" (vv. 16–17).

Every vision of heaven recorded in Scripture highlights that same sense of breathtaking majesty and daunting radiance. No wonder. All of heaven is lit by God's own glory; no other illumination is necessary (Isaiah 60:19; Revelation 21:23; 22:5). It is a luminescence that makes the light of our sun seem dingy and dismal by comparison. And the glory of heaven is infinitely more intricate, transcendent, beautiful, awe-inspiring, full of wonder and delight. If you could observe it for all eternity you would never grow weary of it. If you are a believer, that is precisely what is in store for you.

But the glory of heaven is not a sight that would make any mere mortal giddy or self-assured. Just the opposite. It's such a formidable effulgence that one glimpse of God's glory in its full, unmediated potency would literally be fatal to unglorified human flesh. God told Moses, "You cannot see my face, for man shall not see me and live" (Exodus 33:20). The apostle Paul described it as "unapproachable light, whom no one has ever seen or can see" (1 Timothy 6:16).

Nevertheless, a yearning to see God's glory is one of the hallmarks of true belief in him. This, of course, is the single most powerful attraction and the highest reward of heaven: *God's glory is permanently on display there in all its full resplendence.* We will be able to see it without being destroyed by it. The redeemed will have glorified bodies, perfectly fit for heaven. They will get to behold God's glory, study it, bask in it, reflect it, and enjoy it for all eternity. "Blessed are the pure in heart, for they shall see God" (Matthew 5:8). Their vision of the glory will be unobstructed, unclouded, unmediated, and unhindered by the effects of sin or guilt. "We shall see him as he is" (1 John 3:2). That expectation is an essential aspect of authentic saving faith (Hebrews 11:16).

Moses therefore wanted to see God's glory whether it killed him or not. So the Lord agreed to hide Moses in a cave and let him look for a brief moment as God moved past and away from him. After that shielded encounter with God's back, Moses's own face shone for a time with a fading reflection of the divine glory. But even such a small sample of the glory was utterly terrifying to the Israelites (Exodus 34:30). Moses had to cover his face with a veil!

If the fading, reflected glow on Moses's face was so thoroughly frightening, it is no wonder that every person in the Bible who had a vision of heaven and lived to tell about it said the sight provoked immobilizing fear. *Of course* that's what anyone who has truly seen heaven would talk about.

By contrast, today's gnostic near-death experiences seem to puff up the heavenly visitor's own self-image with delusions of grandeur. Whereas all the prophets and apostles in biblical times who saw heaven were dumbstruck, chagrined, and wishing to hide in the presence of divine glory, Colton Burpo says he was shown high honor by heaven's other inhabitants: "'They brought in a little chair for me,' he said, smiling. 'I sat by God the Holy Spirit.'"[1]

All the currently popular afterlife accounts contain a generous dose of that kind of swagger, and all of them seem similarly insensible to the real glory of heaven. Mary Neal says her arrival in heaven was celebrated by "a large welcoming committee." She says this group included several of her dead friends and neighbors (including "Mrs. Sivits, my old babysitter"). They were "sent by God," she says—and "[they]

---

[1] Quoted in Todd Burpo with Lynn Vincent, *Heaven Is for Real: A Little Boy's Astounding Story of His Trip to Heaven and Back* (Nashville: Nelson, 2010), 102.

greeted me with the most overwhelming joy I have ever experienced and could ever imagine. It was joy at an unadulterated core level."[2]

Kevin Malarkey, in *The Boy Who Came Back from Heaven*, claims his son Alex still makes regular visits to heaven ("mostly in his sleep"):

> He arrives just inside the gates. He talks with the angels who stand guard. . . . Next Alex will enter the Temple and speak to God Himself. On the way, he may speak to other angels, or he may not. . . . Alex converses with God until the Lord tells him the visit is finished. Sometimes other angels are in the meetings, and sometimes it is only God and Alex."[3]

Malarkey's account of his son's experience stands out from the rest on this very point. He *does* mention how God's glory is portrayed in the Bible, and he even cites a couple of instances where heavenly glory inspired fear in biblical figures who saw it. In the end, however, the glory of God is barely a side note, certainly not the centerpiece, of the tale Kevin Malarkey tells. In fact, his whole point in bringing up the subject seems to be to tell how fearless his young son is in the presence of God's glory.[4] According to Kevin, the angels keep telling the child not to fear, but little Alex Malarkey remains childishly intrepid in the midst of all heaven's glory.

Utterly missing from these accounts is the powerful sense of personal unworthiness and ineligibility that dominates every biblical account of people who saw heaven. Also missing is any awestruck description of the glory that is heaven's main feature.

Compare any of those accounts with Ezekiel's detailed description of wheels within wheels (Ezekiel 1:16); with "living creatures dart[ing] to and fro, like the appearance of a flash of lightning" (v. 14); creatures moving "in any of their four directions without turning as they went" (v. 17); their wings making a noise "like the sound of many waters,

---

[2] Mary C. Neal, *To Heaven and Back: A Doctor's Extraordinary Account of Her Death, Heaven, Angels, and Life Again* (Colorado Springs: Waterbrook, 2012), 69.

[3] Kevin Malarkey and Alex Malarkey, *The Boy Who Came Back from Heaven: A Remarkable Account of Miracles, Angels, and Life beyond This World* (Carol Stream, IL: Tyndale, 2010), 182. See appendix 2 for an extended review. Although Kevin and Alex Malarkey are listed as joint authors on the book's cover, Alex has publicly disclaimed the book online, calling it "1 of the most deceptive books ever." Beth Malarkey, Alex's mom and Kevin's wife, describes the book as "a beautiful testimony distorted, twisted, packaged and used as business." http://amomonamission.blogspot.com/2012/11/following-is-post-that-my-son-alex.html

[4] Ibid.

like the sound of the Almighty, a sound of tumult like the sound of an army" (v. 24); and above all, that indescribable glory, "Like the appearance of the bow that is in the cloud on the day of rain, so was the appearance of the brightness all around. Such was the appearance of the likeness of the glory of the LORD" (v. 28).

It's not at all a scene that says, "pull up a chair and make yourself comfortable." In fact, this was the very point where Ezekiel said, "When I saw it, I fell on my face" (v. 28).

Visions of Rapture

The apostle John's vision of heaven is Scripture's most detailed account of the heavenly realm, filling almost the entire book of Revelation. It makes an instructive contrast to the currently popular heavenly travel journals.

John's purpose in writing is not to tell us what heaven is like. This vision is mainly about "the day of wrath when God's righteous judgment will be revealed" (to borrow words from Romans 2:5). The name of the book, *Revelation*, is a translation of the first Greek word that opens John's message: *apokalypsis* (Revelation 1:1). That, of course, is the root of the English word *apocalypse*—which in popular usage is frequently applied to any kind of climactic catastrophe. What John describes in the book of Revelation is literally the catastrophe to end all catastrophes. John's vision is *apocalyptic* in every sense of that word.

What John saw from heaven's perspective was a prophetic revelation of the appalling and awesome outpouring of divine fury that will eventually befall the whole earth. In the aftermath, in the closing chapters, John explains how these apocalyptic events will resolve in the triumph of God, the unveiling of the new heaven and the new earth, and the eternal rest of the faithful in the never-ending bliss of that domain.

Thus the end of the book of Revelation gives us the best, most complete biblical window on the saints' eternal rest. But bear in mind: that is not really the point of John's vision. His real aim is to give us an extended account of how divine wrath and earthly tribulation will be poured out upon all humanity—on a scale unfathomable to our minds and unparalleled in our experience. John clearly wants to provoke wonder, awe, reverence, and fear—and it is in that context that he gives us the Bible's most detailed description of heaven.

Remember that the apostle Paul's vision of heaven was so real and so vivid that he said—twice: "Whether [it was] in the body or out of the body I do not know, God knows" (2 Corinthians 12:2–3). Twice John says, "I was in the Spirit" (Revelation 1:10; 4:2). So this is clearly a Spirit-directed vision. It is not a dream, a hallucination, a near-death experience, or a figment of John's imagination. His spirit was carried by the Holy Spirit out of the material world (fully awake, not in a dream), and he was shown by divine revelation things he could never perceive by his own senses. This is the most detailed, extended prophetic vision of any kind we find anywhere in Scripture. It is (like Paul's vision of heaven) so vivid that John must have felt as if he had been transported physically into the events he describes.

It happened instantaneously. John says, "I looked, and behold, a door standing open in heaven! And the first voice, which I had heard speaking to me like a trumpet, said, 'Come up here, and I will show you what must take place after this.' *At once* I was in the Spirit, and behold, a throne stood in heaven, with one seated on the throne" (Revelation 4:1–2). There was no journey through a dark tunnel, no angelic welcoming committee, and no floating sensation while he looked back down on his own body as his soul left it. This wasn't astral projection; John was immediately transported from the island of Patmos to the heavenly dimension "in the Spirit."

Notice, too, that John's attention is drawn first to the throne of God: "Behold, a throne stood in heaven, with one seated on the throne." John's focus remains there for all of Revelation 4; and throughout the later chapters of the book, he returns again and again to this throne. (The throne is mentioned more than forty times in Revelation, at least once in 14 of the book's 22 chapters.) As we have seen already and shall see again several more times, this throne is the heart and the axis of heaven.

John spends the next few verses describing the creatures, the decorations, the lights, and the colors that immediately surround the throne. In chapter 5, we'll return to this same passage for a closer look at the heavenly throne and its surroundings. What I want to point out in this context, however, is the profound worship that takes place around the throne.

The stage for worship is set with John's description of the four magnificent creatures who stand watch around the throne: "Around the throne, on each side of the throne, are four living creatures, full of eyes in front and behind: the first living creature like a lion, the second living creature like an ox, the third living creature with the face of a man, and the fourth living creature like an eagle in flight" (4:6–7).

These are angels—apparently the same four creatures Ezekiel describes in his vision of heaven. Throughout Ezekiel 10, Ezekiel refers to them as "cherubim." Indeed, Psalms 80:1 and 99:1 describe God as "enthroned upon the cherubim." In Isaiah's vision of heaven, he says, "I saw the Lord sitting upon a throne, high and lifted up; and the train of his robe filled the temple. Above him stood the seraphim" (Isaiah 6:1–2)—and he goes on to describe the seraphim as winged creatures that guard the throne. The word *seraphim* is used only twice in Scripture, both times in Isaiah 6. The root word has the connotation of fire, so these could simply be a fiery order of cherubim, and hence the same creatures Ezekiel calls "cherubim," or they could be a distinct and higher order of angels.

These creatures whom Ezekiel calls "cherubim" are vastly different from Raphael's famous painting of cherubs as dreamy, cute-faced, childlike moppets. They certainly aren't like any ceramic cherub you have ever seen! Ezekiel says they "had a human likeness, but each had four faces, and each of them had four wings" (Ezekiel 1:5–6). So their form was like the human form—presumably with arms and legs and the ability to stand upright. And (according to John) they had eyes all around.

Ezekiel agrees. But his description is more elaborate:

> As I looked at the living creatures, I saw a wheel on the earth beside the living creatures, one for each of the four of them. As for the appearance of the wheels and their construction: their appearance was like the gleaming of beryl. And the four had the same likeness, their appearance and construction being as it were a wheel within a wheel. When they went, they went in any of their four directions without turning as they went. And their rims were tall and awesome, and the rims of all four were full of eyes all around. (Ezekiel 1:15–18)

Picture that, if you can. It is clearly magnificent—certainly not the kind of scenario where you would pull up a little chair and sit down for an informal chat.

Ezekiel and John give similar accounts of the creatures' faces. John describes the creatures from a fixed perspective, "[one] like a lion, the second . . . like an ox, the third . . . with the face of a man, and the fourth . . . like an eagle" (Revelation 4:7). Ezekiel says each of the four creatures had all four faces: "Each had a human face. The four had the face of a lion on the right side, the four had the face of an ox on the left side, and the four had the face of an eagle" (Ezekiel 1:10).

Ezekiel mentions "four wings" on each of the creatures (v. 6). He seems to mean that they had a wing on each side, plus front and back, and he further says that "under their wings on their four sides they had human hands" (v. 8). They also seem to have had an additional set of wings with which they flew, because Revelation 4:8 says, "each of them [had] six wings." That is exactly how Isaiah describes the seraphim: "Each had six wings: with two he covered his face, and with two he covered his feet, and with two he flew" (Isaiah 6:2). Two wings devoted to service and four wings devoted to worship. Thus the priority of worship is well illustrated by these angels.

In Isaiah's account, he famously writes, "One called to another and said: 'Holy, holy, holy is the LORD of hosts; the whole earth is full of his glory!'" (v. 3). John witnessed the same spectacle, and he says it is a never-ending chorus around the heavenly throne. He writes, "Day and night they never cease to say, 'Holy, holy, holy, is the Lord God Almighty, who was and is and is to come!'" (Revelation 4:8).

The praise that ensues is in the form of a cantata—or better yet an oratorio. The seraphic chorus is answered by an antiphonal choir. It swells in a great crescendo and becomes a massive concert of praise that dominates John's vision all the way to the end of chapter 5.

Starting with the first "Holy, holy, holy" of Revelation 4:8, John records five hymns of praise before he gets to the end of the next chapter. These heavenly hymns can be divided into two categories. Some of them sing about *the redemption of creation;* the rest about *the redemption of the human race.*

The praise in Revelation 4 focuses on God as the creator and redeemer of everything: "Worthy are you, our Lord and God, to receive glory and honor and power, for you created all things, and by your will they existed and were created" (v. 11). Chapter 5 focuses on God as the God of salvation, who is going to redeem humanity:

> The twenty-four elders fell down before the Lamb, each holding a harp, and golden bowls full of incense, which are the prayers of the saints. And they sang a new song, saying,
>
> > "Worthy are you to take the scroll
> > and to open its seals,
> > for you were slain, and by your blood you ransomed people
> > for God
> > from every tribe and language and people and nation,
> > and you have made them a kingdom and priests to our God,
> > and they shall reign on the earth." (vv. 8–10)

The praise culminates in this famous song of praise about Christ: "Worthy is the Lamb who was slain, to receive power and wealth and wisdom and might and honor and glory and blessing!" (v. 12). Our congregation sings those very words to a familiar tune practically every time we celebrate the Lord's Table.

The praise is not finished:

> And I heard every creature in heaven and on earth and under the earth and in the sea, and all that is in them, saying,
>
> > "To him who sits on the throne and to the Lamb
> > be blessing and honor and glory and might forever and ever!"
>
> And the four living creatures said, "Amen!" and the elders fell down and worshiped. (vv. 13–14)

It is an oratorio about redemption.

There is a long, steady crescendo in the orchestration of this oratorio. It starts with a quartet (the four angels). To that are added twenty-four voices (the elders, 4:10). Then on top of the angelic quartet and the twenty-four elders, harps are added (5:8). Finally they are joined by every living being in heaven—"myriads of myriads and thousands of thousands" (v. 11). It all crescendos to the very pinnacle of heavenly worship, and the angels add the final cadence: "The four living creatures said, 'Amen!' and the elders fell down and worshiped" (v. 14). Every creature in heaven then collapses in sheer adoration to God.

I want to see that. *I want to be part of it.*

And one thing I know for certain: no one who truly witnessed such a spectacle would ever come back to earth talking about anything else.

4

This World Is Not
My Home

As misleading as these spurious stories about heaven may be to people who are duped by them, far more people lose sight of heaven because they are swept up in worldliness and materialism and push all thoughts of heaven and the afterlife from their minds completely. Despite the high sales and far-reaching influence of today's books about journeys to heaven and back, an attachment to this material world is surely a far more pervasive reason people fail to think rightly about heaven.

Let's be honest, too: materialism is not a problem for pagans only. A look at America's evangelical subculture reveals that materialism is alive and well among Bible-believing Christians. We now have modern megachurch complexes that include high-tech entertainment and special-effects facilities, health spas, fitness centers, bowling alleys, and even food courts. Dispensing material comforts to the flock has become more important for some churches than pursuing the prize of the heavenly calling. Little wonder if the people in the pews miss the point that materialism is sin. And it's hardly a surprise if a heaven utterly dominated by God's glory sounds "boring" to people who have fostered large appetites for worldly amusements in place of worship.

Frankly, most Christians in wealthy Western cultures have things too good right here in this world. Most don't really know what it is to long for heaven. God has blessed us with an abundance of earthly comforts—more than any prior generation in all of recorded history.

We are in danger of becoming so comfortable in this life that we forget we are but strangers and pilgrims in this world. Like Abraham, we're supposed to think of ourselves as vagabonds here on earth, "looking forward to the city that has foundations, whose designer and builder is God" (Hebrews 11:10).

Christians in less affluent and less comfortable cultures than ours tend to think more about heaven, because it promises things so different from what they have known in this world.

I ministered a few years ago in an isolated city south of Siberia and on the back side of Tibet, where I met with fifteen hundred impoverished Christians who had suffered greatly under Russian oppression for three quarters of a century. They were the children of exiles, economically deprived, working hard daily just to find food. They wanted me to teach them from the Bible, and the subject they most desired to study was about their future in the glory of heaven. I had the privilege of doing that over several hours, and many wept with joy.

How different is our response, coming from a more comfortable culture! I often meet Christians who live as if heaven would be an unwelcome intrusion into their busy schedule—an interruption of career goals or holiday plans.

We live in an era of immediate gratification. No generation prior to this has ever had access to so many means of fulfilling fleshly desires in a here-and-now fashion. We have credit cards allowing us to own what we can't afford, go where we wouldn't be able to go, and do what would otherwise be impossible for us. Only after we have had the vacation or consumed the luxury do we have to worry about paying for it. The prevalence of uncontrolled credit card debt is symptomatic of an attitude that says, "I want what I want *when* I want it!" The mind-set of our age is against postponed pleasures of any kind. We prefer instant gratification, and we all too willingly sacrifice the future on the altar of the immediate.

Again, Christians are by no means exempt from this tendency. Rather than setting our affections on things above, we tend to become attached to the things of this earth. It's all too easy to become absorbed in temporal matters and neglect what is eternally important. We spend our energies consuming and accumulating things that may promise fulfillment or enjoyment right now but "perish as they are used" (Colossians 2:22). Jesus reminds us that *all* earthly things—along with any pleasure they bring—will decay and pass away (Matthew 6:19; Luke 12:20; 18:22). That's why we're commanded to lay up for ourselves treasures in heaven, where they can never be destroyed or pass away.

Sadly, having lost sight of the "sweet by and by," too many Christians busy themselves with the harried here and now, and they themselves are consumed by consumable things.

Worse, certain high-profile media ministries, preaching a false gospel of earthly prosperity, give multitudes the disastrous impression that this is what Christianity is all about. They promise people that Jesus wants them healthy, wealthy, and successful in this life. Such teaching is extremely popular because it caters to the spirit of the age—particularly the desire to have everything in this life, right now. People influenced by prosperity preachers tend to think of heaven as the ultimate fulfillment of every material craving. For those with such a view, even the command to "seek the things that are above, where Christ is, seated at the right hand of God" (Colossians 3:1) becomes a justification for carnal covetousness.

Because the church doesn't *really* have heaven on its mind, Christians tend to be self-indulgent, self-centered, weak, and materialistic. Our present comforts consume too much of our thoughts, and if we're not careful, we end up entertaining wrong fantasies about heaven—or thinking very little of heaven at all.

No Christian should ever fall into that trap. From time to time someone will suggest that Christians are too concerned with heaven. I'm sure you have heard the common complaint about people who are "so heavenly minded that they are no earthly good." There is indeed a kind of ersatz spirituality that renders people worthless for good works and mutual edification. But such people are not really *heavenly* minded at all. They are typically like the Pharisees, going through the motions of ritual and public piety for the sake of self, with no real thought about the glory of God. "They do all their deeds to be seen by others" (Matthew 23:5). That's the polar opposite of true heavenly mindedness.

Now and then someone will protest that Christians are so concerned with heaven that they neglect earthly priorities—social justice, the needs of the poor and oppressed, health care for the disenfranchised and underprivileged, and so on. That charge ignores the fact that Christians have always led the way in matters of public welfare, the building of hospitals, emergency relief work, and other expressions of human compassion. Charity work always flourishes where the gospel is boldly proclaimed. But the argument that earthly relief should take priority over spiritual salvation is not a Christian perspective. Jesus summed up the proper order of priorities clearly with the familiar command, "Seek first the kingdom of God and his righteousness, and all these things will be added to you" (Matthew 6:33).

The Preciousness of Heaven

In reality, everything that is truly precious to us as Christians is in heaven.

The Father is there, and that's why Jesus taught us to pray, "Our Father in heaven, hallowed be your name" (Matthew 6:9). *Jesus* himself is at the Father's right hand. Hebrews 9:24 says, "Christ has entered, not into holy places made with hands, which are copies of the true things, but into heaven itself, now to appear in the presence of God on our behalf." So our Savior is also in heaven, where he intercedes on our behalf (Hebrews 7:25).

Many *brothers and sisters in Christ* are there, too. Hebrews 12:22–24 says that in turning to God we have come "to Mount Zion and to the city of the living God, the heavenly Jerusalem, and to innumerable angels in festal gathering, and to the assembly of the firstborn who are enrolled in heaven, and to God, the judge of all, and to the spirits of the righteous made perfect, and to Jesus, the mediator of a new covenant." Our departed loved ones in the faith are there with Christ and with the Father. Every Old and New Testament believer who has died is now in heaven.

Our names are recorded there. In Luke 10:20 Christ tells his disciples, who were casting out demons, "Do not rejoice in this, that the spirits are subject to you, but rejoice that your names are written in heaven." And by saying that our names are written in heaven, Christ assures us that we have a title deed to property there. This is *our inheri-*

tance. First Peter 1:4 says we are begotten in Christ "to an inheritance that is imperishable, undefiled, and unfading, kept in heaven for you."

"*Our citizenship* is in heaven," according to Philippians 3:20. In other words, heaven is where we belong. We're just "strangers and exiles on the earth" (Hebrews 11:13). Our goals therefore should not include the accumulation of material possessions here. Our real wealth—*our eternal reward*—is in heaven (Matthew 5:12). In Matthew 6:19–21 Jesus says that the only treasure we will possess throughout eternity is there.

In other words, everything we *should* love everlastingly, everything we rightly value, everything of any eternal worth is in heaven.

So self-indulgence and materialism foster a worldly atmosphere that has a particularly destructive spiritual bent. It undermines everything the church should stand for. It tears Christians away from their heavenly moorings. And it makes them worldly.

The term *worldliness* almost sounds outdated, doesn't it? Many people think it sounds petty, legalistic, and unnecessarily old-fashioned. Our grandparents heard sermons against "the sin of worldliness." We think *we're* too sophisticated to concern ourselves with such trivia. But the real problem is that we are not sufficiently concerned with heavenly values, so we don't appreciate how wickedly sinful it is to hold on to earthly ones.

And that is the essence of worldliness: it is a love for earthly things, an esteem for earthly values, and a preoccupation with earthly cares. Scripture plainly labels it sin—and it *is* sin of the worst stripe. It is a spiritual form of adultery that sets one against God himself: "You adulterous people! Do you not know that friendship with the world is enmity with God? Therefore whoever wishes to be a friend of the world makes himself an enemy of God" (James 4:4).

I have actually heard Christians say they don't want to go to heaven until they've enjoyed all that the world can deliver. When all earthly pursuits are exhausted, or when age and sickness hamper their enjoyment, then they believe they'll be ready for heaven. *Please, God, don't take me to heaven yet*, they pray. *I haven't even been to Hawaii!*

But if you live your life without cultivating a love for heavenly things, you will never be fit for heaven. First John 2:15–17 makes that very point: "Do not love the world or the things in the world. If anyone loves the world, the love of the Father is not in him. For all that is in the world—the desires of the flesh and the desires of the eyes and pride of life—is not from the Father but is from the world. And the world is passing away along with its desires, but whoever does the will of God abides forever."

Some people who claim to know Christ actually love the world so much that frankly there may be good reason to wonder if they can possibly be citizens of heaven. As one of the old spirituals says, "Everybody talkin' 'bout heaven ain't goin' there."

Sadly, though, it is also true that not everyone who is going to heaven is talking about it the way they should be. "My brothers, these things ought not to be so" (James 3:10). The hope of heaven should fill us with a joy of anticipation that loosens any grip this transitory world might have on our hearts.

A Worldview That Looks toward Heaven

It may sound paradoxical to say this, but heaven should be at the center of the Christian worldview. The term *worldview* is a name for the moral, philosophical, and spiritual framework through which we interpret the world and everything around us. Everyone *has* a worldview, whether consciously or not.

A proper Christian worldview is uniquely focused heavenward. Though some would deride this as "escapism," it is, after all, the very thing Scripture commands: "Set your minds on things that are above, not on things that are on earth" (Colossians 3:2). The King James Version perfectly captures the sense of the command: "Set your *affection* on things above." The apostle Paul penned that verse, by the way, and his approach to life was anything but escapist.

In fact, Paul is a wonderful example of the proper biblical perspective between heaven and earth. He faced overwhelming persecution on earth and never lost sight of heaven. In 2 Corinthians 4:8–10 he says, "We are afflicted in every way, but not crushed; perplexed, but not driven to despair; persecuted, but not forsaken; struck down, but not destroyed; always carrying in the body the death of Jesus, so that the life of Jesus may also be manifested in our bodies." Then in verses 16–17 he adds, "we do not lose heart. Though our outer self is wasting away, our inner self is being renewed day by day. For this light momentary affliction is preparing for us an eternal weight of glory beyond all comparison, as we look not to the things that are seen but to the things that are unseen." Elsewhere he told the church at Rome, "I consider that the sufferings of this present time are not worth comparing with the glory that is to be revealed to us" (Romans 8:18).

Paul was saying exactly what Peter told the scattered and persecuted believers he wrote to: we endure the sufferings of this world for the sake of heaven's glory (1 Peter 1:3–7). Whatever we suffer in this life cannot be compared with the glory of the life to come.

In other words, we don't seek to *escape* this life by dreaming of heaven. But we do find we can *endure* this life because of the certainty of heaven. Heaven is eternal. Earth is temporal. Those who fix all their affections on the ephemeral realities of this passing world are the real escapists, because they are vainly attempting to avoid facing eternity—by hiding in the fleeting shadows of things that are only transient.

The irony is that all the things we can see and touch in this world are less substantive and less permanent than the eternal things of heaven, which things we can grasp only by faith. The apostle Paul wrote, "We look not to the things that are seen but to the things that are unseen. For the things that are seen are transient, but the things that are unseen are eternal. For we know that if the tent that is our earthly home is destroyed, we have a building from God, a house not made with hands, eternal in the heavens" (2 Corinthians 4:18—5:1).

It always amazes me when I encounter someone living as if this life is an unending reality. Nothing is more obvious than the transitory nature of human life. The fact that this earthly tabernacle—the human body—is dissolving becomes obvious at an all too early age. This tent is being torn down. "In this tent we groan" (2 Corinthians 5:2). Moreover, "the whole creation has been groaning together in the pains of childbirth until now" (Romans 8:22). Nothing in this world is permanent. That should be obvious to anyone who contemplates the nature of things, even on the most superficial level.

There are many who mistakenly conclude that the brevity of life is a good justification for unbridled self-indulgence. After all, if there's nothing to life but what we can see and experience in the here and now, why not make the most of personal pleasure? A famous brewery used to advertise its beer by emphasizing the brevity of life: "You only go around once, so grab for all the gusto you can." In a similar vein a popular shoe company advertised, "Life is short. Play hard." How different that is from Jesus's advice to use this earthly life as an opportunity to lay up treasure in heaven!

But if this earthly life were the sum total of human existence, then our existence would be a tragic affair indeed. Nihilism would indeed be the only philosophy that would ultimately make sense: nothing would truly matter, so we might just as well try to gain all the pleasure and self-gratification we can from life before we die and return to nothingness.

As Christians, we naturally deplore that kind of hedonism and lament the despair it breeds. But let's acknowledge that a nihilistic worldview is the most clear and logical alternative to Christianity. If our existence is the product of nothing and will lead to nothing, then life itself is really nothing. Or (as one skeptic expressed it), we are just protoplasm waiting to become manure. If that is the case, then there's really no good reason we should not simply eat, drink, and be merry while we wait to die.

But Scripture tells us that is the worldview of a fool (Luke 12:19–20). How much better to have the eternal perspective! A pamphlet I once read related the following anecdote from the life of John Quincy Adams:

> One day in his 80th year . . . he was approached by a friend who said, "And how is John Quincy Adams today?"
>
> The former President of the United States replied graciously, "Thank you, John Quincy Adams is well, sir, quite well, I thank you. But the house in which he lives at present is becoming dilapidated. It is tottering upon its foundations. Time and the seasons have nearly destroyed it. Its roof is pretty well worn out, its walls are much shattered, and it trembles with every wind. The old tenement is becoming almost uninhabitable, and I think John Quincy Adams will have to move out of it soon; but he himself is quite well, sir, quite well." And with this the venerable statesman, leaning heavily upon his cane, moved slowly down the street.[1]

---

[1] Herbert H. Wernecke, *When Loved Ones Are Called Home* (Grand Rapids, MI: Baker, 1972), 17.

A New Building from God

Paul says that when the earthly tabernacle of our body is gone, we will receive a new building from God, eternal in the heavens. To complete 2 Corinthians 5:2, which I quoted in part a page or two earlier, "in this tent we groan, *longing to put on our heavenly dwelling.*" Romans 8:23 says that in heaven even our failing bodies will be redeemed—glorified. Christ himself "will transform our lowly body to be like his glorious body, by the power that enables him even to subject all things to himself" (Philippians 3:21). Our groaning will be ended when we are finally clothed with a heavenly body, with all the same amazing properties of Christ's resurrection body. (I'll have much more to say about that wonderful reality in chapter 7.)

A glorified body alone would be good reason to fix all our hopes and affections on heaven, wouldn't it? My dear friend Joni Eareckson Tada knows this as well as anyone. Her earthly body was paralyzed from the shoulders down when she dived into shallow water as a teenager. In recent years she has waged a battle against cancer. As long as I've known her, she has had her heart set on heaven. It shows in her conversation, her songs, her radio messages, and her artwork. Often it seems as if talking with her draws one to the very edge of heaven, where we can see in. Joni explains this in her book on the subject:

> I still can hardly believe it. I, with shriveled, bent fingers, atrophied muscles, gnarled knees, and no feeling from the shoulders down, will one day have a new body, light, bright, and clothed in righteousness— powerful and dazzling. . . .
>
> It's easy for me to "be joyful in hope," as it says in Romans 12:12, and that's exactly what I've been doing for the past twenty-odd years. My assurance of heaven is so alive that I've been making dates with friends to do all sorts of fun things once we get our new bodies. . . . I don't take these appointments lightly. I'm convinced these things will really happen.[2]

Whether or not the apostle Paul made appointments with people as he looked ahead to heaven, Scripture does not say. But clearly he had

---

[2] Joni Eareckson Tada, *Heaven* (Grand Rapids, MI: Zondervan, 1995), 53–55.

that very same kind of vivid expectation as he waited for heaven. Look again at these first few verses of 2 Corinthians 5:

> We know that if the tent that is our earthly home is destroyed, we have a building from God, a house not made with hands, eternal in the heavens. For in this tent we groan, longing to put on our heavenly dwelling, if indeed by putting it on we may not be found naked. For while we are still in this tent, we groan, being burdened—not that we would be unclothed, but that we would be further clothed, so that what is mortal may be swallowed up by life. (vv. 1–4)

In this body we groan because we are burdened by sin, sickness, sorrow, and death. Yet we don't want to be unclothed. In other words, we have no ambition to become disembodied spirits. *That's* not what we're yearning for. We want both our spirits and our bodies to enter the presence of God. And that is God's plan, too.

Some people have the notion that heaven is wholly ethereal, spiritual, and unreal. They envision it as a wispy, intangible existence in a dreamlike spiritual dimension. That is not the biblical conception of heaven. In heaven we will have real bodies—changed, glorified, made like Christ's resurrection body (Philippians 3:21)—bodies *more* solid than our current state, because they will not be subject to the effects of aging, injury, illness, or death. "This perishable body must put on the imperishable, and this mortal body must put on immortality. When the perishable puts on the imperishable, and the mortal puts on immortality, then shall come to pass the saying that is written: 'Death is swallowed up in victory'" (1 Corinthians 15:53–54). And when I get my glorified knees I already have an appointment to go for a long run with Joni Tada.

No Place like Home

Paul says, "He who has prepared us for this very thing is God, who has given us the Spirit as a guarantee" (2 Corinthians 5:5). The Greek word translated "guarantee" is *arrabōn*, the same word Paul used in Ephesians 1:14, also referring to the Holy Spirit. In modern Greek a form of this ancient word, *arrabōn*, is used to signify an engagement ring. In New Testament times it usually referred to a down payment or first installment on a debt—earnest money. So, the Holy Spirit is a token of God's pledge to us that even our bodies will be made new and imperishable in the glory of heaven.

Paul goes on to apply this truth in very practical terms: "So we are always of good courage. We know that while we are at home in the body we are away from the Lord, for we walk by faith, not by sight. Yes, we are of good courage, and we would rather be away from the body and at home with the Lord" (2 Corinthians 5:6–8). This world held no fascination for Paul. He longed for the world to come.

Do you find it difficult to say honestly that those verses express the deepest desires of your heart? There is a tendency for most of us to hold tightly to this world because it is all that we know. It is familiar to us. All our dearest relationships are built here. We too easily think of it as home. So we become captive to this life. But notice that Paul says he would rather be "at home" with the Lord. That is precisely what the Greek expression in the original text signifies. It is a form of the verb *endēmeo*, "to be at home." We are most truly "at home" only when we are finally with the Lord. Paul understood this. And the knowledge that he belonged in heaven was the very thing that helped him endure the struggles of this life.

We too should long to be clothed with our heavenly form. We should look forward to being absent from the body and present with the Lord. We should become more preoccupied with the glories of eternity than we are with the afflictions of today.

What Is Heaven?

The English Standard Version of the Bible employs the word *heaven* 493 times in 464 different verses. The Hebrew word usually translated "heaven," *shamayim*, is a plural noun form that literally means "the heights." The Greek word translated "heaven" is *ouranos* (the same word that inspired the name of the planet Uranus). It refers to that which is raised up, or lofty. Both *shamayim* and *ouranos* are used variously in Scripture to refer to three different places. (This explains why in 2 Corinthians 12:2 Paul refers to being caught up into "the *third* heaven.")

The closest heavenly realm to us, of course, is *the atmospheric heavens*. This is the sky, or the troposphere—the region of breathable atmosphere that blankets the earth. For example, Genesis 7:11–12, speaking of the flood in Noah's time, says, "The windows of the heavens were opened. And rain fell upon the earth forty days and forty nights." There the word "heaven" refers to the blanket of atmosphere around the world, which is where the hydrological cycle occurs. Psalm 147:8 says that God "covers the heavens with clouds; he prepares rain for the earth." That is the first heaven.

The planetary heavens, the second heavenly realm, is where the stars, the moon, and the planets are. Scripture uses the very same word for heaven to describe this region. For example, Genesis 1 says,

> And God said, "Let there be lights in the expanse of the heavens to separate the day from the night. And let them be for signs and for seasons, and for days and years, and let them be lights in the expanse of the heavens to give light upon the earth." And it was so. And God made the two great lights—the greater light to rule the day and the lesser light to rule the night—and the stars. And God set them in the expanse of the heavens to give light on the earth (vv. 14–17).

The third heaven, the one Paul speaks of in 2 Corinthians 12, is *the heaven where God dwells* with his holy angels and those saints who have died. The other heavens will completely pass away (2 Peter 3:10). This heaven is eternal. It is the realm where God dwelt before time began—a dimension outside our universe. In Deuteronomy 26:15, the Lord himself instructs the Israelites to address him in prayer with these words: "Look down from your holy habitation, from heaven." So this heaven is uniquely the realm of God.

Someone inevitably asks, If God is omnipresent, how can Scripture say heaven is his habitation? After all, how can an omnipresent being be said to dwell *anywhere*? Solomon, when dedicating the temple in Jerusalem, prayed, "Behold, heaven and the highest heaven cannot contain you; how much less this house that I have built!" (1 Kings 8:27).

It is certainly true that "heaven and the highest heaven" cannot *contain* God. He is omnipresent. There is no realm to which his presence does not reach and no place exists where he is absent. The psalmist, exalting God's omnipresence, said, "If I make my bed in Sheol [hell], you are there!" (Psalm 139:8).

So to say that God *dwells* in heaven is not to say that he *is contained* there. But it is uniquely his home, his center of operations, his command post. It is the place where his throne resides. And it is where the most perfect worship of him occurs. It is in that sense that we say heaven is his dwelling place.

This concept of heaven as the dwelling place of God runs throughout Scripture. In the Old Testament, for example, Isaiah 57:15 says, "Thus says the One who is high and lifted up, who inhabits eternity, whose name is Holy: '*I dwell in the high and holy place.*'" So God specifically declares that he has a real dwelling place. Isaiah 63:15 identifies that place: "Look down from heaven and see, from your holy and beautiful habitation." Psalm 33:13–14 says, "The LORD looks down from heaven; he sees all the children of man; from where he sits enthroned he looks out on all the inhabitants of the earth."

The same idea of heaven as God's dwelling place is stressed throughout the New Testament. In fact, it is a running theme in Jesus's Sermon on the Mount. Our Lord said, "Let your light shine before others, so that they may see your good works and give glory to your Father who is in heaven" (Matthew 5:16). He cautioned those who were prone to make oaths that they should not swear by heaven, "for it is the throne of God" (v. 34). And he instructs his hearers to love their enemies, "so that you may be sons of your Father who is in heaven" (v. 45). Matthew 6:1 says, "Beware of practicing your righteousness before other people in order to be seen by them, for then you will have no reward from your Father who is in heaven." He instructs his disciples to pray this way: "Our Father in heaven, hallowed be your name" (v. 9). Nearing the end of the Sermon, he says, "If you then, who are evil, know how to give good gifts to your children, how much more will *your Father who is in heaven* give good things to those who ask him!" (7:11). And, "Not everyone who says to me, 'Lord, Lord,' will enter the kingdom of heaven, but the one who does the will of my Father who is in heaven" (v. 21).

This same phrase echoes again and again in both the preaching and the private ministry of Jesus. Matthew 10:32–33 says, "everyone who acknowledges me before men, I also will acknowledge before my Father who is in heaven, but whoever denies me before men, I also will deny before my Father who is in heaven." Matthew 12:50 says, "For whoever does the will of my Father in heaven is my brother and sister and mother." Jesus said to Peter, "Blessed are you, Simon Bar-Jonah! For flesh and blood has not revealed this to you, but my Father who is in heaven" (Matthew 16:17). He compared believers to little children and warned people against causing offense to them: "See that you do not despise one of these little ones. For I tell you that in heaven their angels always see the face of my Father who is in heaven" (Matthew 18:10). He added, "So it is not the will of my Father who is in heaven that one of these little ones should perish" (v. 14). And, "Again I say to you, if two of you agree on earth about anything they ask, it will be done for them by my Father in heaven" (v. 19). He constantly referred to God as "my Father in heaven."

The concept of heaven as God's dwelling place is also implicit in the New Testament teaching about the deity and incarnation of Christ. He is described as "the bread of God . . . who comes down from heaven" (John 6:33). Christ's own claim of deity is implicit in this statement: "I have come down from heaven, not to do my own will but the will of him who sent me" (v. 38). He says of himself, "I am the bread that came down from heaven" (v. 41). Numerous times in John 6 alone he makes this same claim (vv. 50–51, 58). Those claims were correctly understood by Jesus's hearers as straightforward assertions that he is God.

In fact, heaven is so closely identified with God in the Jewish conception that it actually became a euphemism for God himself. *Heaven* was substituted for the name of God by people fearful of taking the Lord's name in vain. Particularly during the Intertestamental Period (the four hundred years between the events of the Old Testament and those of the New), the Jewish people developed an almost superstitious fear of using God's name. They believed the covenant name of God (*YHWH*, or as it has been anglicized, Jehovah) was too holy to pass through human lips. So they began substituting other terms in place of God's name, and "heaven" became a common substitute. By New Testament times that practice was so ingrained that the Jewish people understood most references to heaven as references to God himself.

Instead of swearing by God's name, for example, they would swear by heaven. And since "heaven" was merely a substitute reference to

God himself, Jesus pointed out that swearing by heaven was a *de facto* violation of the commandment not to take his name in vain. Thus in Matthew 23:22 he says, "whoever swears by heaven swears by the throne of God and by him who sits upon it." The word *heaven* stood for God himself.

Such usage is common in the New Testament. Luke refers to "the kingdom of God." But Matthew, writing to a predominantly Jewish readership, calls it "the kingdom of heaven" (cf. Luke 8:10; Matthew 13:11). We see another example of the use of *heaven* as a euphemism for God in Luke 15:18, for example, where the prodigal son, rehearsing what he would say to his Father, says, "I will arise and go to my father, and I will say to him, 'Father, I have sinned against heaven and before you.'" He meant, of course, that he had sinned *against God.*

Although the word *heaven* is often used this way in place of God's name, we must not conclude that Scripture intends to equate heaven with God himself. The terms are *not* synonyms. God transcends heaven. Heaven, in the end, is a *place.* It is the place where God dwells, the place where the elect will dwell with him for all eternity, the heaven of heavens—the third heaven.

The Realm of God's Kingdom

This is not to suggest that heaven is limited by the normal boundaries of time and space. We have seen where Scripture teaches clearly that heaven is a real place that can be seen and touched and inhabited by beings with material bodies. We affirm that truth unequivocally.

But Scripture also reveals heaven as a realm not confined to an area delimited by height, width, and breadth. Heaven seems to span all those dimensions—and more. In Christ's message to the Philadelphian church, for example, he speaks of the capital city of the eternal realm as "the city of my God, the new Jerusalem, which comes down from my God out of heaven" (Revelation 3:12). In the closing chapters of Scripture, the apostle John speaks of "the holy city Jerusalem coming down out of heaven from God" (Revelation 21:10). The new heavens and new earth are seen blending together in a great kingdom that incorporates both realms. The paradise of eternity is thus revealed as a magnificent kingdom where both heaven and earth unite in a glory that surpasses the limits of the human imagination and the boundaries of earthly dimensions.

So heaven is not confined to one locality marked off by boundaries that can be seen or measured. It transcends the confines of time-space dimensions. Perhaps that is part of what Scripture means when it states that God inhabits eternity (Isaiah 57:15). His dwelling place—heaven—is not subject to the normal limitations of finite dimensions. We don't need to speculate about *how* this can be; it is sufficient to note that this is how Scripture describes heaven. It is a real place where people with physical bodies will dwell in God's presence for all eternity; and it is also a realm that surpasses our finite concept of what a "place" is.

There's another important sense in which heaven transcends normal time-space dimensions. According to Scripture, in a very real sense the kingdom of God—incorporating all the elements of heaven itself—is the spiritual sphere in which all true Christians live even now. The kingdom of heaven invades and begins to govern the life of every believer in Christ. Spiritually, the Christian enters into heaven with full rights of citizenship here and now, in this life.

That's exactly what Paul was saying when he wrote, "our citizenship is in heaven" (Philippians 3:20). There's a positional sense in which we who believe are already living in the kingdom of God.

In Ephesians 1:3 the apostle Paul says that God "has blessed us in Christ with every spiritual blessing *in the heavenly places*." Ephesians 2:5–6 likewise says, "even when we were dead in our trespasses, [God] made us alive together with Christ . . . and raised us up with him and seated us with him in the heavenly places in Christ Jesus." Note that in both passages, the verbs are past tense. Paul is speaking of an already accomplished reality. We aren't yet in heaven bodily. But in terms of our spiritual privileges and our standing before God, it is as if we were already seated with Christ in the heavenlies. Because of our spiritual union with him, we have already entered into the heavenly realm. We possess eternal life here and now, and the spiritual riches of heaven are fully ours in Jesus Christ.

Christ himself preached that the kingdom of heaven is at hand (Matthew 4:17). Yet he said to those who demanded to know when the *visible* kingdom would come, "The kingdom of God is not coming in ways that can be observed, nor will they say, 'Look, here it is!' or 'There!' for behold, the kingdom of God is in the midst of you" (Luke 17:20–21).

Think about this: heaven is where holiness, fellowship with God, joy, peace, love, and all other virtues are realized in utter perfection. But we can experience all those things—at least partially—even now. The Holy Spirit (the divine down payment on our inheritance) is producing in us the fruit of "love, joy, peace, patience, kindness, goodness, faithfulness, gentleness, self-control" (Galatians 5:22–23). Again, those are the same traits that characterize heaven—heavenly fruit.

Moreover, we have the life of God in us and the rule of God over us. We have been given blessings and stature befitting true citizens of heaven. We have become part of a new family, a new kind of community. We have left the kingdom of darkness for the kingdom of light. We are no longer under the dominion of Satan but have entered God's eternal kingdom alongside Christ. Second Corinthians 5:17 says, "If anyone is in Christ, he is a new creation. The old has passed away; behold, the new has come." We are among the firstfruits of God's new creation (James 1:18), which will culminate in the eternal new heavens and new earth. *That's* what Jesus meant when he said, "The kingdom of God is within you" (Luke 17:21, KJV).

Christ was not denying the reality of a literal, visible, earthly kingdom where he will reign over all the nations. Too many prophecies in both the Old and New Testaments affirm that such a kingdom will one day exist. Nor was he suggesting that heaven is not a real *place*. He was simply teaching that heaven transcends all time-space limitations. He was focusing the Pharisees' attention on the important reality of seeking the heavenly kingdom right here and now. Immediate entrance to the kingdom is the very thing the gospel message offers. That's why it is so often called "this gospel of the kingdom" (cf. Matthew 24:14).

When Jesus preached, he called people to enter the kingdom (Luke 13:24). Sometimes he urged people to be saved (John 5:34). And other times he spoke of inheriting eternal life (Mark 10:30). All three expressions come together in the account of the rich young ruler. He asked Jesus, "Good Teacher, what must I do *to inherit eternal life?*" (Luke 18:18). When the young man turned away without believing, Jesus said, "How difficult it is for those who have wealth *to enter the kingdom of God!*" (v. 24). And the disciples, shocked at what had transpired, asked, "Then who can *be saved?*" (v. 26). All three expressions point to the reality that occurs at conversion. When a person trusts Christ, that person is saved, inherits eternal life, and enters into the kingdom of God. Believers come under God's rule and authority, not physically in heaven, but in every spiritual sense the influence of Christ's government extends to them.

So while we do not yet live physically in heaven, we do have our spiritual citizenship in the heavenly realm. Therefore we should be preoccupied with heavenly things.

Hearts in Heaven

That is the whole point of this study. If my purpose were merely to dispel earthly myths about heaven, I could fill not just a few appendixes, but several volumes, with biblical rebuttals of the claims found in today's best sellers. It is certainly crucial that we recognize the dangers of the gnostic approach to heaven and turn away from it.

But we dare not stop there. We must also seek to understand the *biblical* concept of heaven. We are commanded to contemplate heaven, to pursue it the way Abraham sought the city of God, to fix our affections there.

This means earnestly purging worldliness from our hearts. It means learning to wean ourselves from the preoccupations of this life. It means looking ahead to eternity and living in the expectation of a sure and certain hope. It means looking away from the mundane and temporal, and fixing our eyes steadfastly on him who *is* the glory and the centerpiece of heaven.

Those who live with this heavenly perspective discover abundant life as God intended it here on earth. Ironically, those who pursue earthly comforts are really the most *un*comfortable people on earth. As the Puritan theologian Richard Baxter wrote,

> A heavenly mind is a joyful mind; this is the nearest and truest way to live a life of comfort, and without this you must needs be uncomfortable. Can a man be at a fire and not be warm; or in the sunshine and not have light? Can your heart be in heaven, and not have comfort?

[On the other hand,] what could make such frozen, uncomfortable Christians but living so far as they do from heaven? . . . O Christian get above. Believe it, that region is warmer than this below.[3]

Baxter went on to write,

There is no man so highly honoureth God, as he who hath his conversation in heaven; and without this we deeply dishonour him. Is it not a disgrace to the father, when the children do feed on husks, and are clothed in rags, and accompany with none but beggars? Is it not so to our Father, when we who call ourselves his children, shall feed on earth, and the garb of our souls be but like that of the naked world, and when our hearts shall make this clay and dust their more familiar and frequent company, who should always stand in our Father's presence, and be taken up in his own attendance? Sure, it beseems not the spouse of Christ to live among his scullions and slaves, when they may have daily admittance into his presence-chamber; he holds forth the sceptre, if they will but enter.[4]

Unfamiliarity with heaven makes a dull and worldly Christian. God has graciously bid us sample the delights of the world to come, and it is only a rebellious and perverse mind-set that keeps us mired in the mundane and worldly. God has given us a down payment on heaven. He has transferred our citizenship there. We "are no longer strangers and aliens, but . . . are fellow citizens with the saints and members of the household of God" (Ephesians 2:19). We therefore *cannot* ignore heaven's glory as if it had no significance. In Baxter's words, "There is nothing else that is worth setting our hearts on."[5]

I know few truths in Scripture that are more liberating to the soul than this: "Our citizenship is in heaven, and from it we await a Savior, the Lord Jesus Christ, who will transform our lowly body to be like his glorious body, by the power that enables him even to subject all things to himself" (Philippians 3:20–21).

That is where our hearts should be. The cares of this world are nothing but a snare and a deadly pit. Jesus characterized "the cares

[3] Richard Baxter, *The Saints' Everlasting Rest*, abridged by John T. Wilkinson (1650; repr., London: Epworth, 1962), 110.
[4] Ibid., 118.
[5] Ibid., 121.

of the world and the deceitfulness of riches and the desires for other things" as unholy diversions that "enter in and choke the word, and it proves unfruitful" (Mark 4:19). Similarly, the apostle John writes, "All that is in the world—the desires of the flesh and the desires of the eyes and pride of life—is not from the Father but is from the world" (1 John 2:16).

"But we have the mind of Christ" (1 Corinthians 2:16). We can fix our hearts on the eternal glory of heaven, not on the things of this world, which inevitably come to naught anyway (1 John 2:17). We are members of a new family, having become the children of God (John 1:12). Galatians 4:26 says that "the Jerusalem above is free, and she is our mother." We have a new citizenship (Philippians 3:20), new affections (Colossians 3:2, kjv), and a new storehouse where we are to deposit our treasures (Matthew 6:19–20).

Best of all, we can live in the glow of heaven's glory here and now, with our hearts already in heaven. This is to say that the Christian life is meant to be a foretaste of heaven on earth. Believers can daily partake of the sweet, satisfying benefits of the same heaven to which someday we will go to dwell forever. Praising and loving God with all our being, adoring and obeying Christ, pursuing holiness, cherishing fellowship with other saints—those are just some of the elements of heavenly life believers already savor in this world. Those same pursuits and privileges will occupy us forever, but as we see the fruit of the Holy Spirit come to maturity in our lives, we should begin to enjoy and treasure the goodness of heaven in a very full sense even now.

5

What Heaven
Will Be Like

Gustav Mahler's Fourth Symphony is based on a poem that describes heaven from a child's point of view. The music certainly *sounds* heavenly. The symphony's fourth movement features a soprano singing the German words to the poem *"Das himmlische Leben"*—"The Heavenly Life." English listeners might simply be moved by the serene beauty of the music. But the German words paint a peculiar picture of heaven.

In the first place, the inhabitants of Mahler's heaven are voracious carnivores. The poem speaks of Herod as a butcher who kills unsuspecting little lambs so that the inhabitants of heaven can eat all they want. The oxen are so plentiful that St. Luke slaughters them "without giving it a thought." Angels are there, baking bread. And "if you want roebuck or hare, on the public streets they come running right up."

The lyrics also have the inhabitants of heaven jumping and skipping and singing—but mostly gorging themselves on an endless supply of food. Saint Peter catches fish from the heavenly pond, and Saint Martha (still "distracted with much serving," apparently) must be the cook.

So this child's vision of heaven turns out to be another "paradise" where earthly appetites are indulged.

I'm intrigued by the way the unbelieving world portrays heaven. At one end of the spectrum is this view that heaven exists to gratify earthly lusts. At the other is a cynical suspicion that heaven will be unbearably monotonous. The classic cartoon caricature pictures heaven's inhabitants sitting on clouds and playing harps. I don't know if anyone really imagines heaven will be like that, but I have no doubt that many people think of heaven as a bland, boring place with nothing enjoyable to do.

A skeptic once told me, "I'd rather be in hell with my friends than in heaven with all the church people." Such a flippant attitude betrays a tragic lack of regard for the horrors of hell. More than that, it grossly underestimates the blessedness of heaven.

This deep-seated suspicion that heaven may be an eternal bore reflects the sinful thinking of fallen minds. As sinners we are naturally prone to think a little sin is surely more enjoyable than perfect righteousness. It is hard for us to imagine a realm wholly devoid of sin and yet filled with pure and endless pleasures.

But that is exactly how heaven will be. We will bask in the glory of God, realizing at last our chief end—to glorify God and to *enjoy* him forever. The psalmist wrote, "In your presence there is fullness of joy; at your right hand are pleasures forevermore" (Psalm 16:11).

Such a thought is unfathomable to our finite minds. But Scripture repeatedly makes clear that heaven is a realm of unsurpassed joy, unfading glory, undiminished bliss, unlimited delights, and unending pleasures. Nothing about eternal glory can possibly be boring or humdrum. It will be a perfect existence. We will have unbroken fellowship with all heaven's inhabitants. Life there will be devoid of any sorrows, cares, tears, fears, or pain. "Everlasting joy shall be upon their heads; they shall obtain gladness and joy, and sorrow and sighing shall flee away" (Isaiah 35:10). God himself "will wipe away every tear from their eyes, and death shall be no more, neither shall there be mourning, nor crying, nor pain anymore, for the former things have passed away. And he who was seated on the throne said, 'Behold, I am making all things new.' Also he said, 'Write this down, for these words are trustworthy and true'" (Revelation 21:4–5).

The best of our spiritual experiences here on earth are only small samples of heaven. Our highest spiritual heights, the profoundest of all our joys, and the greatest of our spiritual blessings will be normal in heaven. As we live now in the heavenlies, we are merely tasting the glories of the life to come. When we consider that Christ prayed that all who know him would spend eternity with him in unbroken fellowship (John 17:24), our hearts should overflow with gratitude and expectation.

The preacher of Ecclesiastes said that the day of our death is better than the day of our birth (7:1). He was merely being cynical about the meaninglessness and futility of this earthly life, but there is a valid sense for the Christian in which it is true that our death ushers us into an infinitely greater glory than our birth ever did. This earthly life "is few of days and full of trouble" (Job 14:1). The confidence that heaven awaits us should fill us with a glorious hope. Paul said, "For to me to live is Christ, and to die is gain" (Philippians 1:21). The prospect of heaven made him joyful even in the face of death.

Absent from the Body, Present with the Lord

Paul also said he "would rather be away from the body and at home with the Lord" (2 Corinthians 5:8). This was not a morbid death wish on Paul's part. He was not saying he was burnt out, fed up with living, and eager to die. Rather, he was expressing his confidence that earthly existence is not the end of life at all for the Christian. Death immediately ushers the believer into a fuller, higher realm of more abundant life—in the very presence of the Lord.

If you are a Christian, someone trusting Christ alone for your salvation, Scripture promises that the moment you leave this life you will go to heaven. To be absent from the body is to be present with the Lord. To depart this life is to "be with Christ" (Philippians 1:23). The righteous man who dies "is taken away from calamity; he enters into peace" (Isaiah 57:1–2). "Blessed are the dead who die in the Lord. . . . [They] rest from their labors" (Revelation 14:13). Indeed, "to live is Christ, and to die is gain" (Philippians 1:21).

We need to have a heart like Paul's—yearning to be clothed with our heavenly form and to exchange this transient world for eternal joy. He wrote, "This perishable body must put on the imperishable, and this mortal body must put on immortality." (1 Corinthians 15:53). Our mortality will be swallowed up by a more abundant life (2 Corinthians 5:4).

Someone inevitably asks about the state of believers who die between now and the final consummation of all things. Do believers who die receive temporary bodies between now and the resurrection? What is the intermediate state like? Are there compartments within heaven? Where did Old Testament believers go when they died? And what about purgatory?

Some Wrong Views

A number of speculative views have been proposed to attempt to answer those questions. With regard to the state of Old Testament believers, for example, some teach that in the Old Testament, Hades (the realm of the dead) was divided into two sections—one for the wicked and one for the righteous. They suggest that Old Testament saints who died went to the realm called "Abraham's side" (cf. Luke 16:22–23)—a sort of heavenly holding tank. According to this theory, these believers were kept in that compartment of Hades and not brought into the heaven of heavens until Christ conquered death in his resurrection.

Most of that is sheer conjecture with little if any real biblical support. Wilbur Smith writes, "However abundant the Scriptural data might be regarding the resurrection of believers and their life in heaven, the state of the soul between death and resurrection is rarely referred to in the Bible."[1] Scripture simply does not give much information about the intermediate state. But what we do know from Scripture is enough to debunk some of the wrong theories.

SOUL SLEEP. One view held by many is that the soul of a believer who dies remains unconscious until the resurrection. This view is found in some of the noncanonical writings of the early church. Its best-known advocates today are the Seventh-Day Adventists. They point out that the word "sleep" is often used in Scripture as a synonym for death. For example, Jesus told the disciples, "Our friend Lazarus has fallen asleep, but I go to awaken him" (John 11:11). And Paul described the dead in Christ as "those who have fallen asleep" (1 Thessalonians 4:14).

But the "sleep" referred to in such imagery has to do with the body, not the soul. In his account of the crucifixion, Matthew wrote

---

[1] Wilbur M. Smith, *The Biblical Doctrine of Heaven* (Chicago: Moody, 1968), 155.

of a great earthquake: "The tombs also were opened. And many bodies of the saints who had fallen asleep were raised" (Matthew 27:52). It is the *body*, not the soul, that "sleeps" in death. The body lies in rest utterly devoid of any sensation or awareness. But the soul enters the very presence of the Lord. This was affirmed again and again by the apostle Paul in the verses I cited above, as he described his desire to be absent from the body, so that he could be "away from the body and at home with the Lord" (2 Corinthians 5:8).

The souls of the departed enter into their rest. But it is a rest from labor and strife, not a rest of unconsciousness. The apostle John said of the righteous dead that they "rest from their labors" (Revelation 14:13). Yet he is clearly not describing a "rest" of unconscious sleep; in the scene John witnessed in heaven, the souls of the redeemed were there, actively singing and praising God (vv. 1–4).

Everything Scripture says about the death of believers indicates that they are immediately ushered consciously into the Lord's presence. In the words of the Westminster Confession of Faith, "The bodies of men after death return to dust, and see corruption; but their souls, (which neither die nor sleep,) having an immortal subsistence, immediately return to God who gave them. The souls of the righteous, being then made perfect in holiness, are received into the highest heavens, where they behold the face of God in light and glory, waiting for the full redemption of their bodies" (32.1).

PURGATORY. The Roman Catholic doctrine of purgatory is nowhere taught in Scripture. It was devised to accommodate Catholicism's denial of justification by faith alone. Here's why:

Scripture very clearly teaches that an absolutely *perfect* righteousness is necessary for entry into heaven. Jesus said, "I tell you, unless your righteousness exceeds that of the scribes and Pharisees, you will never enter the kingdom of heaven" (Matthew 5:20). He then added, "You therefore must be perfect, as your heavenly Father is perfect" (v. 48)—thus setting the standard as high as it can possibly be set.

Later in his ministry, when the rich young ruler approached Jesus asking how he might enter heaven, Jesus upheld this same standard of absolute perfection. He began by challenging the clear implication that the young man hoped he could attain a sufficient goodness of his own to merit heaven: "Why do you ask me about what is good? There is only one who is good" (Matthew 19:17). Notice: Jesus did not disclaim that he himself was sinlessly perfect (a lot of people misread this passage as if that's what Jesus was saying). He was simply pointing out plainly that the standard of perfection required to earn heaven is impossible for fallen creatures.

Because the young man was clearly undeterred by this, however, Jesus told him that in order to obtain eternal life, he must have a track record of perfect obedience to the law (vv. 17–21). Again and again, he made the required standard of righteousness impossibly high for all who would seek to earn God's favor on their own.

The young ruler clearly did not understand or acknowledge his own sinfulness. He assured Jesus that he had indeed kept the law from his youth up (v. 20).

Jesus subtly pointed out the young man's covetousness, which was a violation of the tenth commandment. From the outset of his conversation with the young man, the Lord was prodding him to confess that no one but God himself is truly *good*. But the rich young ruler was unwilling to face his own sin, and so he finally went away without salvation.

The disciples marveled at this. The young man was evidently— from the human perspective—one of the most righteous individuals they knew. Notice that no one disputed his claim that he had obeyed the law. There must have been no overt sins in his life that anyone could point to. He was the best of men. So the disciples were floored when he walked away with no assurance of eternal life from Jesus. In fact, Jesus told them as emphatically as possible, "Truly, I say to you, only with difficulty will a rich person enter the kingdom of heaven. Again I tell you, it is easier for a camel to go through the eye of a needle than for a rich person to enter the kingdom of God" (v. 23).

There's no mistaking Jesus's point. He was setting the standard at an impossible height. He was saying that the most fastidious legal observance is not enough. The most flawless external righteousness is not enough. All the worldly advantages of wealth are of no help. Only *absolute perfection* is acceptable to God. Our Lord kept underscoring these things because he wanted people to see the utter futility of trying to earn righteousness by any system of works.

The disciples got the message. They asked, "Who then can be saved?" (v. 25).

And Jesus replied, "With man this is impossible, but with God all things are possible" (v. 26).

We know from Paul's treatise on justification in Romans 4 that God saves believers *by imputing to them the merit of Christ's perfect righteousness*—not in any sense because of their own righteousness. God accepts believers "in Christ." He clothes them with the perfect righteousness of Christ. He declares them perfectly righteous because of Christ. Their sins have been imputed to Christ, who has paid the full penalty. His righteousness is now imputed to them, and they receive the full merit for it. That is what justification by faith means. "For our sake [the Father] made [Christ] to be sin who knew no sin, so that *in him* we might become the righteousness of God" (2 Corinthians 5:21).

In other words, God does not first make us perfect, then accept us on that basis. He *first* legally justifies us by imputing to us an alien righteousness, *then* perfects us by conforming us to the image of Christ. He "justifies the ungodly" (Romans 4:5).

Paul wrote, "Therefore, since we have been justified [past tense] by faith, we have peace with God through our Lord Jesus Christ" (Romans 5:1). And, "There is therefore now [present tense] no condemnation for those who are in Christ Jesus" (Romans 8:1). Those verses describe our justification as something already accomplished. It is a completed reality, not something we are striving for. Jesus himself described justification as an immediate event when he told how the repentant publican was saved after begging God for mercy: "I tell you, this man went down to his house justified"—past tense (Luke 18:14).

Scripture clearly and consistently deals with justification as a settled fact for every believer; it is not an ongoing process. We stand before God in faith right now, fully acceptable to him because of Christ's righteousness—not because of any doings of our own.

Roman Catholic doctrine denies all that. Catholicism teaches that justification is an ongoing process that depends on the degree of real, personal righteousness we achieve. According to Rome, Christ's merit imputed to us is not sufficient to save; we must earn more merit of our own through the sacraments and other good works. Righteousness is *infused* into us (rather than being imputed to us). But it is obvious that we are not perfectly righteous by any practical measure. So the righteousness we obtain by grace must be perfected by our own efforts. According to Catholic teaching, this real, personal righteousness that resides in us is the necessary ground on which God accepts us. And our justification is not complete until we are really and completely perfect—by an inherent righteousness, not merely by a legally imputed righteousness. This actually reverses the biblical order, suggesting that we must *first* be perfected, and only *then* is our justification complete. In other words, in Roman Catholic doctrine, God does not justify the ungodly.

The Catholic view of justification poses an obvious dilemma. We know too well that even the best Christians fall far short of perfection. No one (Catholic teaching actually says *almost* no one) achieves absolute perfection in this life. And if our own perfection is a prerequisite to heaven, it would seem no one could enter heaven immediately upon death. Any remaining imperfections would need to be worked out first.

The doctrine of purgatory is necessary to solve this dilemma. Deny that we are justified by faith alone, and you must devise an explanation of how we can make the transition from our imperfect state in this life to the perfect state of heaven. Purgatory is where Roman Catholics believe most people go after death to be finally purged of their remaining guilt and gain whatever merit they may be lacking to enter heaven. Catholicism teaches that this will involve intense pain and suffering.

Oddly enough, although Catholic doctrine denies that the imputed righteousness of Christ is sufficient to save sinners in this life, it does allow the imputation of righteousness from earthly sinners to those in purgatory. That is why Masses are said for the dead. Supposedly the righteousness earned by way of the sacrament is imputed to the person in purgatory, and that shortens his or her stay there.

The Biblical Response

As I have said, none of this is taught in Scripture. The sufferings of Christ were fully sufficient to atone for our sins. Our own sufferings can add nothing to the merit of Christ. As the writer of Hebrews says, there is no efficacious sacrifice for sin other than what Christ has provided. If Christ's sacrifice is not sufficient, or if we willfully turn away from it, "there no longer remains a sacrifice for sins, but a fearful expectation of judgment, and a fury of fire that will consume the adversaries" (Hebrews 10:26–27).

For all believers, because we are fully justified, there can be no condemnation. No postmortem suffering is necessary to atone for remaining sin; *all* our sins are covered by the blood of Christ. No merit is lacking that must be made up. Every believer will be able to say with the prophet Isaiah, "I will greatly rejoice in the LORD; my soul shall exult in my God, for he has clothed me with the garments of salvation; he has covered me with the robe of righteousness, as a bridegroom decks himself like a priest with a beautiful headdress, and as a bride adorns herself with her jewels" (Isaiah 61:10).

Some claim that 1 Corinthians 3 describes purgatory, where the believer is put through a fiery judgment to purge out the dross of sin. But read that passage again. It describes the judgment of the believer's *works*, to see if they are "wood, hay, straw" or "gold, silver, precious stones" (v. 12). At issue is whether our works endure or are burned up. And it is the works, not the saints themselves, that are tested in the purging fire. This is the judgment that will take place in the eschatological future at the judgment seat of Christ. It is not describing an ongoing state of purgatory that believers pass through on their way to heaven:

> Each one's work will become manifest, for the Day will disclose it, because it will be revealed by fire, and the fire will test what sort of work each one has done. If the work that anyone has built on the foundation survives, he will receive a reward. If anyone's work is burned up, he will suffer loss, though *he himself will be saved, but only as through fire.* (vv. 13–15).

Notice again, that only the works, not the believers themselves, must go through the fire. Also note that rewards are what is at issue—not entrance to heaven.

Everything in Scripture indicates that the believer's entrance to heaven occurs immediately upon death. Let's examine a few key passages:

PSALM 16. Here we find the psalmist hopeful even as he faced death: "You will not abandon my soul to Sheol, or let your holy one see corruption. You make known to me the path of life; in your presence there is fullness of joy; at your right hand are pleasures forevermore" (vv. 10–11). The psalmist anticipated that when he left this world, he would enter the presence of God, finding eternal pleasure and fullness of joy. He had no fear of purgatorial sufferings. And he left no place for the notion of soul sleep.

PSALM 23. The final verse of this familiar psalm says, "Surely goodness and mercy shall follow me all the days of my life, and I shall dwell in the house of the LORD forever." David was certain that once his life was over, he would dwell for all eternity in the house of the Lord (which in this context can refer only to heaven). Notice that he goes immediately from "all the days of my life" to "dwell[ing] in the house of the LORD." The hope he expresses here is exactly the same as Paul's: to "be away from the body and at home with the Lord" (2 Corinthians 5:8).

LUKE 16. When the beggar Lazarus died, Jesus says he "was carried by the angels to Abraham's side" (v. 22). As we noted earlier, some think this expression "Abraham's side" describes a sort of holding tank where Old Testament saints went while awaiting heaven. That seems an unnecessary imposition on the text. Based on the psalmist's statements, there is no reason to doubt that Old Testament saints went directly to heaven. I believe both Abraham and Lazarus were in the presence of God. In any case, this account rules out both soul sleep and purgatory.

To shed light on the expression "Abraham's side," we turn to a parallel expression that occurs in John 13. This is part of the apostle John's description of that final Passover celebration in the upper room. He writes, "One of his disciples, whom Jesus loved, was reclining at table at Jesus' side" (v. 23). The scene is a low table, where guests had to recline. Verse 25 says "that disciple, leaning back against Jesus," asked who the betrayer would be. This disciple (who we know was John himself—John 21:20, 24) was clearly in a position so that his head was near Jesus's side. Tables in that culture were very low, and reclining was a typical position for people who were sharing a meal.

So when Jesus says Lazarus was carried to "Abraham's side," he indicates that the former beggar was reclining at a banquet table in a celebration of joy, next to Abraham, the father of the faithful. In other words, Lazarus was in the guest of honor's place. Imagine the dismay of the Pharisees when Jesus portrayed an ordinary beggar reclining at the table next to the greatest of the Jewish Fathers!

Again, I'm convinced we are supposed to understand this as heaven, not some kind of holding chamber remote from God's celestial throne and adjacent to hell. Scripture never suggests Old Testament believers went to temporary quarters in the realm of the dead to wait for Christ to carry them into glory. In fact, the evidence points to a different conclusion.

MATTHEW 17. For example, when Christ was transfigured, Moses and Elijah appeared with him (v. 3). Remember, Elijah had been caught up bodily to heaven (2 Kings 2:1, 11). Moses and Elijah were summoned from there to the Mount of Transfiguration, where they conversed with Jesus about "his departure, which he was about to accomplish at Jerusalem" (Luke 9:31). Obviously, Christ's death and resurrection hadn't yet occurred, so if Old Testament saints were being kept in a place of confinement, that is where Moses would have needed to be brought from.

It seems obvious that Moses had not been shut away for ages in some intermediate compartment of Hades. He was intimately familiar with Christ, a partaker of his glory, and knowledgeable enough about his earthly work to discuss the details of what he was about to do. This is an amazing passage, a clear window into the kind of close fellowship we will share with Christ in eternity.

LUKE 23. This familiar text describes that touching moment during the crucifixion when one of the thieves next to Jesus repented. "He said, 'Jesus, remember me when you come into your kingdom.'

And he said to him, 'Truly, I say to you, today you will be with me in Paradise'" (vv. 42–43).

The word translated "Paradise" in the Greek text is exactly the same word the apostle Paul uses to describe the third heaven in 2 Corinthians 12:3. *Paradise* is a synonym for heaven. It cannot be a reference to purgatory. And the promise of Paradise *today* rules out not only purgatory, but soul sleep as well.

If anyone were a candidate for purgatory, this thief certainly would have been. Moments before, he had taunted Christ along with the unrepentant thief (Mark 15:32). His repentance was a last-minute change—while he was literally in his death throes. Yet Jesus promised to see him that very day in Paradise.

Biblical Glimpses of Heaven

Scripture contains many descriptions of heaven. Some of them are cast in apocalyptic language filled with symbolism and mystery. Apocalyptic symbolism in Scripture always means that something of great consequence is under discussion. Don't make the error of thinking symbolic language means the thing described is unreal. As we have already established, the Bible asserts that heaven is a real place. And the descriptions of heaven, even the most apocalyptic ones, describe a real place.

Ezekiel's Wheel

One of the most dramatic descriptions of heaven in all Scripture comes from the prophet Ezekiel. Ezekiel was wonderfully transported to the very heart of heaven in a vision, and he describes in vivid detail what heaven and the throne room of God are like.

Here is Ezekiel 1 in its totality:

> In the thirtieth year, in the fourth month, on the fifth day of the month, as I was among the exiles by the Chebar canal, the heavens were opened, and I saw visions of God. On the fifth day of the month (it was the fifth year of the exile of King Jehoiachin), the word of the LORD came to Ezekiel the priest, the son of Buzi, in the land of the Chaldeans by the Chebar canal, and the hand of the LORD was upon him there.

As I looked, behold, a stormy wind came out of the north, and a great cloud, with brightness around it, and fire flashing forth continually, and in the midst of the fire, as it were gleaming metal. And from the midst of it came the likeness of four living creatures. And this was their appearance: they had a human likeness, but each had four faces, and each of them had four wings. Their legs were straight, and the soles of their feet were like the sole of a calf's foot. And they sparkled like burnished bronze. Under their wings on their four sides they had human hands. And the four had their faces and their wings thus: their wings touched one another. Each one of them went straight forward, without turning as they went. As for the likeness of their faces, each had a human face. The four had the face of a lion on the right side, the four had the face of an ox on the left side, and the four had the face of an eagle. Such were their faces. And their wings were spread out above. Each creature had two wings, each of which touched the wing of another, while two covered their bodies. And each went straight forward. Wherever the spirit would go, they went, without turning as they went. As for the likeness of the living creatures, their appearance was like burning coals of fire, like the appearance of torches moving to and fro among the living creatures. And the fire was bright, and out of the fire went forth lightning. And the living creatures darted to and fro, like the appearance of a flash of lightning.

Now as I looked at the living creatures, I saw a wheel on the earth beside the living creatures, one for each of the four of them. As for the appearance of the wheels and their construction: their appearance was like the gleaming of beryl. And the four had the same likeness, their appearance and construction being as it were a wheel within a wheel. When they went, they went in any of their four directions without turning as they went. And their rims were tall and awesome, and the rims of all four were full of eyes all around. And when the living creatures went, the wheels went beside them; and when the living creatures rose from the earth, the wheels rose. Wherever the spirit wanted to go, they went, and the wheels rose along with them, for the spirit of the living creatures was in the wheels. When those went, these went; and when those stood, these stood; and when those rose from the earth, the wheels rose along with them, for the spirit of the living creatures was in the wheels.

Over the heads of the living creatures there was the likeness of an expanse, shining like awe-inspiring crystal, spread out above their heads. And under the expanse their wings were stretched out straight, one toward another. And each creature had two wings covering its body. And when they went, I heard the sound of their wings like the sound of many waters, like the sound of the Almighty, a sound of tumult like the sound of an army. When they stood still, they let down their wings. And there came a voice from above the expanse over their heads. When they stood still, they let down their wings.

And above the expanse over their heads there was the likeness of a throne, in appearance like sapphire; and seated above the likeness of a throne was a likeness with a human appearance. And upward from what had the appearance of his waist I saw as it were gleaming metal, like the appearance of fire enclosed all around. And downward from what had the appearance of his waist I saw as it were the appearance of fire, and there was brightness around him. Like the appearance of the bow that is in the cloud on the day of rain, so was the appearance of the brightness all around.

Such was the appearance of the likeness of the glory of the LORD. And when I saw it, I fell on my face, and I heard the voice of one speaking.

That is Ezekiel's description of God's throne in heaven. We can't fully understand all he described, and neither did he. But under the inspiration of the Holy Spirit he attempted to describe what he saw: blazing light reflected off polished jewels and colored wheels of light mingled with angelic beings (the "living beings"). Around the throne of the eternal, glorious God, he saw a flashing, sparkling, spinning rainbow of brilliance.

How do we interpret such mysterious language? Some strive to find meaning in every facet of Ezekiel's vision. (One source I consulted, for example, explains the faces of the angelic creatures like this: the lion refers to majesty and power; the man represents intelligence and will; the ox stands for patient service, and the eagle speaks of swift judgment.) But we must be cautious not to get carried away reading meaning into symbols that are not explained to us. This is not a secret message to be decoded; it is a large picture designed to display the sovereignty, majesty, and glory of God and the incredible beauty, symmetry, and perfection of his heaven. Although it's impossible to interpret the specifics definitively, we *can* understand that Ezekiel's aim was to put the glory of heaven on display. The wheels that moved in concert, the flashing lightning, the sparkling jewels, and the brilliant light—all picture God's glory.

So although Ezekiel's picture of heaven may be beyond our ability to fathom, we can certainly grasp the main idea: heaven is a realm of inexpressible glory.

John's Apocalypse

We return now to John's extended vision of heaven as it is described in the book of Revelation. As we saw in chapter 3, the book of Revelation is the story of how God's wrath will finally be poured out upon the earth. Evil will be conquered forever and vanquished from the universe. It is a graphic and troubling vision, not primarily a lesson about heaven.

Still, we learn a lot about heaven from John's vision. The Greek word translated "heaven" occurs more than fifty times in the book of Revelation. Twice God is called "the God of heaven" (11:13; 16:11)—a phrase used twenty-two times in the Old Testament. The entire book of Revelation is written from heaven's perspective, though it deals largely with events that occur on earth.

There are many striking similarities between John's vision and Ezekiel's. John's is a fuller account, of course, but it blends beautifully with what Ezekiel described. The throne of God figures large in both accounts.

In Revelation 4, where John describes how he was caught up into heaven, the very first thing he mentions is God's throne: "After this I looked, and behold, a door standing open in heaven! And the first voice, which I had heard speaking to me like a trumpet, said, 'Come up here, and I will show you what must take place after this.' At once I was in the Spirit, and behold, a throne stood in heaven, with one seated on the throne" (vv. 1–2).

Ezekiel ended his vision of heaven with a description of the throne and the inexplicable glory that emanates from it. John *begins* by describing that same throne. Repeatedly in this passage he mentions the throne, which is the hub of all heaven and the focal point of God's presence. From the throne of God emanates all the glory of heaven.

Verse 3 says, "He who sat there had the appearance of jasper and carnelian." Jasper is an opaque, translucent crystalline quartz of differing colors, especially shades of green. (But the jasper of ancient times may actually have been a transparent stone.) The word translated "carnelian" is *sardion*—"sardius" in some translations. It is a red ruby-like stone. Some suggest that the red sardius may speak of God as Redeemer, the One who provided a blood sacrifice—thus stressing the glory of God's redemptive character. Jasper and sardius were the first and last of the twelve stones on the breastplate of the high priest (Exodus 28:17, 20).

It is impossible to ignore the fact that both Ezekiel and John are describing a scene of breathtaking grandeur and dazzling beauty—a glory that far surpasses the limits of human language. John, like Ezekiel, is painting a big picture that portrays heaven as a bright, colorful realm of inexpressible splendor and delight. Again, let's not get so caught up in trying to read meaning into the symbols that we miss that rather obvious point.

Language fails when humans try to describe divine glory, so John is using these comparisons to precious jewels to picture the breathtaking beauty of heavenly glory. The jewels he mentions were the most stunning, glorious images he could picture, so he resorts to them to make his point. Remember, though, that he is actually describing a glory that far exceeds that of any jewel dug out of the earth. If the scene is hard for you to visualize, that's fine. John is purposely painting a picture of glory that exceeds our ability to imagine.

Sounding much like Ezekiel, John continues, "around the throne was a rainbow that had the appearance of an emerald. . . . From the throne came flashes of lightning, and rumblings and peals of thunder" (vv. 3–5). Again the imagery is designed to inspire awe and fear. It speaks of an immeasurable glory, power, and majesty.

The thunder and lightning are reminiscent of another scene in Scripture: Mount Sinai, where God came down to give the law. The Israelites saw the divine glory in the form of thunder and lightning (Exodus 19:16). This language seeks to describe the indescribable. The sense it conveys is a holy awe that transcends any earthly amazement.

John continues his description of the scene around the throne, giving another detail we ought to note carefully: "before the throne were burning seven torches of fire, which are the seven spirits of God" (Revelation 4:5).

That verse confuses a lot of people. It does not suggest that there are seven Holy Spirits. The apostle Paul makes that clear in 1 Corinthians 12:4: "there are varieties of gifts, but the same Spirit" (cf. v. 11)—and in Ephesians 4:4: "There is one body and one Spirit" (cf. Ephesians 2:18). So this cannot be a reference to seven distinct Spirits of God. Obviously, that would violate what Scripture teaches elsewhere about the personality of the Holy Spirit.

The expression "seven spirits" is typical apocalyptic language and imagery. John links it to seven lamps, which echo the lampstands of the churches in Revelation 2–3. And those in turn seem to have some relationship to the seven lamps in the original tabernacle (see Exodus 25:31–37). These were actually seven candles atop a *single* gold lampstand. The imagery the seven lamps conveys is therefore that of a sevenfold menorah. And the reference to "seven spirits" should be interpreted as a reference to the *one* Spirit of God, who is represented here with a sevenfold symbol.

In what sense is the Spirit "seven"? This could be a reference to the Spirit's sovereignty over the seven churches named in chapters 2–3. In all of Scripture, the expression is used only here and in Revelation 1:4; 3:1; and 5:6. The first two times it appears, it is specifically in reference to the seven churches.

It could also be a reference to Isaiah 11:2, which depicts the Holy Spirit with a seven-faceted description: "the Spirit of [1] the LORD . . . the Spirit of [2] wisdom and [3] understanding, the Spirit of [4] counsel and [5] might, the Spirit of [6] knowledge and [7] the fear of the LORD." Whatever the expression in Revelation 4:5 means, it does not suggest that there is more than "one Spirit" by whom we are baptized into the body of Christ (1 Corinthians 12:13). That would run counter to the rest of Scripture (cf. also Ephesians 2:18; John 14:16–17).

Look again at Revelation 4. Verse 6 says, "Before the throne there was as it were a sea of glass, like crystal." Picture the beauty of that scene: a brilliant rainbow and the flashing colors of emerald, sardius, and jasper all splashing off a sea of crystal!

Again, all this color, light, and crystal reflect the splendor and majesty of God's throne. This is familiar imagery in Scripture. In Exodus 24 we read, "Moses and Aaron, Nadab, and Abihu, and seventy of the elders of Israel went up, and they saw the God of Israel. There was under his feet as it were a pavement of sapphire stone, like the very heaven for clearness" (vv. 9–10). The flashing and sparkling light of God's glory is reflected by this crystal-clear, brilliant, sparkling sea of glass. Notice that the crystal sea is described as "pavement of sapphire stone" in Exodus 24—possibly because of the color reflecting off it. But both passages speak of its extraordinary "clearness." Ezekiel says it is "like awe-inspiring crystal, spread out above [the angels'] heads" (1:22). All of these passages picture heaven as a realm of unimaginable beauty, where every element of everything is designed as a backdrop to reflect and magnify the divine glory.

All this emphasis on brightness and clarity suggests that heaven is not a land of shadows and mists. In the biblical accounts, there is no hint of the long, dark tunnel that features so prominently in many near-death experience stories (see appendix 1). Instead, everything is described in terms of light and brilliance and clarity!

Even when John describes the other inhabitants of heaven, the focus remains on the glory of God. The seats of twenty-four "elders"—no doubt representing the whole body of the redeemed church—encircle the throne (Revelation 4:4). Verse 6 adds that four living creatures also encircled the throne—undoubtedly a reference to angelic creatures, perhaps the cherubim. So surrounding the throne are the angelic host and the church; occupying the throne is God himself in all the glory of his majestic power and holiness.

As we noted in chapter 3, the book of Revelation alone mentions the throne of God at least forty-one times. All activity in heaven focuses in this direction, and all the furnishings of heaven reflect the glory that emanates from here.

Is There a Temple in Heaven or Not?

In the ancient world, the two most important buildings of any national capital were the palace and the temple. They represented civil and spiritual authority. In heaven the centrality of the throne of God emphasizes both his sovereignty and his worthiness to be worshiped. All heaven is his palace, and all heaven is also his temple.

In Revelation 3:12 Christ says, "The one who conquers, I will make him a pillar in the temple of my God. Never shall he go out of it, and I will write on him the name of my God, and the name of the city of my God, the new Jerusalem, which comes down from my God out of heaven, and my own new name." In Johannine writings "the one who conquers" is every true believer.[2] So every redeemed person is pictured here as a pillar of the temple ceremonially inscribed with three names. In Revelation 7:15 one of the twenty-four elders, speaking of saints who have come out of the great tribulation, tells the apostle, "They are before the throne of God, and serve him day and night in his temple; and he who sits on the throne will shelter them with his presence."

In other words, those verses teach that Christians will serve God forever in a heavenly temple. Other passages also speak of a temple in heaven. For example, Revelation 11:19 speaks of "God's temple in heaven" and "the ark of his covenant . . . within his temple." Later John describes "the sanctuary of the tent of witness in heaven" (15:5). Those passages make it clear that there is a temple in heaven.

In Revelation 21:22, however, describing New Jerusalem, John writes, "I saw no temple in the city." Attempting to reconcile Revelation 21:22 with the rest of Revelation, some interpreters argue that presently there *is* a temple in heaven, but when God constructs the new heavens and earth, there *won't be.* That does not seem to capture the most obvious meaning of John's description. The temple in heaven is not a building; it is the Lord God Almighty himself. Revelation 7:15 implies this when it says "he who sits on the throne will shelter them with his presence." And Revelation 21:22–23, continuing the thought of "no temple," adds, "Its temple *is* the Lord God the Almighty and the Lamb. And the city has no need of sun or moon to shine on it, for the glory of God gives it light, and its lamp is the Lamb."

The glory of God both illuminates heaven and defines the boundaries of its temple. One might say all heaven is the temple, and the glory and presence of the Lord permeate it.

A misunderstanding of these verses, unfortunately, has contributed to the notion that heaven is a dull, monotonous place. After all, who wants to be a pillar in a temple we can never leave? (cf. Revelation 3:12). But don't miss the import of what John is saying here. The

---

[2] For more on this theme, see the subsection titled "The One Who Conquers" in chapter 6.

point is not that we become immovable support posts in a building, but that we enter the very presence of the Lord and never again leave *him*. Remember, *he* is the temple of which we are pillars. The imagery is tremendously rich, echoing Jesus's promise, "I will come again and will take you to myself, that where I am you may be also" (John 14:3)—and the apostle Paul's great hope, "so we will always be with the Lord" (1 Thessalonians 4:17). Our place will forever be in the very presence of God.

Bear in mind that both Ezekiel and the apostle John are struggling to describe the indescribable—and you and I are not capable of unscrewing the inscrutable. Even if God had revealed all the details about heaven, we wouldn't be able to know or understand them. It is unlike anything we know. But in Ephesians 2, Paul gives some insight into heaven from a slightly different perspective. Here Paul is describing our utter dependence on God for salvation, saying that before we were redeemed we were dead in our trespasses and sins (v. 1), by nature children of wrath (v. 3). Then he describes God's mercy and love toward us in saving us from our sins. The thought of God's grace reaching out to save us when we deserved the opposite ought to overwhelm us with gratitude and humility.

Now notice what Paul says in Ephesians 2:7: God saved us "so that in the coming ages he might show the immeasurable riches of his grace in kindness toward us in Christ Jesus." That verse won't satisfy people curious to understand what heaven *looks* like, but note the vivid description of what heaven will *be* like: it is a place where the riches of God's grace shine even more brightly than they do here on earth. That is what makes me long for heaven most.

Stop and think of it. Every good thing we know here on earth is a product of God's grace (see James 1:17). And we who know Christ are going to heaven for this express purpose: so that God can showcase the infinite riches of his grace by showering his goodness on us endlessly. Does that not make your heart prefer the glory of heaven to the meager pleasures of earth?

6

New Jerusalem

Eternal heaven will be vastly different—expanded—from the heaven where God now dwells. As we saw briefly in chapter 4, in the consummation of all things, God will remake the heavens and the earth, merging his heaven with this earth in a perfect dwelling place that will be our home forever. In other words, heaven, the realm where God dwells, will expand to encompass the entire universe of creation, which will be fashioned anew in a manner fit for the glory of heaven. The apostle Peter described this as the hope of every redeemed person: "According to his promise we are waiting for new heavens and a new earth in which righteousness dwells" (2 Peter 3:13).

Even in the Old Testament that was what the righteous hoped for. We know that earthly Canaan was the Promised Land of the nation of Israel. But Hebrews 11 tells us that Abraham, to whom the promise was originally made, actually had his heart set on something more than a mere earthly land-promise. "By faith he went to live in the land of promise, as in a foreign land, living in tents with Isaac and Jacob, heirs with him of the same promise. For he was looking forward to the city that has foundations, whose designer and builder is God" (vv. 9–10). Abraham's eyes were set on the eternal promised land, not merely on earthly real estate. He made himself a nomad in this life, willing by faith to seek his only permanent dwelling in God's eternal city in the world to come. According to the biblical record, the only actual land Abraham ever owned was the small burial plot he bought to lay Sarah's body to rest (Genesis 23:20). It ended up being the final resting place for him and the rest of the Hebrew patriarchs. Heaven was the only inheritance he really desired anyway.

The Old Testament prophesied a massive renovation of heaven and earth that would eventually result in the saints' eternal dwelling place. Psalm 102:25–26 pictures the Lord changing our universe as if it were a worn-out garment: "Of old you laid the foundation of the earth, and the heavens are the work of your hands. They will perish, but you will remain; they will all wear out like a garment. You will change them like a robe, and they will pass away." (Interestingly, Hebrews 1:10–12 quotes this passage, attributing the words to God the Father, who is speaking to the Son. This is one of the great proofs of Jesus's eternal deity.)

Clearly, a major cosmic remodeling has always been the plan of God. This was also God's gracious promise to his people through the Old Testament prophets. Speaking in Isaiah 65:17–19, God says,

> For behold, I create new heavens
>   and a new earth,
> and the former things shall not be remembered
>   or come into mind.
> But be glad and rejoice forever
>   in that which I create;
> for behold, I create Jerusalem to be a joy,
>   and her people to be a gladness.
> I will rejoice in Jerusalem
>   and be glad in my people;
> no more shall be heard in it the sound of weeping
>   and the cry of distress.

There God states that he will alter the present heaven and earth in a way that amounts to a whole new creation. Notice that in the new universe, New Jerusalem will be the focus of everything. The new heaven and new earth will be so glorious that it makes the first fade into insignificance ("the former things shall not be remembered or come into mind"—v. 17). In the next and final chapter of Isaiah's prophecy, the Lord promises that this new heaven and new earth will remain forever, as will all the saints of God: "'For as the new heavens and the new earth that I make shall remain before me,' says the LORD, 'so shall your offspring and your name remain'" (66:22).

Revelation 21 gives what amounts to a full exposition of Isaiah's promise. Here the apostle John describes his vision of the final consummation of all things. This chapter contains the Bible's most exhaustive description of the new heaven and new earth—along with the holy city, New Jerusalem. What we see in microcosm at the end of Isaiah is spelled out more fully at the end of Revelation.

Here's the setting: The battle of Armageddon has been fought (Revelation 19), the earthly, millennial reign of Christ has come to an end (20:7), and at the great white throne judgment God has sentenced Satan and all the ungodly to eternal hell (20:11–15). Then the whole universe will be dissolved ("the first heaven and the first earth had passed away, and the sea was no more"—21:1). Everything we know will be made perfect. Evil will be purged from the universe. Death and sin and sadness and pain will be entirely done away with. The new heavens and new earth that take the place of the old will be the glorious realm in which we will dwell eternally.

The Old Universe Dissolves

Before we look closely at the description of heaven in Revelation 21, however, let's examine the process by which all things are made new. The apostle Peter goes into detail on this, in a familiar passage that is well worth examining.

Peter writes, ". . . knowing this first of all, that scoffers will come in the last days with scoffing, following their own sinful desires. They will say, 'Where is the promise of his coming? For ever since the fathers fell asleep, all things are continuing as they were from the beginning of creation.'" (2 Peter 3:3–4). This predicts a time of apostasy and spiritual apathy when unbelief and skepticism are prevalent. What Peter describes is a common brand of mocking skepticism in our own time. You have no doubt heard skeptics who claim that if Jesus hasn't returned after two millennia, he's not going to return at all! (Which is something akin to thinking that because I haven't died yet, I'm never going to.)

The skepticism Peter describes has special reference to cataclysmic judgment. These scoffers hold a belief similar to what geologists call *uniformitarianism*—the theory that all natural phenomena have operated uniformly since the origin of the earth. (Uniformitarianism is the belief that undergirds the most popular evolutionary timetables.) The scoffers' brand of uniformitarianism is metaphysical, however.

They insinuate that God (if they acknowledge him at all) has left the scene. "All we can observe are natural phenomena," they say. "The earth has continued to revolve, the rains have come and the sun has shone, and the water cycle has operated since the beginning of recorded history. There's no reason to think it can't go on evolving slowly forever, and certainly no reason to think God will intervene in any sort of judgment on a cosmic scale."

But theirs is an arrogant, flippant false security. Peter continues: "For they deliberately overlook this fact, that the heavens existed long ago, and the earth was formed out of water and through water by the word of God, and that by means of these the world that then existed was deluged with water and perished" (vv. 5–6). Those who say there has been no cataclysmic judgment on the earth forget (actually, they *willfully* reject God's revelation) about the great flood, when God drowned the entire human race, sparing only Noah and his family.

Peter speaks of "the earth . . . formed out of water and through water" (v. 5). Many believe that prior to the flood, a canopy of water or water vapor encircled the earth (cf. Genesis 1:7), protecting it from the sun's ultraviolet rays. Because of that protection, plant life flourished, and men and animals lived hundreds of years. (This would explain why, immediately after the flood, the ages of people listed in the biblical genealogies began to decline sharply. Life expectancy was altered dramatically by the cataclysm.) Evidently the very canopy that was the earth's protection became the means of its judgment as the breaking up of the canopy inundated the earth.

According to Scripture, the flood was the last great catastrophe on a cosmic scale, right down to our own time. Things *have* pretty much continued as they have always been, despite the fact that Jesus said God's judgment was imminent even in *his* day (cf. Matthew 3:2, 10–12).

Peter says, however, that no one should misinterpret God's delay as apathy, unfaithfulness, or slackness. In the first place, time is of no consequence to the Lord. A thousand years is no different from a single day to him. What Jesus said was imminent two thousand years ago is still imminent today.

But more important than that, the only reason God delays his final judgment is because of his grace: "But do not overlook this one fact, beloved, that with the Lord one day is as a thousand years, and a thousand years as one day. The Lord is not slow to fulfill his promise as some count slowness, but is patient toward you, not wishing that any should perish, but that all should reach repentance" (2 Peter 3:8–9).

"The LORD is good to all, and his mercy is over all that he has made" (Psalm 145:9). Remember that in the aftermath of the flood, God made a gracious promise never again to destroy the earth in such a way (Genesis 9:12–16)—and he confirmed his covenant with a rainbow. His grace, not his wrath, is currently on display.

However, we dare not presume that his grace rules out the day of his wrath. The wrath will come as well, when the day of the Lord is unleashed. Peter reminds us, just as "the world that then existed was deluged with water and perished," even so shall *this* world one day suffer cataclysmic destruction: "the heavens and earth that now exist are stored up for fire, being kept until the day of judgment and destruction of the ungodly" (2 Peter 3:6–7).

So next time, instead of water, it will be fire—and fire unlike any known to humanity: "The day of the Lord will come like a thief, and then the heavens will pass away with a roar, and the heavenly bodies will be burned up and dissolved, and the earth and the works that are done on it will be exposed" (v. 10). Atomic science has demonstrated to us that such destruction can occur. By splitting the atom, man unleashed the potential for unbelievable destruction—a chain reaction of atomic explosions could literally disintegrate this earth. Moreover, our earth has tremendous potential for fire. We live on the crust of a fireball; most of the earth's approximately 8,000-mile diameter is molten flame. The earth's core is a flaming, boiling, liquid lake of fire, which when it gets too close to the earth's crust, bursts through as a volcano.

But the fire Peter describes is no mere nuclear bomb. It is a meltdown of universal proportions. The heavens pass away with a great noise. The elements melt with fervent heat. Everything we know will be instantly burned up. This is the culmination of an eschatological period known as "the day of the Lord," which is always associated in Scripture with the outpouring of divine wrath and judgment. The sudden fiery demolition of the universe is the consummation of it all.

Peter's whole point has an intensely practical application: "Since all these things are thus to be dissolved, what sort of people ought you to be in lives of holiness and godliness, waiting for and hastening the coming of the day of God, because of which the heavens will be set on fire and dissolved, and the heavenly bodies will melt as they burn!" (2 Peter 3:11–12). The point is obvious: if everything in this life is perishable, we need to set our hearts on things that are imperishable. Like Abraham, the father of the faithful, we need to fix our hopes on a more permanent city—one whose architect and builder is God, and one that will never pass away. And so, Peter concludes, "According to his promise we are waiting for new heavens and a new earth in which righteousness dwells" (v. 13).

But even this greatest of God's judgments ultimately has a gracious purpose, for only then will the universe stop groaning under the curse of sin (see Romans 8:19–22).

A New Heaven and a New Earth

We return to Revelation 21 for a biblical description of the "new heaven and a new earth," which will come when "the first heaven and the first earth [have] passed away" (v. 1). The Greek word translated "new" (*kainos*) stresses that the earth God will create will not just be "new" as opposed to "old." It will also be *different*. Paul uses the same Greek word twice in 2 Corinthians 5:17: "If anyone is in Christ, he is a new creation. The old has passed away; behold, the new has come." The word denotes a change in quality. The new heavens and earth, like our newness in Christ, will be glorified, free from sin's curse, and eternal.

Scripture doesn't tell us what the new earth will look like, but we have reason to believe that it will in many respects seem familiar. Jerusalem will be there—albeit an all-new Jerusalem. John's description concentrates on the holy city, which has streets, and walls, and gates. John also mentions a high mountain, water, a stream, and trees. Best of all, it is populated with the people of God—real people whom we will know and with whom we will have eternal fellowship.

All Things New

The new earth will also be utterly different, unfamiliar. John says, for example, "the sea was no more" (v. 1). That's a large difference immediately, because the current earth is mostly covered with water. Some Bible scholars think this stresses the erasure of all national boundaries. Others point out that the sea symbolized fear to the ancients, so they believe the absence of sea implied the absence of fear. Both may contain an element of truth. In the new heaven and earth nothing will make us afraid, and nothing will separate clans or nations of people from one another. The only water described in heaven is the "the river of the water of life, bright as crystal, flowing from the throne of God and of the Lamb" (Revelation 22:1). This crystal-clear river flows right down heaven's main street (v. 2).

Verses 3–7 of Revelation 21 outline the most remarkable features of the new heavens and new earth:

> And I heard a loud voice from the throne saying, "Behold, the dwelling place of God is with man. He will dwell with them, and they will be his people, and God Himself will be with them as their God. He will wipe away every tear from their eyes, and death shall be no more, neither shall there be mourning, nor crying, nor pain anymore, for the former things have passed away."
>
> And he who was seated on the throne said, "Behold, I am making all things new." Also he said, "Write this down, for these words are trustworthy and true." And he said to me, "It is done! I am the Alpha and the Omega, the beginning and the end. To the thirsty I will give from the spring of the water of life without payment. The one who conquers will have this heritage, and I will be his God and he will be my son.

Here Scripture promises that heaven will be a realm of perfect bliss. Tears, pain, sorrow, and crying will have no place whatsoever in the new heavens and new earth. It is a place where God's people will dwell together with him eternally, utterly free from all the effects of sin and evil. God is pictured as personally wiping away the tears from the eyes of the redeemed.

Heaven is a realm where death is fully conquered (1 Corinthians 15:26). There is no sickness there, no hunger, no trouble, and no tragedy. Just consummate delight and eternal blessings. It is frankly hard for our minds to imagine, having never known anything in this life that is free from the taint of sin and its calamities.

How Can Heaven Be Perfect When There Is Such a Place As Hell?

Many people wonder how they can endure eternity knowing that some of their earthly loved ones will not be there. What about parents whose wayward son has departed from Christ and died in immorality and unbelief? How can heaven be perfect for them? What about someone whose earthly father died in sin, not knowing the Lord? How can that person endure the pain of eternal separation? What about the widow who comes to Christ after her beloved spouse has already died in a state of unbelief? How can heaven be pure bliss with no hope of reunion with these loved ones?

Scripture does not give a direct answer to that question. Some suggest that our memories of relationships on this earth will eventually fade. And there is a hint in Scripture that this may be a factor: In the Isaiah 65 passage describing the new heavens and new earth, God says, "Behold, I create new heavens and a new earth, and *the former things shall not be remembered or come into mind*" (v. 17). However, I don't think this can possibly mean we will forget everything about this earth and our relationships here. After all, we will continue many of those same relationships eternally. And we will spend eternity reciting the glory of how Christ has redeemed us. Since our redemption was accomplished by his work *on earth*, it is impossible that we will completely lose our memory of all earthly events and relationships.

But we will have a much clearer understanding of things from heaven's perspective. Now we see all things as in a cloudy mirror. Then we will know exactly as we are known (1 Corinthians 13:12). All our earthly attachments will be overwhelmed by more satisfying relationships and more perfect affections. Just as God promises to be father to the fatherless here on earth (Psalm 68:5), so he will personally fill the void left by any broken earthly relationships—and in an even more perfect way, because our feelings and our desires will be untainted by the effects of our sin. We will see and understand better the perfect justice of God, and we shall glorify him for every detail of the outworking of his eternal plan—including his dealings with the wicked.

The final verses of Isaiah's prophecy indicate that the destruction of the wicked will ultimately be something for which we will worship

God (Isaiah 66:23–24). The existence of hell will not dim the glory of heaven or dilute its bliss in the least.

As for how this will work out in the hearts and minds of the redeemed, Scripture simply does not tell us. We're promised only that God himself will dry our tears. For now, it is enough to know that we can trust implicitly his infinite goodness, compassion, and mercy.

Furthermore, notice that when God says he will make all things new, he adds a message to the apostle John: "Write this down, for these words are trustworthy and true" (Revelation 21:5)—as if to add an exclamation mark to the reliability of these great promises. We who truly know the Lord know we can trust him even with our unanswered questions. *All* his words are true and faithful, so when he says he is making all things new, it is a promise we can cling to, despite our inability to know precisely how all the difficulties will resolve. Heaven will be utterly perfect, no matter how impossible it may be for us to understand everything now.

One other thing is perfectly clear: God cannot be faulted for any lack of mercy or goodness, even though people perish eternally. He cannot be charged with any blame for their destruction. He freely offers the water of life to all who thirst (v. 6).

The One Who Conquers

The redeemed have a further promise. God says, "The one who conquers will have this heritage, and I will be his God and he will be my son" (Revelation 21:7). For those who emerge from this life victorious over sin and death, God will elevate them to a position of unimaginable privilege—and will bestow on them an inheritance beyond any earthly standard of measure.

"The one who conquers" is a description of *every* redeemed person. There is no partition in heaven between the "overcomers" and the "defeated Christians"—though some have attempted to teach this. One surprisingly popular view, for example, even goes so far as to claim that the "outer darkness" spoken of in Matthew 8:12 (where "there will be weeping and gnashing of teeth") is a realm of heaven reserved for believers who do *not* conquer![1] The conquering ones, in this view,

[1]Joseph Dillow, *The Reign of the Servant Kings* (Miami Springs, FL: Schoettle, 1992), 347.

are "a separate class of Christians who persevere."[2] Christians who are non-conquerors are banished to the outer regions of heaven, unable to share in its full blessedness.

But that view is patently unbiblical. According to Scripture there is no such thing as a true believer who does *not* persevere in the faith—because God himself promises to keep us. We are "kept by the power of God through faith unto salvation ready to be revealed in the last time" (1 Peter 1:5, KJV). And therefore all true Christians are ultimately conquerors. Those who depart from the faith demonstrate that they were never really in Christ to begin with (1 John 2:19). This is the doctrine known as the "perseverance of the saints."[3]

"The one who conquers," "you have overcome," and other parallel expressions are common in the Johannine writings. The apostle John quite plainly uses the concept of the "overcomer" as a synonym for the believer. He addresses both spiritual young men and spiritual fathers as those who have "have overcome the evil one" (1 John 2:13–14). He warns all believers about the spirit of antichrist, then writes, "Little children, you are from God and have overcome them, for he who is in you is greater than he who is in the world" (4:4). And to make it perfectly clear that he means *all* believers are overcomers, he writes, "Everyone who has been born of God overcomes the world. And this is the victory that has overcome the world—our faith. Who is it that overcomes the world except the one who believes that Jesus is the Son of God?" (5:4–5). There is therefore no such thing as a believer who is not an overcomer. This identification of believers as overcomers is also used in Christ's letters to the churches (cf. Revelation 2:7, 11, 17, 26; 3:5, 12, 21).

If Children, Then Heirs

It ought to be clear, then, that when God says, "The one who conquers will have this heritage, and I will be his God and he will be my son," this is a promise to all believers. He will be our God; we shall be his children. Heaven will be our home, and we will dwell there not as mere guests, but with all the privileges of family members—children of the Lord of the heavenly domain.

---

[2] Ibid., 481.
[3] See John MacArthur, *Faith Works* (Dallas: Word, 1992), 175–192.

A study of the biblical passages related to our inheritance could be a book in itself. Scripture teaches that all who are believers are children of God (John 1:12)—"and if children, then heirs—heirs of God and fellow heirs with Christ" (Romans 8:17).

Perhaps not surprisingly, those who think heaven is divided between "overcomers" and run-of-the-mill Christians often suggest that only the "overcomers" share in the inheritance of the kingdom. Those left in "outer darkness" are disinherited, put outside the Father's house, cast out of the banquet hall, relegated to a secondary existence in the eternal realm—and not permitted in God's immediate presence.[4] This is a curious, and wholly unbiblical, idea of heaven! It makes the Christian's inheritance something to be merited by the believer's own works.[5] The notion that someone could get to heaven in that kind of spiritual limbo—devoid of any inheritance—is altogether foreign to everything Scripture has to say about heaven.

There are, of course, passages of Scripture that indicate there will be differing levels of greatness in heaven. The parable in Luke 19:16–19, for example, portrays God as a nobleman who rewards two of his faithful servants by making them rulers over ten cities and five cities, respectively. Also, Jesus speaks of the "least in the kingdom of heaven" (Matthew 11:11)—implying that there are varying degrees of standing in heaven. Our Lord taught repeatedly that believers will receive rewards for their faithfulness—and those rewards vary from person to person (Matthew 25:21–24).

How are these rewards determined? Our *works* will be tested for this very purpose. In that day when we stand before the judgment seat of Christ, the whole edifice of our earthly lives will be tested by the fire of God to determine the quality of our works. Some impressive superstructures will be reduced to rubble, because they are built only for show—not out of lasting material. Like sets on a movie lot, these "buildings" may be magnificent and *appear* genuine even on close inspection, but the fire will test them for what they are made of, not for what they look like. All the wood, hay, and straw will be burned away. Scripture promises, "If the work that anyone has built on the

---

[4] Dillow, *Reign of the Servant Kings*, 348.
[5] Ibid., 48–49.

foundation survives, he will receive a reward" (1 Corinthians 3:14). What about the person whose works are burned up? "He will suffer loss, though he himself will be saved, but only as through fire" (v. 15). That evokes the notion of someone who is pulled from a burning building alive. He may be unharmed by the fire, but the smell of smoke is all over him—he has barely escaped destruction.

But don't be quick to relegate such a person to the confines of outer darkness, where there will be weeping and gnashing of teeth. Like the thief on the cross, like the workman hired at the last hour, that person will receive infinitely more than he or she has merited. Even those who barely escape the flames remain heirs of God and fellow heirs with Christ, sharing fully in the eternal blessing of heaven. The least in the kingdom of heaven is still greater than the greatest on earth (Matthew 11:11). In that realm the last are first and the first last—indicating that, as far as our *inheritance* is concerned, everyone finishes in a dead heat. And since whatever rewards we may earn will be cast before the throne of the Lamb (see Revelation 4:10), there cannot be a very pronounced hierarchy among the saved in the eternal state. Certainly there is no justification for teaching that some will be kept out of the heavenly banquets and consigned forever to the exterior realms of the kingdom.[6]

Our inheritance is something entirely different from our rewards. Our eternal inheritance is not merited by works, nor is it apportioned according to them. The apostle Paul ties our inheritance to our adoption as sons (Romans 8:15–17). An *inheritance* by definition is not a reward for merit earned. It is a birthright.

Furthermore, there was a significant difference between Roman law and Jewish practice on the matter of a child's inheritance. By Jewish law, the eldest son always received a double portion of the inheritance. Under the Roman system, all children could receive equal shares. When Paul wrote, "if children, then heirs—heirs of God and fellow heirs with Christ" (Romans 8:17), he was addressing a Roman audience. The context indicates his emphasis was on the equality of God's children and the security of every Christian's inheritance.

---

[6] Matthew 8:12 says, "*The sons of the kingdom* will be thrown into the outer darkness. In that place there will be weeping and gnashing of teeth." "The sons of the kingdom" refers not to Christians, but to unbelieving Israelites. Their relationship to "the kingdom" is only a line of physical descent—an earthly tie, and not enough to make them spiritually fit for the heavenly kingdom. So Jesus tenderly warns that if they do not repent they will be judged along with the rest of the unbelieving world.

Writing to the Galatians, Paul made a similar point: "*If you are Christ's*, then you are Abraham's offspring, heirs according to promise" (Galatians 3:29). He echoed the thought a chapter later: "And because you are sons, God has sent the Spirit of his Son into our hearts, crying, 'Abba! Father!' So you are no longer a slave, but a son, and *if a son, then an heir* through God" (4:6–7). The inheritance is not a reward for a faithful servant (as were the rewards in most of Jesus's parables). It is a birthright for every child of the Father.

Plainly, Scripture is teaching that all Christians will receive a full share of the inheritance of heaven. *Every* believer will "inherit all things" (Revelation 21:7, KJV), so the inheritance isn't carved up and apportioned on the basis of worthiness. And when God says, "I will be his God and he will be my son"—he is saying that heaven will be not only our dwelling place, but also our possession. We will be there not as boarders, but as full-fledged members of the family. What an inexpressible privilege that is!

The Holy City

Now look back at Revelation 21:2 for another important perspective on the heavenly realm. John writes, "I saw the holy city, new Jerusalem, coming down out of heaven from God, prepared as a bride adorned for her husband."

Prepared As a Bride

As John watches, an entire city, magnificent in its glory, descends whole from heaven and becomes a part of the new earth. Heaven and earth are now one. The heavenly realm has moved its capital city intact to the new earth. Pay special attention to the key terms in this verse:

"*Prepared*" seems to imply that New Jerusalem had somehow been made ready before the creation of the new heavens and new earth. John does not say he saw the city being created. When he laid eyes on it, it was complete already. In other words, it was brought to the new earth from another place. Where is this other place?

"*Coming down out of heaven from God*" indicates that the city—already complete and thoroughly furnished—descended to the new earth from the heavenly realm, no doubt from the place Paul called "the third heaven." Again, this occurs immediately after the new heaven and earth are created. New Jerusalem, the capital city of the eternal realm, descends right before John's eyes, out of the very realm of God, where it has already been "prepared." Who "prepared" it? Evidently this incredible heavenly city is precisely what our Lord spoke of when he told his disciples that he was going away to "prepare a place" for them (John 14:3). Now at the unveiling of the new heavens and new earth, the city is finally prepared and ready—

"As a bride adorned for her husband." This speaks of the glory of this unimaginable city. Just think, when our Lord fashioned the material universe at the beginning of time, he did it in seven days. He has been working on this feature of heaven for nearly two millennia. What a wonder it must be! The surpassing glory of this city is too rich to express in words.

You Have Come to Mount Zion

New Jerusalem is the very city Abraham was seeking, "whose designer and builder is God" (Hebrews 11:10). The writer of Hebrews says to all the redeemed, "You have come to Mount Zion and to the city of the living God, the heavenly Jerusalem, and to innumerable angels in festal gathering, and to the assembly of the firstborn who are enrolled in heaven, and to God, the judge of all, and to the spirits of the righteous made perfect" (12:22–23).

That's a fascinating verse about heaven. The earthly *Mount Zion* is adjacent to the Temple Mount in old Jerusalem. To dwell in Zion is to have one's residence right next to the Lord's own holy dwelling. This heavenly Zion will be the eternal home of all *"who are enrolled in heaven"*— all the redeemed of all ages. (Again this destroys the notion that some of the redeemed will be banished to a place outside the main core of heaven.) Here *"the spirits of the righteous"* will finally be *"made perfect."* We will be made fit to dwell amid such unimaginable glory (1 John 3:2).

The Crown Jewel of Heaven

Revelation 21:10–27 describes in even more vivid detail John's vision of the holy city as it descended from heaven. An angel took John in his vision to a mountain on the new earth from which he could watch

God's masterpiece, the capital city of the infinite heaven, descend from God, out of the third heaven, and become the crown jewel of the new heavens and new earth.

Notice that John describes the city as "having the glory of God, its radiance like a most rare jewel, like a jasper, clear as crystal" (v. 11).

As we have already seen, this theme of light and glory is woven through everything Scripture has to say about the eternal realm. Heaven itself is an infinite, eternal expression of divine glory. We might say that the essence of heaven is God's glory manifest in its midst. Isaiah 60:19 says, "The sun shall be no more your light by day, nor for brightness shall the moon give you light; but the Lord will be your everlasting light, and your God will be your glory." Revelation 21:23 echoes an identical thought: "The city has no need of sun or moon to shine on it, for the glory of God gives it light, and its lamp is the Lamb." God himself will light all of the infinite heaven, beginning with this sparkling celestial jewel called New Jerusalem.

When I was growing up, I used to go roller-skating in Pasadena. Hanging in the middle of the rink was a sphere covered with small, mirrored squares. When lights were aimed at it, the whole rink flashed and sparkled with light. I realize that's a poor and tawdry comparison, but in a very small and mundane way the manner in which those mirrors gathered up, magnified, and dispersed illumination may picture what John is trying to communicate in this description of lights and jewels. He saw the eternal city coming down from heaven, and it resembled a sparkling, crystal, diamond-like stone blazing with the glory of God's very nature. And the splashing light of God's glory literally covered the infinite new universe with breathtaking beauty.

Glorious Walls and Gates

Verse 12 says the city "had a great, high wall." Why would the heavenly city have a wall? Walls are for defense against one's enemies. But there will be no enemies in this realm; all the enemies of God will have already been cast into the lake of fire (Revelation 20:14–15). So this wall serves no *functional* purpose. Like everything else in heaven, it is a display of the glory of God. It also symbolizes the inviolable security of heaven.

Speaking of these same walls, Revelation 22:14–15 says, "Blessed are those who wash their robes, so that they may have the right to the tree of life and that they may enter the city by the gates. Outside are the dogs and sorcerers and the sexually immoral and murderers and idolaters, and everyone who loves and practices falsehood." That does not mean dogs and sorcerers and liars are camped just outside the gates of the city. Again, all who fit that description have already been banished to hell eternally (Revelation 21:8; 20:15).

The walls and gates merely stand as a silent testimony that some can enter and others cannot. Those who cannot enter are not some kind of second-class Christians. They are the unbelievers, who are already consigned to eternal destruction.

John's description of the wall and its gates is interesting:

> It had a great, high wall, with twelve gates, and at the gates twelve angels, and on the gates the names of the twelve tribes of the sons of Israel were inscribed—on the east three gates, on the north three gates, on the south three gates, and on the west three gates. And the wall of the city had twelve foundations, and on them were the twelve names of the twelve apostles of the Lamb (21:12–14).

So the gates are named after the tribes of Israel and the foundations after the twelve apostles. This will be the dwelling place for all the people of God redeemed out of every era of human history. Israel and the church are brought together in the eternal realm to form one people of God for all eternity.

The existence of gates implies that people are able to leave and enter the city. Don't think the city *contains* us. It will be our home, but we will not be confined there. We will have the infinite universe to travel, and when we do, we will go in and out through those gates.

Heavenly Measurements

In 21:15–16 John says, "The one who spoke with me had a measuring rod of gold [probably about ten feet long] to measure the city and its gates and walls. The city lies foursquare, its length the same as its width. And he measured the city with his rod, 12,000 stadia. Its length and width and height are equal." So the city is perfectly symmetrical, a massive cube, fifteen hundred miles square and fifteen hundred miles high. Some have suggested that this could actually describe a pyramid. While that is indeed a possible interpretation of these dimensions, it seems unlikely that Scripture would not say so if that's what it meant to convey. I take this as a description of a cube.

What is the significance of a cube-shaped city? Remember that in Solomon's temple the Most Holy Place was a cube of twenty cubits (1 Kings 6:20). The New Jerusalem is the Most Holy Place for eternity. This *is* the very sanctuary of God himself. It is his house, and our dwelling place is likewise part of the Father's own house (see Psalm 23:6; John 14:2). God has brought the very heart of the heavenly tabernacle—the Most Holy Place—to earth.

A height of fifteen hundred miles is frankly difficult to envision. On the current earth, something fifteen hundred miles high would extend well out of earth's atmosphere (which is only about a hundred miles deep). But remember that heaven and earth are now merged, and atmosphere ceases to be an issue.

Are these great heights and distances merely symbolic? I'm inclined to think not. John describes the angel's measurement of the city wall: "He also measured its wall, 144 cubits by human measurement, which is also an angel's measurement" (v. 17). The fact that such precise measurements are given seems to suggest that this describes a real place with real earthly dimensions. Indeed, the expression "by human measurement" could hardly mean anything else.

According to these measurements, the New Jerusalem covers a surface area of 2.25 million square miles. By comparison, all of greater London is only 621 square miles. The actual City of London proper is an area of only one square mile, densely packed, but with a population of about 5,000. On that basis, the New Jerusalem would be able to house over a hundred billion people! And that does not even begin to take into account the towering height of the city! Heaven will certainly be large enough for the "few" who find the narrow way (Matthew 7:13–14). And we'll discover in the glory of eternity that the "few" are really "a great multitude that no one could number, from every nation, from all tribes and peoples and languages" (Revelation 7:9). Heaven will have plenty of room for all of them.

How far is fifteen hundred miles? It is about the same as the distance from Maine to Florida. Imagine such an area squared off, then cubed, with multiple levels and millions of intersecting golden avenues. New Jerusalem is a place of unearthly majesty and beauty!

The Building Materials

Revelation 21:18 tells us that the walls are made of jasper. That is a translucent, semiopaque stone of varying colors. Some have suggested that in biblical times "jasper" was the name for a transparent, diamond-like semiprecious stone. In any case, the jasper stone allows the glory of God, radiating from the center of the city, to shine through. The city itself is "pure gold, like clear glass" (Revelation 21:18). Of course, the gold we're familiar with is not transparent. The expression could refer to gold that is polished to a perfect sheen so that it reflects like a clear mirror. More likely it describes a variety of the precious metal so pure that it is translucent. Both Ezekiel and John describe much of heaven as being transparent like precious gems. The radiance of God's glory reflects the beauty of his presence through every diamond facet. That is what John saw. It must have sparkled with an unearthly brilliance and heavenly glow, but with a golden tone—so he recognized it as pure gold.

Verses 19–20 say, "The foundations of the wall of the city were adorned with every kind of jewel. The first was jasper, the second sapphire, the third agate, the fourth emerald, the fifth onyx, the sixth carnelian, the seventh chrysolite, the eighth beryl, the ninth topaz, the tenth chrysoprase, the eleventh jacinth, the twelfth amethyst." Those are all colored jewels—various greens, sky blue, red, golden, violet, and other radiant hues. Along with the glasslike gold and translucent walls, this forms a picture of unbelievable and indescribable beauty. God has planted within us a love of beauty—and heaven's surpassing beauty will satisfy that love forever.

John adds, "And the twelve gates were twelve pearls, each of the gates made of a single pearl, and the street of the city was pure gold, like transparent glass" (v. 21). It is hard to imagine gates that big, each made of a single pearl. But that is what John describes. These won't be pearls from some giant variety of oysters, but perfect pearls made by God's own hand.

What Heaven Lacks

One is tempted to say nothing will be lacking in heaven, but happily that is not the case. The apostle John lists a number of things utterly missing from heaven. You may be surprised by some of them:

No Temple

We already noted in chapter 5 that there is no physical temple in heaven. John writes, "I saw no temple in the city, for its temple is the Lord God the Almighty and the Lamb" (v. 22). So in one sense there is no temple in heaven. In another sense, however, God himself *is* the temple.

In what sense is God the "temple" of heaven? A temple is where you go to worship. John is suggesting that in heaven when we worship, we will worship in the very presence of God. He is the place of worship and the sanctuary for heaven's worshipers. He "will shelter them with his presence" (Revelation 7:15). They serve him day and night. The worship never stops.

Unfortunately, some people tend to think of worship as starchy, formal, perhaps even a bit uncomfortable. Use the word *worship* to a Sunday school boy in my generation, and he would most likely think of something that makes him feel confined and somewhat awkward— a stuffy ceremony where he has to sit still and be quiet. Other people (more and more nowadays) think of worship as totally *in*formal self-expression, with a driving musical crescendo and lots of passionate physical gestures. Neither idea comes close to a true understanding of the biblical concept of worship.

I did a book-length study exploring the biblical concept of worship a few years ago and discovered that the real essence of worship is neither liturgy nor raw passion. Nor is worship an activity that can be relegated to a weekly event or the musical numbers in our order of service. True worship (according to the Bible) incorporates all of life. That's why Paul could write to the Corinthians, "whether you eat or drink, or whatever you do, do all to the glory of God" (1 Corinthians 10:31). "Whatever you do, in word or deed, do everything in the name of the Lord Jesus, giving thanks to God the Father through him" (Colossians 3:17). There's nothing *necessary* and *legitimate* in life that cannot be done to the glory of God. And since worship is simply glorifying God, this means there is nothing required of us that cannot be done as an act of worship. Therefore if we were perfect beings, sinless in every regard, our lives would be nonstop worship.

That is exactly what heaven will be! To cite once more the familiar words of the first question from the Westminster Shorter Catechism, we will *glorify God and enjoy him forever*. Far from being stuffy and uncomfortable, our worship in heaven will bring us sheer pleasure. It will be unhindered, unadulterated enjoyment of God, never dampened by any pangs of guilt, any fear of insecurity, or any strains of weariness. None of our earthly pleasures can compare with the perfect delight we will derive from heavenly worship. All the joys we associate with earthly love, earthly beauty, and other earthly blessings are nothing in comparison to the pure bliss of heavenly worship before the very face of him from whom all true blessings flow.

Only those who know him can even begin to appreciate the unadulterated pleasure this will be.

And the privilege of such perfect worship is part of the saints' inheritance. The psalmist wrote, "Whom have I in heaven but you? And there is nothing on earth that I desire besides you. My flesh and my heart may fail, but God is the strength of my heart and my portion forever" (Psalm 73:25–26).

Isn't that the fulfillment of our very deepest desires? As the Psalmist wrote, "One thing have I asked of the LORD, that will I seek after: that I may dwell in the house of the LORD all the days of my life, to gaze upon the beauty of the LORD and to inquire in his temple" (Psalm 27:4). In heaven that will be precisely our inheritance, and we will dwell forever in the house of the Lord (Psalm 23:6)—a more glorious temple than we could ever imagine.

No Light Source

A temple building is not all that will be missing from heaven. As we noted earlier in this chapter, there will be no need of cosmic light sources. Revelation 21:23 says, "the city has no need of sun or moon to shine on it, for the glory of God gives it light, and its lamp is the Lamb."

The glory of heaven is a far more brilliant light than anything we currently know or imagine. Isaiah wrote, "Then the moon will be confounded and the sun ashamed, for the LORD of hosts reigns on Mount Zion and in Jerusalem, and his glory will be before his elders" (24:23). Next to the glory of God, the light of the sun and moon are paltry, flickering candles. Revelation 21:24 adds: "By its light will the nations walk, and the kings of the earth will bring their glory into it." John is saying that even the kings of the earth will yield up their own glory in the face of the glory of heaven. All nations will walk in the light of God's presence, and all men, regardless of their position, will bow to his glory.

I once received a letter from an atheist who wanted to argue that if we take Scripture at face value, heaven will be hotter than hell. "Hell must be at or below the boiling temperature of brimstone (sulfur)—around 450 kelvins," he wrote. "And Isaiah 30:26 says that 'the light of the sun shall be sevenfold, as the light of seven days, in the day that the Lord bindeth up the breach of his people, and healeth the stroke of their wound.' Any competent physicist will tell you that a light source seven times the sun's brightness would cause the earth's surface to be well in excess of 450 kelvins. So if the Bible is true, heaven will be much hotter than hell."

But that argument does not really take Scripture at face value. In the first place, Isaiah 30:26 describes God's judgment on the earth, not the heavenly state. In the second place, the whole point of this passage in Revelation 21 is that there is no "light source" in heaven. The light there is not a radiant light, subject to Kelvin's scale. The only light is the glory of God. It permeates all heaven; it does not shine from any "source." It is a light *unlike* any light known on earth. It is the very light of him who "is light, and in him is no darkness at all" (1 John 1:5). No reason exists to think the glow of divine glory emits heat.

Again, this description pushes human language to the limit and aims to convey an idea that we cannot possibly imagine. But it is clear that the glory of heaven will be unimaginably brilliant.

Years ago Lutheran scholar J. A. Seiss wrote these beautiful words about the light of heavenly Jerusalem:

> That shining is not from any material combustion,—not from any
> consumption of fuel that needs to be replaced as one supply burns
> out; for it is the uncreated light of Him who is light, dispensed by and

through the Lamb as the everlasting lamp, to the home, and hearts, and understandings, of His glorified saints. When Paul and Silas lay wounded and bound in the inner dungeon of the prison of Philippi, they still had sacred light which enabled them to beguile the night-watches with happy songs. When Paul was on his way to Damascus, a light brighter than the sun at noon shone round about him, irradiating his whole being with new sights and understanding, and making his soul and body ever afterward light in the Lord. When Moses came down from the mount of his communion with God, his face was so luminous that his brethren could not endure to look upon it. He was in such close fellowship with light that he became informed with light, and came to the camp as a very lamp of God, glowing with the glory of God.

On the Mount of Transfiguration, that same light streamed forth from all the body and raiment of the blessed Jesus. And with reference to the very time when this city comes into being and place, Isaiah says, "The moon shall be ashamed and the sun confounded,"—ashamed because of the out-beaming glory which then shall appear in the New Jerusalem, leaving no more need for them to shine in it, since the glory of God lights it, and the Lamb is the light thereof.[7]

No Security System

The apostle John further writes, "its gates will never be shut by day—and there will be no night there" (v. 25). In an ancient city the gates were shut at night to protect the people from robbers, bandits, and invading armies. Gates that are always open speak of perfect security and protection. There will be absolutely no threat to the security of heaven, so there will be no need of closed gates.

Verse 26 repeats the thread of thought from verse 24—the idea of kings bringing their glory to the throne of God: "They will bring into it the glory and the honor of the nations." In other words, there will be no rival to the glory or the authority of God. The cosmic conflict of the ages will be finally ended forever, and God and his people will dwell in utter security.

John says, "Nothing unclean will ever enter it, nor anyone who does what is detestable or false, but only those who are written in the Lamb's book of life" (v. 27; cf. 22:15). Only the elect of God—those

[7] J. A. Seiss, *The Apocalypse: Lectures on the Book of Revelation* (1865; repr., Grand Rapids, MI: Zondervan, 1970), 499.

who have put their trust in Christ—will enter that great city. Satan and his wicked minions will already have been banished forever from the scene.

No Needs

In Revelation 22:1–2 the angel shows John the "river of the water of life, bright as crystal, flowing from the throne of God and of the Lamb through the middle of the street of the city; also, on either side of the river, the tree of life with its twelve kinds of fruit, yielding its fruit each month. The leaves of the tree were for the healing of the nations." This crystal-clear, celestial river flows out of the throne and through the middle of the New Jerusalem. Imagine what a river meant to someone living in a barren place like the wilderness of Sinai. It was a welcome place of comfort and rest, refreshment and sustenance. A river meant cool water to a mouth parched by the desert heat. And imagine the joy of someone who lived in the desert finding a tree with fruit! The New Jerusalem will be the epitome of everything precious— a city, a river, and trees.

Psalm 46:4–5 speaks of the same river: "There is a river whose streams make glad the city of God, the holy habitation of the Most High. God is in the midst of her; she shall not be moved."

In Eden also there was a beautiful river that watered the garden (Genesis 2:10). Eden had "the tree of life . . . in the midst of the garden" (Genesis 2:9). So the scene in heaven seems to be the final perfection of everything Eden represented.

"The tree of life" might actually describe one, two, or three trees. The Greek expression lacks a definite article, so this could actually be translated, "In the middle of the street and on either side of the river was a tree of life"—signifying three trees, one in the street and two on either side of the river. Alternatively (and more likely), "In the middle of the street" might describe the position of the river, "and on either side of the river, a tree of life" (Revelation 22:2).

In any case, the fruit of the tree of life is indescribably wonderful. It bears twelve kinds of fruit, one for each month—like a "fruit-of-the-month" tree. The privilege of eating from this tree is granted to all overcomers (Revelation 2:7).

In heaven we will eat for enjoyment, not sustenance. Nevertheless, the tree has a wholesome, beneficial effect on those who partake. Even its leaves are "for the healing of the nations" (v. 2). The Greek word translated "healing" is *therapeia*, from which we get the English word *therapeutic*. John is saying that the leaves of the tree of life somehow enrich heavenly life—if only through the pure joy of eating. The water of life is also there for the sheer pleasure of drinking. No food will be *needed* in heaven, but incredible gourmet delights will nonetheless be enjoyed. Again this underscores the truth that God's design for us is that we may *enjoy* him forever. Much of heaven is designed for sheer pleasure—both the pleasure of God and the pleasure of his people.

No Curse

If any aspect of heaven stirs my heart with eager anticipation, it is this:

> No longer will there be anything accursed, but the throne of God and of the Lamb will be in it, and his servants will worship him. They will see his face, and his name will be on their foreheads. And night will be no more. They will need no light of lamp or sun, for the Lord God will be their light, and they will reign forever and ever. (Revelation 22:3–5)

The curse, with all its painful and detestable ramifications, will be overturned and erased forever. Pain, the agony of toil, sweat, thorns, disease, sorrow, and sin will have no place whatsoever in heaven.

As the apostle Paul wrote, "What no eye has seen, nor ear heard, nor the heart of man imagined, what God has prepared for those who love him" (1 Corinthians 2:9). The delights of heaven are beyond the scope of our wildest imaginations. But for the believer, we can taste it even now: "These things God has revealed to us through the Spirit" (v. 10). We "have tasted the heavenly gift" (Hebrews 6:4). And having had a foretaste of heaven, we ought to have our hearts fixed firmly there.

Unfortunately, many Christians think close fellowship with God and enjoyment of heaven is impossible until we actually arrive there. But the real truth is that for Christians, eternal life is a present possession, not merely a future hope. We're supposed to live as if our hearts are in heaven already. We can commune and fellowship with God even now—not face-to-face, but through prayer and the study of his Word.

In heaven the difference will be that we will be with him on a face-to-face basis (1 Corinthians 13:12). First Thessalonians 4:17 says that from the time we are caught away to be with the Lord, through all eternity, "we will always be with the Lord." "He has said, 'I will never leave you nor forsake you'" (Hebrews 13:5).

So when the apostle John says that in heaven we will see his face (Revelation 22:4), this implies the ultimate perfection of our intimacy, communion, and fellowship with the Lord. Having his name on our forehead speaks of both his ownership of us and our unflagging commitment to him.

These, then, are the consummate blessings of the eternal state: We will be forever in the presence of the eternal, holy God. We will have intimate, unbroken fellowship with Christ. We will be fellow heirs with Christ. We will rule and reign with Christ. The full riches of heaven will be ours to possess and enjoy however we please.

All those statements would be blasphemous if God himself had not promised these things to us.

7

What *We* Will Be Like in Heaven

Perfection.

Most of us understand the concept but have a hard time envisioning anything truly perfect. Everything in our earthly experience is flawed, imperfect.

And for those who know and love the Lord, the imperfections we are most deeply aware of often tend to be our own. I'm not speaking of the frailties of our bodies—though we feel those all too well. But the imperfections that trouble us most are not that superficial. The real problem is a sinfulness that comes straight from the heart (see Mark 7:21–23).

Of course, we have a tendency to be more tolerant of our *own* imperfections than of the failings of others. We try to cover for ourselves, but in our hearts we know all too well that we are woefully and sinfully imperfect. What Christian cannot echo the sentiment Paul expresses in Romans 7:24: "Wretched man that I am! Who will deliver me from this body of death?"

We're not alone in this. The entire universe suffers the effects of human sin. Paul also writes, "We know that the whole creation has been groaning together in the pains of childbirth until now" (Romans 8:22). That's why *all* we can know on earth is imperfection. All creation agonizes under the cruel effect of sin's curse, waiting for the consummation of all things, when the curse will be finally removed.

At that time, everything will be perfect. Pain, sorrow, and the groaning of creation will finally be no more. "The ransomed of the Lord shall return and come to Zion with singing; everlasting joy shall be upon their heads; they shall obtain gladness and joy, and sorrow and sighing shall flee away" (Isaiah 35:10).

Not only that, but *we* shall be gloriously perfected. The whole person—body and soul—will be made completely new, flawless. As the apostle John wrote, "Beloved, we are God's children now, and what we will be has not yet appeared; but we know that when he appears we shall be like him, because we shall see him as he is" (1 John 3:2).

We can't envision it now—"what we will be has not yet appeared"—but we will finally be wholly and completely Christlike. This is the very purpose for which God chose us in eternity past: "to be conformed to the image of his Son, in order that he might be the firstborn among many brothers" (Romans 8:29). "He chose us in him before the foundation of the world, that we should be holy and blameless before him" (Ephesians 1:4). He has already begun this good work in us, and he will faithfully "bring it to completion at the day of Jesus Christ" (Philippians 1:6). And when we see Christ, we will instantly and summarily be made utterly perfect, because we shall see him as he is.

Heaven is a perfect place for people made perfect. Perfection is the goal of God's sanctifying work in us. He's not merely making us better than we are; he is conforming us to the image of his Son. He is making us fit to dwell in his presence forever. The utter perfection of heaven is the consummation of our salvation. It is the purpose for which he chose us before the foundation of the world.

Changed from the Inside Out

God begins the process of perfecting us from the moment we are converted from unbelief to faith in Christ. The Holy Spirit regenerates us. He gives us a new heart with a new set of holy desires (Ezekiel 36:26). He transforms our stubborn wills. He opens our hearts to embrace the truth rather than reject it. He enables us to believe rather than doubt. He gives us a hunger for righteousness and a desire for him. And thus the new birth transforms the inner person. From that point on, everything that occurs in our lives—good or bad—God uses to make us like Christ (Romans 8:28–30).

In terms of our moral and legal status, believers are judged perfect immediately—not on the basis of who we are or what we have done, but because of what Christ has done for us. We are fully justified the moment we believe. We are forgiven of all our sin. We are clothed with a perfect righteousness (Isaiah 61:10; Romans 4:5), which instantly gives us a standing before God without any fear of condemnation (Romans 5:1; 8:1). This is the great position of privilege Scripture refers to when it says God has "blessed us in Christ with every spiritual blessing in the heavenly places" (Ephesians 1:3). And when Paul writes that God has "raised us up with him and seated us with him in the heavenly places in Christ Jesus" (Ephesians 2:6), he is again speaking of this position of favor with God that we have been granted by grace alone. We are not literally, physically seated with Christ in the heavenlies, of course. We are not mystically present there through some kind of spiritual telepathy. But legally, in the eternal court of God, we have been granted full rights to heaven. That is the high legal standing we enjoy even now.

But God does not stop there. Having judicially declared us righteous (Scripture calls that *justification*), God never stops conforming us to the image of his Son (that is *sanctification*). Although our legal standing is already perfect, God is also making *us* perfect. Heaven is a place of perfect holiness, and we would not be fit to live there unless we too could be made holy. In a sense, then, the blessing of justification is God's guarantee that he will ultimately conform us to the image of his Son. "Those whom he justified he also glorified" (Romans 8:30).

The seeds of Christlikeness are planted at the moment of conversion. Colossians 2:9–10 says that in Christ "the whole fullness of deity dwells bodily, and you have been filled in him"—filled up with all the fullness of God. Peter adds that believers have been granted "all things that pertain to life and godliness" (2 Peter 1:3). If you are a Christian, the life of God dwells in your soul, and with it all that you need for heaven. The principle of eternal life is already in you, meaning you *have* title to heaven as a present possession. You have already passed from death to life (John 5:24). You are a new person (2 Corinthians 5:17). Whereas you were once enslaved to sin, you have now become a slave of righteousness (Romans 6:18). Instead of receiving the wages of sin—death—you have received God's gift of eternal life (Romans 6:23). And eternal life means *abundant* life (John 10:10). It is like an artesian well of spiritual power within us, satisfying and enabling us to live the life we are called to (John 7:38). That is what Paul means when he writes, "If anyone is in Christ, he is a new creation. The old has passed away; behold, the new has come" (2 Corinthians 5:17).

Now let's be honest. Even for the most committed Christian, it doesn't always seem like "the new has come." We don't always *feel* like a "new creation." Usually we are more keenly aware of the sin that oozes from within us than we are of the rivers of living water Christ spoke of. Although we "have the firstfruits of the Spirit, [we] groan inwardly as we wait eagerly for adoption as sons, the redemption of our bodies" (Romans 8:23). And we groan this way all our lives. Remember that it was a mature apostle, not a fragile new Christian, who cried out in Romans 7:24, "Wretched man that I am! Who will deliver me from this body of death?"

Here's the problem: Like Lazarus, we came forth from the grave still bound in grave clothes. We are incarcerated in human flesh. "Flesh" in the biblical sense refers not just to the physical body, but to the sinful thoughts and habits that remain with us until our bodies are finally glorified. When Paul speaks of "flesh" and "spirit" he is not contrasting the material body and the immaterial spirit—setting up a kind of dualism, the way gnostic and New Age doctrines do. He uses the word *flesh* to speak of a tendency to sin—a sin principle—that remains even in the redeemed person.

Paul clearly spells out the problem from his own experience in Romans 7. Here Paul writes,

> For I do not understand my own actions. For I do not do what I want, but I do the very thing I hate. Now if I do what I do not want, I agree with the law, that it is good. So now it is no longer I who do it, but sin that dwells within me. For I know that nothing good dwells in me, that is, in my flesh. For I have the desire to do what is right, but not the ability to carry it out. For I do not do the good I want, but the evil I do not want is what I keep on doing. Now if I do what I do not want, it is no longer I who do it, but sin that dwells within me.

So I find it to be a law that when I want to do right, evil lies close
at hand. (vv. 15–21)

If you are struggling to understand how the apostle Paul employs the term *flesh*, this last phrase can virtually be taken as his definition: *The flesh* is "a law that when I want to do right, evil lies close at hand" (v. 21). Paul goes on to say that this law is embedded in him—"in my members" (v. 23), "waging war against" his desire to obey the righteousness of the law, thus "making me captive to the law of sin that dwells in my members." That indwelling principle of sin includes all the wicked habits and thought patterns that we acquired in our lives before being born again. These fleshly influences have yet to be done away with, and we are severely troubled by them all our lives. Christians spend their lives "putting to death" the deeds of the flesh (Romans 8:13), but the sin principle will never be fully eliminated until we are glorified.

As believers we *are* new creatures—reborn souls—vested with everything necessary for life and godliness, but we cannot appreciate fully the newness of our position in Christ because of the persisting presence of sin in us.

Like Paul, we "delight in the law of God, in [our] inner being" (7:22). Only the principle of eternal life in us can explain such love for the law of God. But at the same time, the flesh constricts and fetters us, like tightly bound grave clothes on someone just up out of the grave. This flesh principle is at war against the principle of new life in Christ. So we feel like captives to the law of sin in our own members (v. 23).

How can this be? After all, Paul earlier wrote in this very epistle that our bondage to sin is broken. We are supposed to "have been set free from sin" (6:22). How is it that just one scant chapter later, he says we are "captive to the law of sin that dwells in my members" (7:23)?

But being a captive is not quite the same thing as being enslaved. As unredeemed sinners, we were full-time slaves of sin—willing servants, in fact. As Christians who are not yet glorified, we are "captives," unwilling prisoners of an already-defeated enemy. Although sin can buffet and abuse us, it does not own us, and it cannot ultimately destroy us. Sin's authority and dominion are broken. It "lies close at hand" in the believer's life (7:21), but it is no longer our master. Our real allegiance is now to the principle of righteousness (v. 22). It is in this sense that "the new has come" (2 Corinthians 5:17). Even though we still fall into old patterns of sinful thinking and behavior, those things no longer define who we are. Sin is now an anomaly and an intruder, not the sum and substance of our character.

God is changing us from the inside out. He has planted the incorruptible seed of eternal life deep in the believer's soul. We have a new desire and a new power to please God. We have a new heart and a whole new love for God. And all those are factors that contribute to our ultimate growth in grace.

Paul makes a fascinating point about the inside-out transformation of believers. In 2 Corinthians 3, he contrasts the effects of our salvation with what happened to Moses when he encountered God's glory on Sinai. Remember that when Moses came down from the mountain after the giving of the law, the glow on his face was so terrifying that he had to put a veil over his face (Exodus 34:29–33). Yet that was a relatively weak and diminishing glory (2 Corinthians 3:7). It was also a *reflected* glory.

In contrast, "the glory which shall be revealed in us" (Romans 8:18, KJV) is an ever-growing glory that is not reflected, but comes straight from within. Paul writes, "We all, with unveiled face, beholding the glory of the Lord, are being transformed into the same image from one degree of glory to another. For this comes from the Lord who is the Spirit" (2 Corinthians 3:18). In other words, the indwelling Spirit of God personally conveys us from one level of glory to another.

The Greek word translated "beholding" means "looking at a reflection." In the familiar King James Version, it says "beholding as in a glass" (or "mirror"). Unlike the Israelites, we require no veil to shield us from the reflection of glory. ("Not like Moses, who would put a veil over his face so that the Israelites might not gaze at the outcome of what was being brought to an end"—v. 13.) We get a full-on look at undiluted glory: "God, who said, 'Let light shine out of darkness,' has shone *in our hearts* to give the light of the knowledge of the glory of God *in the face of Jesus Christ*" (4:6).

We don't literally look directly at the face of Christ, of course. The glory we see is a reflection of "Christ in [us], the hope of glory"

(Colossians 1:27). As we fix our hearts and aspirations on his glory, the glow of Christlikeness grows brighter in us. One day we shall literally see him—not merely as a dim reflection. We will stand bodily in his presence: "For now we see in a mirror dimly, but then face to face" (1 Corinthians 13:12). And with one face-to-face glance at the person of Christ, we will be instantly transformed into his likeness. "We shall be like him, because we shall see him as he is" (1 John 3:2).

Meanwhile, his glory is transforming us from the inside out. That's why (unlike the reflected glow on Moses's face) the glory doesn't fade; it grows "from one degree of glory to another."

Although sin has crippled our souls and marred our spirits—though it has scarred our thoughts, will, and emotions—we who know Christ have already had a taste of redemption. As we set our hearts on heaven and mortify the remaining sin in our members, we can experience the transforming power of Christ's glory on a daily basis. And we long for that day when we will be completely redeemed. We yearn to reach that place where the seed of perfection that has been planted within us will bloom into fullness and we will be completely redeemed, finally made perfect (Hebrews 12:23). That is *exactly* what heaven is all about.

A Redeemed Soul

In heaven we will finally lose all traces of human fallenness. In fact, no one will ever enter heaven or dwell there who isn't absolutely perfect. This is often symbolized in Scripture by the imagery of white robes that are worn by the redeemed in heaven. Revelation 6:11 says this about the martyrs of the apocalypse: "They were each given a white robe and told to rest a little longer, until the number of their fellow servants and their brothers should be complete, who were to be killed as they themselves had been." The white robes symbolize holiness, purity, and absolute perfection. In Revelation 7:14 one of the elders says, "These are the ones coming out of the great tribulation. They have washed their robes and made them white in the blood of the Lamb." Repeatedly, the Bible emphasizes the perfection of those who enter heaven.

Scripture tells us that apart from holiness, "no one will see the Lord" (Hebrews 12:14). God doesn't merely justify us, clothing us with imputed righteousness, then leave us bound in the grave clothes of the flesh. He lovingly, graciously conforms us heart, soul, mind, and flesh to a standard befitting the lofty position he has elevated us to.

But don't misunderstand. This is not to say our own personal holiness is the ground on which we are granted entrance into heaven or acceptance with God. If that were the case, none of us could ever gain enough merit to deserve heaven. We are graciously granted entry into heaven solely and exclusively because of Christ's perfect righteousness, which is imputed to us in our justification. The holiness gained in our sanctification is by no means meritorious.

Moreover, the holiness our sanctification produces could never be sufficient to fit us for heaven by itself. In heaven we will be *perfectly* Christlike. Sanctification is the earthly process of growth by which we press toward that goal; *glorification* is the instantaneous completion of it. God graciously, summarily glorifies us and admits us into his presence. As we noted in chapter 5, there is no waiting period, no soul sleep, and no purgatory.

Misunderstanding on this point runs deep. No less a scholar than C. S. Lewis wrote,

> Our souls *demand* purgatory, don't they? Would it not break the heart if God said to us, "It is true, my son, that your breath smells and your rags drip with mud and slime, but we are charitable here and no one will upbraid you with these things, nor draw away from you. Enter into the joy"? Should we not reply, "With submission, sir, and if there is no objection, I'd *rather* be cleaned first." "It may hurt, you know."— "Even so, sir."[1]

Lewis was no theologian. He was prone (like too many Anglicans) to water down the clarity of biblical truth with Roman Catholic tradition. But this is surely one of his most glaring and baffling errors. It is as if he were totally oblivious to the biblical promise of glorification.

Once more: Nothing in Scripture even hints at the notion of purgatory, and nothing indicates that our glorification will in any way be drawn out or painful. On the contrary, as we have seen repeatedly from Scripture, the moment a believer dies, his soul is instantly glorified and he enters God's presence. To depart this world is to be with Christ

---

[1] C. S. Lewis, *Letters to Malcolm: Chiefly on Prayer* (New York: Harcourt, 1964), 108–109.

(Philippians 1:23). And upon seeing Christ, we become like him. It is a graceful, peaceful, painless, instantaneous transition. Paul says to be absent from the body is to be "at home with the Lord" (2 Corinthians 5:8).

Notice that Paul indicates Christians in heaven at this moment are "away from the body." The body goes to the grave; the soul is admitted immediately to heaven. Hebrews 12:23 also suggests that all the saints who have died and are now in heaven are there without their bodies; it describes heaven as the dwelling place of "*the spirits* of the righteous made perfect." But we do not remain mere spirits throughout eternity. Our glorified spirits will be united with glorified bodies at the final resurrection. (We'll return to that subject later in this chapter.)

What will the perfected soul be like? The most obvious truth is that it will finally be perfectly free from evil forever. We will never again have a selfish desire or utter useless words. We will never perform another unkind deed or think a sinful thought. We will be perfectly liberated from our captivity to sin and finally able to think and act in a way that is perfectly righteous, holy, and honorable in God's sight. Can you imagine yourself in consummate perfection forever? I frankly have a hard time envisioning myself as utterly impeccable. But there will be no imperfection in heaven!

Revelation 21:27 says, "Nothing unclean will ever enter it, nor anyone who does what is detestable or false." No one who has any stain of sin will ever enter the heavenly city; therefore sin will never again pose any threat whatsoever.

What about the stain of *our* past sins? Revelation 22:14–15 says, "Blessed are those who wash their robes, so that they may have the right to the tree of life and that they may enter the city by the gates. Outside are the dogs and sorcerers and the sexually immoral and murderers and idolaters, and everyone who loves and practices falsehood." Sin may define who we once were, but no longer. We are now new creatures in Christ, completely forgiven, thoroughly washed, and forever made perfect. As Paul wrote the Corinthians,

> Do you not know that the unrighteous will not inherit the kingdom of God? Do not be deceived: neither the sexually immoral, nor idolaters, nor adulterers, nor men who practice homosexuality, nor thieves, nor the greedy, nor drunkards, nor revilers, nor swindlers will inherit the

kingdom of God. And such were some of you. *But you were washed, you were sanctified*, you were justified in the name of the Lord Jesus Christ and by the Spirit of our God. (1 Corinthians 6:9–11)

All believers can rest in this confidence: God has already justified us in order to free us from the guilt of sin. He is now sanctifying us in order to deliver us from the corruption of sin. And one day he will glorify us in order to liberate us from the very presence of sin—forever!

If you are not a Christian, you need to lay hold of this truth by faith: *the sin that will keep you out of heaven has no cure but the blood of Christ.* If you are weary of your sin and exhausted from the load of your guilt, he tenderly holds forth the offer of life and forgiveness and eternal rest to you: "Come to me, all who labor and are heavy laden, and I will give you rest" (Matthew 11:28). No one will be turned away. Jesus said, "Whoever comes to me I will never cast out" (John 6:37). All are invited: "The Spirit and the Bride say, 'Come.' And let the one who hears say, 'Come.' And let the one who is thirsty come; let the one who desires take the water of life without price" (Revelation 22:17).

In heaven there will be no sin, suffering, sorrow, or pain. We will never do anything to displease God. There will be no temptation because the world, the flesh, and the devil will all be conspicuously absent. There will be no persecution, division, disunity, or hate. In heaven there will be no quarrels or disagreements. There will be no disappointments. Prayer, fasting, repentance, and confession of sin will cease because the need for them will cease. There will be no weeping because there will be nothing to make us sad. With sin and its effects erased forever, it will be a life of unimaginable blessing!

We will then know *perfect pleasure*. In Psalm 16:11, the psalmist addresses God: "In your presence there is fullness of joy; at your right hand are pleasures forevermore." In heaven, everything that now makes us groan will finally be done away with. We will find ourselves in the very presence of God, where the purest and truest kind of pleasure is possible. Whatever pleasures we have known here on earth while living under the curse of sin, they are trivial, paltry diversions compared to the pure delights of heaven. When our souls are made new we will finally be able to glorify God perfectly and enjoy him forever, as he intended. Since nothing is better or greater than God, the pure enjoyment of him must be the very essence of bliss.

In heaven we will also have *perfect knowledge.* Paul writes, "Now I know in part; then I shall know fully, even as I have been fully known" (1 Corinthians 13:12). Since we are known comprehensively by God (Psalm 139:1–3), this must mean that in some sense we will have comprehensive knowledge. It cannot mean we will have absolute omniscience, for omniscience is one of the incommunicable attributes of God. To embrace all knowledge, one would have to *be* God. But this does indicate that our knowledge will be as complete as we could ever desire. We will have no more unanswered questions, no confusion, no ignorance, and no more need to walk by faith rather than by sight.

We will live in *perfect comfort.* We will never experience one uncomfortable moment. In Jesus's account of the beggar Lazarus and the rich man, Abraham says to the rich man in hell, "Child, remember that you in your lifetime received your good things, and Lazarus in like manner bad things; but now he is comforted here, and you are in anguish" (Luke 16:25). Hell is agony; heaven is eternal consolation.

We will finally know *perfect love.* First Corinthians 13:13 says, "Now faith, hope, and love abide, these three; but the greatest of these is love." Why is love the greatest of virtues? Because it is eternal. In heaven all our hopes will be realized. "Hope that is seen is not hope. For who hopes for what he sees?" (Romans 8:24). All that we have laid hold of by faith will be ours to enjoy forever. Faith will be swallowed up by sight. But we will love perfectly and will be loved perfectly for all eternity. John 13:1 says Christ loved his disciples *eis telos*—literally, "to the end," to utter perfection. That same love will engulf us forever. And we will finally be able to love perfectly in return.

We could summarize by saying that heaven is a place of *perfect joy.* Our joy in this life is always mixed with sorrow, discouragement, disappointment, or worry. Sin, grief, and sorrow inevitably dampen happiness. An honest look at life in this world produces more tears than real joy. Our lives here begin with the joy of childbirth, but inevitably end in the sorrows of death and separation. In heaven things will be different. Heaven is a place of undiluted joy. At the end of the parable of the talents in Matthew 25, the master tells the faithful steward, "Well done, good and faithful servant. . . . Enter into the joy of your master." (v. 23).

Jesus's choice of that terminology indicates that one of the dominant characteristics of heaven is joy. Best of all, it's an unending and never-diminishing joy. It *must* be, because heavenly perfection is never altered.

A Glorified Body

As we have already stressed, however, heaven is not merely a state of mind. It is a real place, where the redeemed will have real bodies, exactly like the resurrection body of Jesus Christ.

The Necessity of Our Resurrection

God made human beings body and soul together. He "formed the man of dust from the ground and breathed into his nostrils the breath of life, and the man became a living creature" (Genesis 2:7). We consist of an inner self and an outer self (2 Corinthians 4:16). Therefore our ultimate perfection demands that *both* body and soul be renewed. Even the creation of a new heaven and earth demands that we have bodies—a physical earth calls for its inhabitants to have physical bodies. An honest approach to Scripture does not permit these realities to be spiritualized or allegorized away. Eternal life as a mere state of mind would defeat the whole point of many of the promises of Scripture.

Death results in separation of the body and the soul. Our bodies go to the grave, and our spirits go to the Lord. The separation continues until the resurrection: "Do not marvel at this, for an hour is coming when all who are in the tombs will hear his voice and come out, those who have done good to the resurrection of life, and those who have done evil to the resurrection of judgment" (John 5:28–29). Right now the souls of believers who have died are in heaven. Someday their bodies will be resurrected and joined to their spirits, and they will enjoy the eternal perfection of body and soul.

Similarly, the bodies of unbelievers who have died are in the grave, and their souls are in hell. There will also be a day when the bodies of the ungodly will be raised from the graves and joined to their spirits. They will then stand, body and soul, before the judgment throne of God, and will then be cast bodily into the lake of fire (cf. Matthew 5:30).

Christians need not dread that judgment. There is no possibility of condemnation for those who are in Christ Jesus (Romans 8:1). We *eagerly* await the redemption of our bodies (v. 23). "For in this [body] we groan, longing to put on our heavenly dwelling" (2 Corinthians 5:2). Precisely what does this mean? Does it imply that we will receive all-new bodies? Will they be anything like our current bodies? Will we look anything like we do now?

First of all, note that our resurrection bodies *are* our earthly bodies, glorified. The bodies we receive in the resurrection will have the same qualities as the glorified resurrection body of Christ. "We know that when he appears we shall be like him" (1 John 3:2).

Christ's resurrection body was the same body as before, not a whole new one. After he arose, the tomb was empty. The body itself was resurrected—the very same body, but in a glorified state. The wounds from his crucifixion were still visible (John 20:27). He could be touched and handled—he was not merely an apparition or a phantom (Luke 24:39). He looked human in every regard. He conversed a long time with the disciples on the road to Emmaus, and they never once questioned his humanity (Luke 24:13–18). He ate real, earthly food with his friends on another occasion (vv. 42–43).

Yet his body also had otherworldly properties. He could pass through solid walls (John 20:19). He could appear in different forms so his identity was not immediately obvious (Mark 16:12). He could suddenly appear out of nowhere (Luke 24:36). And he could ascend directly into heaven in bodily form, with no adverse effect as he went through the atmosphere (Luke 24:51; Acts 1:9).

Our bodies will be exactly like that. They will be real, physical, genuinely human bodies—the very same bodies we have while on this earth—yet wholly perfected and glorified. Second Corinthians 5:1 calls the resurrection body "a building from God, a house not made with hands, eternal in the heavens."

First Thessalonians 4 describes the resurrection of believers who have died, and the simultaneous catching away to heaven of believers who are still alive:

We do not want you to be uninformed, brothers, about those who are asleep, that you may not grieve as others who have no hope. For since we believe that Jesus died and rose again, even so, through Jesus, God will bring with him those who have fallen asleep. For this we declare to you by a word from the Lord, that we who are alive, who are left until the coming of the Lord, will not precede those who have fallen asleep. For the Lord himself will descend from heaven with a cry of command, with the voice of an archangel, and with the sound of the trumpet of God. And the dead in Christ will rise first. Then we who are alive, who are left, will be caught up together with them in the clouds to meet the Lord in the air, and so we will always be with the Lord (vv. 13–17).

Paul speaks of this same reality in 1 Corinthians 15:51–52, where he says,

"Behold! I tell you a mystery. We shall not all sleep, but we shall all be changed, in a moment, in the twinkling of an eye, at the last trumpet. For the trumpet will sound, and the dead will be raised imperishable, and we shall be changed."

First, believers who are dead are united with their perfected bodies; then those who are still alive will be caught up and instantly "changed"—glorified. So every Christian still living on the earth when Christ comes will be instantly perfected. And, again, notice that both the living and the dead will have their old bodies made new, glorified.

This doctrine of bodily resurrection is absolutely essential to the Christian message. First Corinthians 15 is the definitive chapter on the subject. There Paul severely rebukes anyone who would doubt or question this reality: "But someone will ask, 'How are the dead raised? With what kind of body do they come?'" To which Paul responds, "You foolish person!" (vv. 35–36). That is one of the most caustic retorts in all the Pauline writings. But in Paul's estimation, this doctrine is fundamental. To deny it is to embrace something other than genuine Christianity: "For if the dead are not raised, not even Christ has been raised. And if Christ has not been raised, your faith is futile and you are still in your sins" (vv. 16–17).

Resurrection Illustrated

Paul uses a series of comparisons to explain the resurrection of the body. The first is an illustration borrowed from Christ's own teaching. Jesus said, "Truly, truly, I say to you, unless a grain of wheat falls into the earth and dies, it remains alone; but if it dies, it bears much fruit" (John 12:24).

The apostle applies the same imagery to the bodily resurrection: "What you sow does not come to life unless it dies. And what you sow is not the body that is to be, but a bare kernel, perhaps of wheat or of some other grain" (1 Corinthians 15:36–37). When you plant a seed, the first thing a seed does is die. It goes into the ground, begins the process of fermentation and decomposition, and that is what triggers the new life. Similarly our bodies will die, be placed in a grave, and then be raised, just as a seed dies and produces a plant that is far more glorious than the seed.

Also, the seed contains the pattern for the plant that grows. All the genetic code for an entire oak tree is contained inside the kernel of the acorn. Likewise, our resurrection bodies will bear a resemblance to the body that is buried—but with a far greater glory. We will be ourselves, only perfect. And the decomposition of the earthly will only facilitate the remaking of a glorified resurrection body—with none of the flaws of the old, but with all that is necessary for a perfect existence in heaven.

That answers the question "How are the dead raised?" (v. 35). Paul employs a second illustration to reply to the doubter's second challenge, "With what kind of body do they come?" The scoffer's question suggests that it is absurd to think normal human flesh would be fit for life in heaven. Paul's reply points out that it is absurd to think of the resurrection body as "normal" human flesh.

After all, even in our limited earthly knowledge, "Not all flesh is the same, but there is one kind for humans, another for animals, another for birds, and another for fish" (v. 39). The resurrected body will no doubt be a different variety of flesh than we know from earthly experience. It will be literal human flesh, but gloriously and perfectly so. It will be as different from our earthly flesh as fish flesh is from bird flesh.

Continuing in a similar mode of thought, Paul says, "There are heavenly bodies and earthly bodies, but the glory of the heavenly is of one kind, and the glory of the earthly is of another. There is one glory of the sun, and another glory of the moon, and another glory of the stars; for star differs from star in glory" (vv. 40–41). Since God made everything from the tiniest microscopic creature to a massive galaxy full of star systems, he can make any kind of body he wants. God's creation is rich with infinite variety. Why question his ability to create human flesh that is fit for heaven?

Tying all these illustrations together, Paul concludes, "So is it with the resurrection of the dead. What is sown is perishable; what is raised is imperishable. It is sown in dishonor; it is raised in glory. It is sown in weakness; it is raised in power. It is sown a natural body; it is raised a spiritual body. If there is a natural body, there is also a spiritual body" (vv. 42–44).

Like a seed, the resurrection body is sown and is raised. Human graveyards are seed plots for the resurrection of the dead. But the resurrection body is new, changed in virtually every way imaginable. It was sown in death and decay; it is raised to be *imperishable*. It was buried as a thing of defilement, ingloriously placed under the earth; but it is raised as something *glorious*. When entombed it is dead, utterly inanimate and impotent; but it is raised to be *powerful*. It is planted as a lifeless material thing, yet raised as something full of life and *spiritual*.

All of this is to say that in heaven we will have real bodies that are permanently and eternally perfect. You will never look in a mirror and notice wrinkles or a receding hairline. You will never have a day of sickness. You won't be susceptible to injury, or disease, or allergies. There will be none of those things in heaven. There will only be absolute, imperishable perfection.

We will no doubt have otherworldly abilities in heaven. Remember that the heavenly city is fifteen hundred miles high. Don't think you'll be waiting for elevators to get you to the top. You'll no doubt have the ability to take flight—or if you desire, simply be transported there in an instant—in the same way that Christ's resurrection body could seemingly disappear and reappear in another place at will.

Above all, we will be *Christlike*. Paul writes,

> Thus it is written, "The first man Adam became a living being"; the last Adam became a life-giving spirit. But it is not the spiritual that is first but the natural, and then the spiritual. The first man was from the earth, a man of dust; the second man is from heaven. As was the man of dust, so also are those who are of the dust, and as is the man of heaven, so also are those who are of heaven. (vv. 45–48)

In that passage Paul contrasts the heads of two families. Adam is our father according to the flesh, meaning that he is the head of the human race. Christ is our spiritual head, and the first among the redeemed race. Just as our earthly bodies are descended from Adam's so that we resemble him, so in heaven we will be like Jesus Christ, who is incorruptible, eternal, glorified, powerful, and spiritual. According to Philippians 3:21, God will "will transform our lowly body to be like his glorious body."

So the best picture of what we'll be like in heaven is the resurrection body of Jesus Christ. We will have a body fit for the full life of God to indwell and express itself forever. We'll be able to eat but won't need to. We will have bodies that can move at will through space and matter. Our bodies will be ageless and incorruptible; we will know nothing of pain, tears, sorrow, sickness, or death.

Our resurrection bodies will be brilliant in their splendor. Christ's glorified body is described as shining like the sun in its strength (Revelation 1:16). In an Old Testament promise, Scripture compares our glorified bodies to the shining of the moon and stars: "Those who are wise shall shine like the brightness of the sky above; and those who turn many to righteousness, like the stars forever and ever" (Daniel 12:3).

Do you see why it is irrational to seek our highest joy and comfort in this life? God's plan, to make us like Christ, is infinitely better. Why would we ever set our affections on the fleeting things of this earth? To have such a perspective is only to seek what will never satisfy. That kind of thinking only aggravates our misery.

Perfect Relationships

So far we have barely touched on the question of relationships in heaven. Yet this is one of the major issues most Christians wonder about. Will we recognize our loved ones? Will we remember our earthly relationships? What kind of relationships will we have? Will we have family love and fellowship in heaven? Will our relationships in heaven be anything like they are here?

The question I'm most often asked about heaven is, *"Will I be married to the same spouse in heaven?"* Most are saying, "I don't want to lose my relationship with my wife; I can't imagine going to heaven and not being married to her." (Others, however, may be secretly hoping for a different answer!)

Scripture speaks specifically to many of these questions. On the issue of marriage and family, for example, Paul said,

> This is what I mean, brothers: the appointed time has grown very short. From now on, let those who have wives live as though they had none, and those who mourn as though they were not mourning, and those who rejoice as though they were not rejoicing, and those who buy as though they had no goods, and those who deal with the world as though they had no dealings with it. For the present form [Gk. *schēma*] of this world is passing away. (1 Corinthians 7:29–31)

The apostle lists several of the things that are passing away: marriage, weeping, earthly rejoicing, and ownership. All the *schēma* of the world is passing away. *Schēma* refers to fashion, manner of life, and a way of doing things.

Paul was saying we should take what this life brings, yet keep from being engulfed in it, because many of the distinctive features of ownership and partnership in this world are part of a *schēma* that is temporary. Although the privileges of marriage are wonderful and its responsibilities enormous, don't allow your marriage to become an excuse for failure to serve God, to put treasure in heaven, or to set your affections on things above.

Paul is not questioning the legitimacy of these earthly blessings such as marriage, normal human emotions, and earthly ownership.

But he is saying that we must never allow our emotions and possessions to control us so that we become entangled by this passing world.

Marriage and other business of this life can sometimes intrude on more important matters of eternal concern. Paul writes, "I want you to be free from anxieties. The unmarried man is anxious about the things of the Lord, how to please the Lord. But the married man is anxious about worldly things, how to please his wife, and his interests are divided" (vv. 32–34). So if you can remain single, do. Concentrate on the things of the Lord, because marriage is only a temporary provision.

If you're already married, however, this does not mean you should become indifferent to your marriage. Too much elsewhere in Scripture elevates the importance of marriage and commands husbands and wives to seek to honor God through the marriage relationship. This passage simply underscores the temporal nature of marriage. While married couples are heirs together of the grace of *this* life (1 Peter 3:7), the institution of marriage is passing away. There are higher eternal values.

Jesus himself expressly taught that marriage is an earthly union only. Matthew 22 records an incident when some Sadducees came to him to try to trick him with a puzzle. The Sadducees did not believe in the afterlife. They had a running dispute with the Pharisees about this very issue. The Pharisees taught that after the resurrection each person would have the same relationships he has here. They believed men would remain married to their earthly wives and retain their earthly families forever.

The Sadducees had undoubtedly heard Jesus speak of eternal life, and they no doubt assumed he shared the Pharisees' views on these questions. So they tried to trap him with a theological brain-twister that utterly perplexed the Pharisees. It was the most difficult theological conundrum the Sadducees could conceive—an absurd moral dilemma based on the Pharisees' view of the afterlife.

They said, "Teacher, Moses said, 'If a man dies having no children, his brother must marry the widow and raise up offspring for his brother'" (v. 24). That was indeed a Mosaic principle taught in Deuteronomy 25. It was known as the law of levirate marriage. It was designed to protect a family's line of inheritance.

The Sadducees presented a hypothetical scenario:

> Now there were seven brothers among us. The first married and died, and having no offspring left his wife to his brother. So too the second and third, down to the seventh. After them all, the woman died. In the resurrection, therefore, of the seven, whose wife will she be? For they all had her." (Matthew 22:25–28)

Jesus's reply was a sharp rebuke for their ignorance of the Scriptures: "You are wrong, because you know neither the Scriptures nor the power of God. For in the resurrection they neither marry nor are given in marriage, but are like angels in heaven" (vv. 29–30).

In other words, angels don't procreate. Neither will redeemed humans in heaven. All the reasons for marriage will be gone. Here on earth man needs a helper, woman needs a protector, and God has designed both to produce children. In heaven, glorified men will no longer require wives as helpers because they will be perfect. Women will no longer need husbands as protectors because they will be perfect. The population of heaven will be a fixed number. Thus marriage as an institution will be utterly unnecessary.

Some believe Jesus's reply to the Sadducees means we will all become genderless creatures in heaven. But that is not a necessary conclusion from what Jesus actually said. Nor does Scripture elsewhere picture the redeemed in heaven as without gender. Certainly the resurrected body of Christ does not appear to have been turned into an androgynous figure. When Mary saw him after the resurrection, she supposed that he was the gardener—a man's occupation in that culture (John 20:15). Others recognized him for who he was. Our gender is part of who we are. Nothing in Scripture suggests that men will cease to be men or that women will cease to be women. But there will be no marrying or giving in marriage. Marriage as an institution will pass away.

But what are those of us who are happily married supposed to think of this? I love my wife. She's my best friend and my dearest companion in every area of life. If those are your thoughts about your spouse as well, don't despair! You will enjoy an eternal companionship in heaven that is more perfect than any earthly partnership. The difference is that you will have such a perfect relationship with every other person in heaven as well. If having such a deep relationship with your spouse here is so wonderful, imagine how glorious it will be to enjoy a perfect relationship with every human in the whole expanse of heaven—forever!

"Will we really know each other?" may be the second most frequently heard question about heaven. And the answer is yes. We will forever be who we are now—only without any of our faults or infirmities. Everything in Scripture seems to confirm this.

For example, in the Old Testament, when a person died, the biblical writers said he was "gathered to his people" (see Genesis 25:8; 35:29; 49:29; Numbers 20:24; Judges 2:10). In 2 Samuel 12, when David's infant child died, David confidently said, "I shall go to him, but he will not return to me" (v. 23). David evidently expected to see the child again—not just a nameless, faceless soul without any clear identity—but that very child.

The New Testament indicates even more clearly that our identities will remain unchanged. While sharing the Passover meal with his disciples, Christ said, "Take this [cup], and divide it among yourselves. For I tell you that from now on I will not drink of the fruit of the vine until the kingdom of God comes" (Luke 22:17–18). Christ was promising that he and his disciples *would* drink the fruit of the vine together again—in heaven. Elsewhere Jesus makes a similar, but even more definite, promise: "I tell you, many will come from east and west and recline at table with Abraham, Isaac, and Jacob in the kingdom of heaven" (Matthew 8:11).

All the redeemed will maintain their identity forever, but in a perfected form. We will be able to have fellowship with Enoch, Noah, Abraham, Jacob, Samuel, Moses, Joshua, Esther, Elijah, Elisha, Isaiah, Daniel, Ezekiel, David, Peter, Barnabas, Paul—or any and all of the saints we know from Scripture.

Remember that Moses and Elijah appeared with Christ on the Mount of Transfiguration. It had been centuries since Elijah was famously transported into heaven in a chariot of fire. Centuries more had passed since Moses died in the wilderness. They had been all that time in heaven, yet they still maintained their clear identities (Matthew 17:3). They had not been changed into some sort of generic beings, devoid of distinctive characteristics; they retained their essential personalities—only in glorified and perfected form.

When the Sadducees tried to trap Jesus about the resurrection, he cited God's words to Moses in Exodus 3:6: "I am the God of your father, the God of Abraham, the God of Isaac, and the God of Jacob." Then Jesus commented, "He is not God of the dead, but of the living" (Matthew 22:32). His plain meaning was that Abraham, Isaac, and Jacob are still living *as* Abraham, Isaac, and Jacob, not in some nameless or indistinct identities. Moreover, Jesus's account of the rich man and Lazarus indicates that *both* men not only maintained their identities, but they remembered and recognized one another (even though Lazarus was in heaven and the rich man in hell).

Another common question is this: *"Will I be reunited with my family and friends in heaven?"* Obviously, the answer to this question is implied by all that we have seen so far. The answer is yes, of course. We will be reunited not only with our own families and loved ones, but with the people of God from all ages. In heaven we will all be one loving family. The immense size of the family will not matter in the infinite perfection of heaven. There will be ample opportunity for close relationships with everyone, and our eternity will be spent in just that kind of rich, unending fellowship.

Describing the Lord's appearing and the resurrection of the saints who have died, Paul writes, "we who are alive, who are left, will be caught up *together with them* in the clouds to meet the Lord in the air, and so we will always be *with the Lord*" (1 Thessalonians 4:17). Paul's purpose in writing was to comfort some of the Thessalonians who evidently thought their dying loved ones would miss the return of Christ and that they would then be separated from them forever. Paul says in verse 18, "Encourage one another with these words." The *encouragement* lies in the promise of reunion. Little encouragement this would be if in the reunion we could not even recognize one another. But Paul's promise that we will all be "together with them [and with] the Lord" forever implies that we shall renew fellowship with every redeemed person whom we have known.

Theologian A. A. Hodge wrote,

Heaven, as the eternal home of the divine Man and of all the redeemed members of the human race, must necessarily be thoroughly human in its structure, conditions, and activities. Its joys and its occupations must all be rational, moral, emotional, voluntary, and active. There must be the exercise of all faculties, the gratification of all tastes, the development of all talent capacities, the realization of all ideals. The reason, the intellectual curiosity, the imagination, the aesthetic instincts, the holy affections, the social affinities, the inexhaustible resources of strength and power native to the human soul, must all find in heaven exercise and satisfaction.[2]

If you're worried about feeling out of place in heaven, don't. Heaven will seem more like home than the dearest spot on earth to you. It is uniquely designed by a tender, loving Savior to be the place where we will live together for all eternity and enjoy him forever—in the fullness of our glorified humanity.

Is it any wonder that the psalmist said, "Precious in the sight of the LORD is the death of his saints"? (Psalm 116:15).

Unbroken Fellowship with God

Without question, the most marvelous thing of all about heaven—heaven's supreme delight—will be that we get to have unbroken fellowship with God himself.

First John 1:3 defines our salvation in terms of fellowship with God: "Our fellowship is with the Father and with his Son Jesus Christ." When we become believers, we enter into close spiritual fellowship with God through our union with Christ. The very life of God becomes ours. His will becomes our will, and his purpose our purpose. Even though sin hinders our walk with Christ on earth, the deepest part of our regenerated soul is united with the resurrected Christ through the indwelling Spirit and thereby in intimate fellowship with the living God.

In other words, salvation brings us into communion with every member of the Godhead. We can talk and commune with YHWH. We are adopted as his children (Romans 8:15). We pray to him as our dear Father—"Abba," in Paul's favorite terminology. We hear him speak to

---

[2] A. A. Hodge, *Evangelical Theology* (Carlisle, PA: Banner of Truth, 1976), 400.

us in his Word. He moves providentially in our lives to reveal himself. We enjoy real spiritual communion with eternal God.

But that communion nonetheless seems incomplete from this earthly perspective. It is shrouded from our plain view. As Paul writes, "Now we see in a mirror dimly, but then face to face. Now I know in part; then I shall know fully, even as I have been fully known" (1 Corinthians 13:12). He's talking about our fellowship with God. In heaven it will be perfect, unhindered, unclouded by any sin or darkness.

This is one of the main things that was on Jesus's heart and mind as he prayed during the night of his betrayal. John 17 records our Lord's high-priestly prayer. It was a prayer for the disciples—and also for every believer of all time. Jesus says so plainly (v. 20).

Anticipating the completion of his work on earth, our Lord asked the Father to return him to the glory he had before the world began. He prayed, "Father, I desire that they also, whom you have given me, may be with me where I am, *to see my glory* that you have given me because you loved me before the foundation of the world" (v. 24). He wants us to be *with him*. But that's not all. Notice the kind of relationship he prays for among all believers: "That they all may be one; as thou, Father, art in me, and I in thee, that they also may be one in us" (v. 21, KJV). His design for us is perfect fellowship both with him and with one another—much like the unity that exists between Father and Son!

This is such an incredibly profound concept that there's no way our finite minds can begin to appreciate it. But it was obviously the foremost thought on Jesus's mind whenever he spoke of the promise of heaven to the disciples. Earlier that same night on the eve of his crucifixion, he told them, "Where I am going you cannot follow me now, but you will follow afterward" (John 13:36). Later, knowing the disciples were troubled at the thought of his leaving them, he expanded the same promise:

> Let not your hearts be troubled. Believe in God; believe also in me. In my Father's house are many rooms. If it were not so, would I have told you that I go to prepare a place for you? And if I go and prepare a place for you, I will come again and will take you to myself, that where I am you may be also. (John 14:1–3)

Simply put, we're going to be with a person as much as we are going to live in a place. The presence of Christ is what makes heaven heaven. "The glory of God gives it light, and its lamp is the Lamb" (Revelation 21:23). Perfect fellowship with God is the very essence of heaven.

Notice how crucial is this principle of *fellowship with God* in the Bible's final summary of heaven: "Behold, the dwelling place of God is with man. He will dwell with them, and they will be his people, and God himself will be with them as their God" (Revelation 21:3). That verse emphasizes God's intimate presence "with man"—among humanity. The idea is that God himself will pitch his tent among the redeemed of the human race and make his dwelling among them. All believers will forever enjoy the pleasure of God's company.

This will not be in the same manner that God had his tabernacle among the Israelites in the wilderness. There, God's tent—the tabernacle—was in the middle of the camp, but it was such a holy place that strict rules governed when and how people could come and go into the tabernacle. No one was permitted into the Most Holy Place, where God himself dwelt—except for the high priest, and that was only once a year. But Revelation 7:15 tells us that "they are before the throne of God, and serve him day and night in his temple; and he who sits on the throne will shelter them with his presence"—indicating that God actually brings us into his own dwelling.

Jesus told the disciples, "In my Father's house are many rooms," then added, "I go to prepare a place for you" (John 14:2). He is personally preparing rooms in the Father's own house for each one of the elect! That promises us the most intimate imaginable fellowship with the living God.

And bear in mind that in heaven we will actually see the Lord face-to-face. There is no way to overstate the wonder and privilege this affords us. John 1:18 and 1 John 4:12 both say, "No one has ever seen God." First Timothy 6:16 declares that God "alone has immortality, who dwells in unapproachable light, whom no one has ever seen or can see." In Exodus 33, when Moses was craving a glimpse of God's glory (v. 18), God agreed to show only his back, and said, "You cannot see my face, for man shall not see me and live" (v. 20). Indeed, God is "of purer eyes than to see evil and cannot look at wrong" (Habakkuk 1:13).

As long as we are tainted by sin, we cannot see God's face. The view of such perfect righteousness would destroy us.

God is therefore inaccessible to mortal man on a face-to-face basis. That is what made Christ's incarnation so wonderful: although "No one has ever seen God; the only God, who is at the Father's side, he has made him known" (John 1:18). Christ "dwelt [Gk. *skenoō*; lit. "encamped" or "tabernacled"] among us" (John 1:14)—"and we have seen his glory, glory as of the only Son from the Father, full of grace and truth."

He came to our world to tabernacle among us, and he did it in order to redeem us and take us to Heaven, where Father, Son, and Holy Spirit will encamp in our midst in perfect fellowship with us forever. What a breathtaking reality!

In heaven, since we will be free from sin, we will see God's glory unveiled and in its fullness. That will be a more pleasing, spectacular sight than anything we have known or could ever imagine on earth. No mere earthly pleasure can even begin to measure up to the privilege and the ecstasy of an unhindered view of the divine glory.

Matthew 5:8 says, "Blessed are the pure in heart, for they shall see God." The Greek verb translated "see" (*horaō*) is in a tense that denotes a future continuous reality. In heaven we will continually be beholding God, face-to-face. Kings generally seclude themselves from direct contact with their people. It is a rare privilege to have an audience with a king. But believers in heaven will forever have perfect, unbroken fellowship with the King of kings!

This has always been the deepest longing of the redeemed soul. The psalmist said, "As a deer pants for flowing streams, so pants my soul for you, O God. My soul thirsts for God, for the living God. When shall I come and appear before God?" (Psalm 42:1–2). And Philip, speaking for all the disciples, said to Christ, "Lord, show us the Father, and it is enough for us" (John 14:8). Moses's petition, "Please show me your glory" (Exodus 33:18) reflects the true desire of every reborn heart. David expresses it beautifully in Psalm 17:15: "As for me, I shall behold your face in righteousness; when I awake, I shall be *satisfied* with your likeness."

David knew every station in life from that of a lowly shepherd, to the honor of being a great warrior, to the status of being king. He tasted every earthly pleasure. And he knew ultimate satisfaction would come only when he could see the face of God and be like him in holiness.

What would really satisfy you? New clothes? A new job? A promotion? A new house or car? A great meal? A fun time? A vacation? Don't set your heart on such paltry earthly pleasures. The redeemed will be able to *see God*. Revelation 22:3–4 seals the promise: "The throne of God and of the Lamb will be in it, and his servants will worship him. They will see his face."

As Christians, our highest satisfaction will come when we see our God and his Son, Jesus Christ, and when we stand before them in perfect uprightness. Heaven will provide us with that privilege: the unclouded, undiminished, uninterrupted sight of his infinite glory and beauty, bringing us infinite and eternal delight. We can begin to understand why Peter, after seeing only a faint glimpse of that glory, wanted to make a camp on the Mount of Transfiguration and stay there permanently! (Matthew 17:4).

Nineteenth-century songwriter Fanny Crosby expressed the hope of every believer in a well-loved gospel song titled "My Savior First of All":

> When my life work is ended, and I cross the swelling tide,
> When the bright and glorious morning I shall see,
> I shall know my Redeemer when I reach the other side,
> And His smile will be the first to welcome me. . . .
>
> Thru the gates of the city in a robe of spotless white,
> He will lead me where no tears will ever fall;
> In the glad song of ages I shall mingle with delight
> But I long to meet my Savior first of all.

Those words have special significance—Fanny Crosby was blind from infancy. She knew that literally the first person she would ever see would be Jesus Christ.

In a way, the same thing is true of us all. Our sight here on earth is virtually like blindness compared to the clearer vision we will have in heaven (1 Corinthians 13:12). We ought to be eagerly looking for that day when our vision will be enlightened by the glory of his presence. I sincerely hope that's your deepest desire.

8

The Heavenly Host

Our study of heaven would not be complete without giving some attention to the angels.

Angels are a familiar presence in popular culture these days. Beginning at least in the early 1970s with the sudden rise of the New Age movement, various myths, superstitions, and occult ideas about angels began to come into mainstream fashion. A couple of extremely popular television series, "Highway to Heaven" (1984–1989) and "Touched by an Angel" (1994–2003) helped fuel the explosion of interest. Hollywood has further stoked the obsession. Literally dozens of major motion pictures featuring stories of angelic visitations have been made over the past three decades or so. Angel artwork, angel figurines, and angel jewelry are all immensely popular and quite commonplace in greeting card shops and gift boutiques. A colleague of mine describes a store near my home. Their entire inventory is nothing but angel merchandise:

> About an hour's drive from my office is a New Age establishment that bills itself as "the world's largest Angel store." The shelves there are well-stocked with paintings, statuettes, and New Age books ostensibly teaching people how to communicate with angels. They also have a large selection of gewgaws called "shelf angels"—porcelain figurines designed to sit on the edge of a shelf—mostly winged women and cherubic toddlers sporting diminutive angel-wings of their own.[1]

Countless books about angels and tales about encounters with angels are being written and published. Most of them have strong New

---

[1] Phil Johnson, "Angels: Messengers and Ministers of God," http://www.ligonier.org/learn/articles/angels-messengers-and-ministers-god/.

Age or occult overtones. A recent search for "angels" in the book category on Amazon.com turned up more than 80,000 results. (A search
for "angels" in all categories at Amazon.com yields more than half a
million listings.) Angels are big business.

The most popular books seem to be those that purport to instruct
readers on how to recognize and communicate with angels. Some of
the best-selling books in the genre are *Where Angels Walk: True Stories
of Heavenly Visitors*[2] (a book that has spawned at least fourteen sequels,
many of which have seen sales figures in the millions); *Angels 101: An
Introduction to Connecting, Working, and Healing with the Angels*;[3] *How to
Hear Your Angels*;[4] *Angelspeake: How to Talk With Your Angels*;[5] and *Your
Angel Journey: A Guide to Releasing Your Inner Angel.*[6]

Communicating with angels is serious business, according to
books like these. One mega–best seller on this subject for the past two
decades is a book called *Ask Your Angels.*[7] According to the promotional
material issued by the publishers, "The authors [of *Ask Your Angels*]
show us how we can draw on the power of angels to reconnect with
our lost inner selves and to achieve our goals, whether they be better
relationships, healing an illness, or recovery from addiction." Supposedly this book will teach the reader "how to align with the angelic
energy field and learn to talk with your angels."

Here are some other verbatim quotations from various publishers' comments about their guidebooks for communicating with the
angelic realm:

> Through the easy techniques presented in this book, you can learn
> to access and attune to beings such as guardian angels, nature spirits
> and elementals, spirit totems, archangels, gods and goddesses—as
> well as family and friends after their physical death. Also reveals
> which acupressure points stimulate your intuitive faculties, how to
> protect yourself from lower-level discarnates, and how to conquer
> fears of the unknown.

[2] Joan Wester Anderson, *Where Angels Walk: True Stories of Heavenly Visitors* (New York: Ballantine, 1992).
[3] Doreen Virtue, *Angels 101: An Introduction to Connecting, Working, and Healing with the Angels* (Carlsbad, CA: Hay, 2006).
[4] Doreen Virtue, *How to Hear Your Angels* (Carlsbad, CA: Hay, 2007).
[5] Barbara Mark and Trudy Griswold, *Angelspeake: How to Talk with Your Angels* (New York: Simon & Schuster, 1995).
[6] Joylina Goodings, *Your Angel Journey: A Guide to Releasing Your Inner Angel* (Ropley, UK: O Books, 2008).
[7] Alma Daniel, Timothy Wyllie, and Andrew Ramer, *Ask Your Angels* (New York: Ballantine, 1992).

Everyone has a Spirit Guide or guardian angel who assists him in keeping on a chosen Karmic path. [This cassette tape] helps you get in touch with yours.

[You can learn to] contact your guardian angel and be receptive to the angelic realm in your daily life. Learn how to attune to the higher frequencies of Spirit, to be more aware of angels and nature spirits, and to communicate with these loving beings in order to develop a deeper appreciation of our own place in Creation.

[This book] enables us to begin to open our hearts to these joyful and comforting protectors, so we can raise our consciousness to a new dimension.

All the pieces in this unique collection stress the cooperation between humans and angels in the creation of our inner life and even of nature. The reader experiences a rich and variegated view of these ancient, elusive spirits that have inspired us for so long.

The authors teach you nine specific ways your personal angel protects you, how to call out to your guardian angel, and how to get your angel to answer your cry for help and assistance in matters big and small. You'll also find out about the Angelic Hierarchy and learn the actual language of the Angelic Kingdom!

Shows us how to co-create with the angels and the Kingdom of Heaven on Earth. Specific exercises and meditations help you communicate with angels who are waiting to be invited into your life!

Inspiration from the angels and Muses is always available. Along with writing and art exercises, the reader will explore the angelic realm through guided journeys, focusing on mandalas, knowing how to use the seasonal forces, learning how colors influence us and how the angels use color and light as their own language. Case histories of how many people became aware of their creative talents when they began playing with the angels are included.

Offers a complete method for bringing the healing light of the soul, the Solar angel, and the angelic healers into the physical body. Taught in workshops for the past eight years, these easy-to-learn processes have helped thousands to heal and upgrade the cells in their body. The healing angels will work with whatever healing path or healing treatment you are now using. Includes a chart of healing questions, colors, and images for use with specific illnesses.

By utilizing a combination of your birth sign and a specific colored candle, you can obtain the magic and wisdom you want in life by calling upon the angels. This book contains many spiritual secrets that will guide the reader to success and power.

Much of this, of course, is little more than occult divination, sorcery, and typical New Age mysticism. Everything we have said about the dangers of mystical inquiry into the realm of the dead applies equally to deliberate attempts to consort with spirit beings. Both activities are occult practices, even if garnished with Christian language and embellished with biblical proof texts. Either kind of investigation into the spiritual realm opens a person up to serious demonic deception.

Indeed, I have no doubt that some who claim to commune with angels really have been able to establish a link with angelic beings—though not in the way they seek. Scripture warns us plainly that Satan and his messengers often appear as angels of light (2 Corinthians 11:13–15). In other words, demonic beings take advantage of the gullibility of people who are actively seeking to communicate with the spirit world. What they are doing is pure shamanism, and it exposes them to all the horrible effects of the black arts. I know people who have been drawn into serious demonic bondage by these practices, and Christians should be strongly warned against such inquiry.

Unfortunately, the evangelical response to these trends has been weak. There is, of course, a plethora of books from evangelical publishers featuring mildly Christianized tales of angelic encounters, enthusiastically recounting "Real-Life Stories about Angels" and glowing tales of Christians who claim to communicate regularly with angels. As usual, evangelicals are addicted to following the world's fads. Unfortunately, this one poses some particularly serious hazards.

As 2 Corinthians 11:15 suggests, "it is no surprise" when a demon disguises himself as a good angel. Furthermore, despite the prevalence of stirring tales about angelic interventions (angels who rescue missionaries from cannibals and similar tales), there is no way any of these stories can be verified—except for the biblical ones. That doesn't mean it *wasn't* an angel whose invisible hand mysteriously steadied you when you were about to take a tumble down the stairs. But it means you cannot possibly know for sure whether it was an angel or not. We *do* know for sure that it is God whose providence preserves us from various disasters. Whether in a given instance he employs angels as his instruments or not, God is the One who should be the focus of our praise and gratitude, not the angelic beings.

Scripture does teach that *some* "have entertained angels unawares" (Hebrews 13:2). And for that very reason we are instructed to show kindness and hospitality to strangers. But the language of Scripture indicates that these incidents are rare, and the key to understanding this verse is the word *unawares*. The verse is describing people who have hosted angels *without knowing it*. It is certainly possible, according to Scripture, that you might play host to an angel. But in all likelihood, if that occurs, it will be without your knowing it. Nowhere does Scripture encourage us to have an angel fetish, to look for evidence of angels in everyday life, or to have such an expectation of entertaining angels that we imagine them in every serendipitous encounter.

The tales that fill today's rendezvous-with-angels books are unverifiable stories—extraordinary displays of divine providence, perhaps, but not necessarily authentic accounts of angelic intervention. The whole fixation is of questionable value. Certainly it is causing far more spiritual harm than good.

What Does Scripture Say about Angels?

In early 1995 I clipped an article from *Moody* magazine that analyzed the angel craze. It included some interesting statistics that gave some measurements to the rapid growth of interest in the subject. The publishing statistics at the time were stunning, showing explosive growth in the number of books about guardian angels, angelic communication, and so on. Of course, those statistics, amazing as they were, would be dwarfed by today's numbers.

But one line I highlighted in the article was a quotation from Moody Bible Institute theology professor Ed Glasscock, who stated, "The Bible never really explains angels. It just makes casual references to their activities."[8] That is absolutely true. Gleaning our information solely from the biblical data, we come up with far more unanswered questions about angels than detailed knowledge. We know that angels minister to humans and even intervene from time to time in human affairs, but as to *how* this happens, we know very little. And (as we have already noted) we are strictly discouraged from looking into any spiritual matters beyond what is revealed for us in Scripture: "The secret things belong to the LORD our God, but the things that are revealed belong to us and to our children forever, that we may do all the words of this law" (Deuteronomy 29:29).

Nevertheless, a considerable body of information *can* be gleaned from Scripture about these wonderful creatures. And since we will spend eternity with the angels in heaven, it will be helpful in our study of heaven to learn all we can from Scripture about the angels and their role.

Scripture uses several expressions to describe the angels. They are called "the sons of the mighty" in the King James Version of Psalm 89:6; "sons of God" (Job 1:6; 2:1; 38:7); *elohim* in the Hebrew of Psalm 8:5 (translated "the heavenly beings" in the ESV); "the holy ones" (Psalm 89:5); "the morning stars" (Job 38:7), "princes" (Daniel 10:13); and "the rulers and authorities in the heavenly places" (Ephesians 3:10).

Study the Bible and you will find angels in the third heaven, where God dwells. There they worship him continuously. You'll find them in the second heaven, traversing the universe, serving God in various ways. And you'll find them in the first heaven, even intervening from time to time in human affairs.

How Angels Were Created

Angels are created beings. They are not demigods. They do not have any of the incommunicable attributes of deity, such as omniscience or omnipresence. They did not exist in eternity past. They are creatures. Nehemiah 9:6 says, "You are the LORD, you alone. You have made heaven, the heaven of heavens, with *all their host*, the earth and all that is on it, the seas and all that is in them; and you preserve all of

---

[8] Quoted in Bill Deckard, "Angels We Have Heard?" *Moody*, April 1995, 46.

them; and *the host of heaven worships you*." That means the angels were created by God. It also suggests the angels—like all other intelligent creatures—were designed to render worship to God, not to receive worship themselves. In fact, in both instances in Scripture where angels are offered worship, they rebuke the worshiper and redirect all worship to God alone (Revelation 19:10; 22:8–9).

Psalm 148 confirms that the angels are created beings who worship the Creator:

> Praise him, all his angels;
> praise him, all his hosts!
> Praise him, sun and moon,
> praise him, all you shining stars!
> Praise him, you highest heavens,
> and you waters above the heavens!
> Let them praise the name of the LORD!
> *For he commanded and they were created.* (vv. 2–5)

Notice that both Nehemiah 9:6 ("You are the LORD [*YHWH*], you alone. You have made heaven, the heaven of heavens, with all their host") and Psalm 148:5 ("the LORD [*YHWH*] . . . commanded and they were created") identify *Jehovah* as the One who created the angels.

One of the strongest proofs of Jesus's deity is the biblical assertion that *he* is the one who created all things, including the angels. Colossians 1:16 says, "By him all things were created, in heaven and on earth, visible and invisible, whether thrones or dominions or rulers or authorities—all things were created through him and for him." There Paul is explicitly defending Christ's deity against the teaching of some who said he was merely a created being. (To this day, the Jehovah's Witness sect teaches that Christ is an archangel—the highest of created beings.) Paul carefully refutes all such teaching by declaring that Christ himself is the One who created everything—*including* all angelic beings and everything else that exists. Therefore Christ *is* YHWH incarnate. He cannot be a mere angel himself. Hebrews 1:4 says he is "as much superior to angels as the name he has inherited is more excellent than theirs," and in verse 6, the Father says, "Let all God's angels worship him."

Paul often refers to the angels as "cosmic powers" (or in the King James Version, "principalities" and "powers") who dwell and rule in heavenly places (Ephesians 6:12). We're not told many precise details about the hierarchy of heaven, but it is clear that the angels are organized in a divinely ordered chain of command:

> The angelic host includes at least one archangel, the seraphim, and the cherubim. The archangel, Michael, is named in Daniel 10:13, 21; Jude 9; and Revelation 12:7. He seems to be the highest of all angelic creatures. Only one other holy angel, Gabriel, is explicitly named (Daniel 8:16; 9:21; Luke 1:19, 26). Some think he is therefore similar in rank to Michael, but Scripture doesn't actually designate Gabriel as an archangel.
>
> The seraphim are mentioned only in the heavenly vision recounted in Isaiah 6:2–6, where the prophet describes them as glorious and imposing figures who stand before God's throne and praise Him constantly, guarding the holiness of His throne.
>
> The cherubim, far from the chubby-faced childlike figures often pictured in popular art, seem to represent the power and majesty of the angelic host. They were positioned as guards by the entrance of Eden (Genesis 3:24). They were also the symbolic guardians of the ark of the covenant (Exodus 37:7). And they formed a living chariot of fire on which the Lord would ride (2 Samuel 22:11; Psalm 18:10; cf. Ezekiel 10:1–22). They are always described as fearsome and awe-inspiring creatures.
>
> Other angelic beings are called thrones, dominions, principalities, and powers (Colossians 1:16). Similar terms are applied even to the fallen angels (Ephesians 6:12; Colossians 2:15).[9]

The angelic host is described throughout Scripture as a huge heavenly army. And as their creator, Christ is set far above them in authority. He alone is at the Father's right hand, "far above all rule and authority and power and dominion, and above every name that is named, not only in this age but also in the one to come" (Ephesians 1:21). Again Scripture repeatedly makes this stark distinction between Christ, who is eternal (John 1:1), and the angels, who are merely created beings. Christ "is before all things, and in him all things hold together" (Colossians 1:17).

---

[9]Johnson, "Angels: Messengers and Ministers of God."

Moreover, the doctrine that angels are created beings is in perfect harmony with 1 Timothy 6:15–16, which states that Jesus Christ is "the blessed and only Sovereign, the King of kings and Lord of lords, who alone has immortality."

It appears that the angels were brought into existence early in the process of creation. Job 38 describes the laying of earth's foundation, "when the morning stars sang together and all the sons of God shouted for joy" (v. 7). So the angels were there to witness the formation of our world. And since there is no procreation among angels (Matthew 22:30), they must have been created all at once—in a sweeping creative act. God commanded, and untold numbers of creatures instantly came into existence, each one independently unique. They do not reproduce, so there can never be any increase in the number. They do not die, so there's no decrease.

How many angels are there? Scripture doesn't tell us a number. But at the birth of Christ there appeared "a multitude of the heavenly host" (Luke 2:13). At his arrest Jesus said if he wanted to, he could simply pray to the Father and immediately call forth "more than twelve legions of angels" (Matthew 26:53). A Roman legion in Jesus's time ranged from 3,000 to 6,000, so that would be 72,000 (or more) angels. Think of it: if Jesus needed thousands of angels, they'd be there instantly. But there's no reason to think "twelve legions" exhausts the ranks of the angels. In fact, there is biblical evidence that the number is much higher.

Scripture often describes the immense number of angels by comparing them to the stars. The angels and the stars are even spoken of in terms that are used interchangeably. "The host of heaven" sometimes speaks of the stars (Deuteronomy 17:3), and sometimes speaks of the angels (1 Kings 22:19). The angels are even called "the morning stars" in Job 38:7. No doubt the emphasis is on their glory and innumerable expanse. Scientists say there are multiplied billions of stars in the universe. Could there be such a large number of angels as well?

Yes. In Revelation 5:11, the apostle John writes, "Then I looked, and I heard around the throne and the living creatures and the elders the voice of many angels, numbering myriads of myriads and thousands of thousands." If we take the numbers literally, it figures to more than a billion. But this is probably an expression the apostle uses to convey the idea of a number so large that it simply cannot be counted.

That is precisely what Hebrews 12:22 indicates: "You have come to Mount Zion and to the city of the living God, the heavenly Jerusalem, and to *innumerable angels* in festal gathering." Like the stars of heaven and the grains of sand on a beach, the number is simply too high to count meaningfully. No doubt God himself knows the precise number. But it is a number so high we would not be able to comprehend the immensity of it.

When Angels Fell

Satan and the demons are fallen angels. All that is known about Satan's fall is conveyed to us rather subtly by Scripture. Satan seems to be the real target of a couple of messages addressed to earthly rulers. These rulers are themselves so evil that we may assume they were indwelt by Satan. Thus the messages addressed to the evil kings seem actually to be meant for Satan. For example, the words of Isaiah 14:12–15, though addressed to the king of Babylon, actually refer to Satan, addressing him as "Lucifer" (KJV), or "Day Star, son of Dawn." (The Hebrew word literally means "Star of the Morning"):

> How you are fallen from heaven,
>   O Day Star, son of Dawn!
> How you are cut down to the ground,
>   you who laid the nations low!
> You said in your heart,
>   "I will ascend to heaven;
> above the stars of God
>   I will set my throne on high;
> I will sit on the mount of assembly
>   in the far reaches of the north;
> I will ascend above the heights of the clouds;
> I will make myself like the Most High."
> But you are brought down to Sheol,
>   to the far reaches of the pit.

Evidently Satan aspired to usurp God's very throne, and as a result he was cast out of heaven.

Ezekiel 28 includes a message to the king of Tyre that clearly goes beyond the king himself and applies to Satan, who must have indwelt him. We know the actual target of the message is the devil, because it alludes to his deception of Eve in the garden:

Thus says the Lord God:

> "You were the signet of perfection,
>   full of wisdom and perfect in beauty.
> You were in Eden, the garden of God;
>   every precious stone was your covering,
> sardius, topaz, and diamond,
>   beryl, onyx, and jasper,
> sapphire, emerald, and carbuncle;
>   and crafted in gold were your settings
>   and your engravings.
> On the day that you were created
>   they were prepared.
> You were an anointed guardian cherub.
>   I placed you; you were on the holy mountain of God;
>   in the midst of the stones of fire you walked.
> You were blameless in your ways
>   from the day you were created,
>   till unrighteousness was found in you.
> In the abundance of your trade
>   you were filled with violence in your midst, and you sinned;
> so I cast you as a profane thing from the mountain of God,
>   and I destroyed you, O guardian cherub,
>   from the midst of the stones of fire." (vv. 12–16)

When Lucifer fell, he took a third of the angels with him (Revelation 12:3–4). These fallen angels are now nothing but demonic beings, some of whom are still troubling the earth to this very day—and will continue to do so until they are destroyed by the hand of God's judgment (Revelation 20:10).

What Angels Are Like

Angels are persons. That is, they are beings with all the attributes of personality: intellect, feelings, and volition. They have personalities. They are intelligent creatures. They act and move and feel.

In the Ezekiel 28 passage that describes the fall of "an anointed guardian cherub," God says to him: "You were the signet of perfection, full of wisdom and perfect in beauty" (v. 12). Evidently this creature who fell and became Satan was the most intelligent of all God's creatures and very likely the highest ranking angel of all.

Angels are almost always portrayed in Scripture as highly intelligent beings. In Matthew 28:5, when the two Marys found Jesus's tomb empty on the morning of the resurrection, the angel guarding the tomb said to them, "Do not be afraid, for I *know* that you seek Jesus who was crucified." The angels communicate. They have conversations. They know things. They obviously are creatures of intellect.

Angels are not omniscient, however. First Peter 1:12 says the gospel contains truths "into which angels long to look." So there are some things they do not understand. Yet even their desire to know more proves that they are intelligent beings.

Angels also express emotion. Remember that they sang together at creation (Job 38:7). Luke 15:10 says, "There is joy before the angels of God over one sinner who repents." I believe that verse speaks of *God's* joy over the salvation of his elect. But surely that joy is also shared by angels. The parable Jesus tells in this context describes a woman who has lost a coin. She sweeps the house, takes a candle, and looks everywhere until she finds it. Then "she calls together her friends and neighbors, saying, 'Rejoice with me, for I have found the coin that I had lost'" (v. 9). Then verse 10 says, "*Just so*, I tell you, there is joy before the angels of God over one sinner who repents." This clearly implies that God rejoices in the angels' presence so that they may share his joy! There is every reason to think they are emotional creatures.

Meaningful worship is impossible apart from emotion, I believe. Of course, sheer blind emotion does not equate to real worship, but "worship . . . in spirit and truth"—the kind of worship God seeks (John 4:23)—is not possible apart from authentic feelings. The purest worship involves rejoicing in the truth (cf. 1 Corinthians 13:6). And the fact that angels are often seen worshiping around the throne of God indicates that they do have emotions. Look at Isaiah's description of angelic worship around the throne of God:

> I saw the Lord sitting upon a throne, high and lifted up; and the train
> of his robe filled the temple. Above him stood the seraphim. Each had

six wings: with two he covered his face, and with two he covered his feet, and with two he flew. And one called to another and said:

> "Holy, holy, holy is the LORD of hosts;
> the whole earth is full of his glory!" (Isaiah 6:1–3)

Isaiah's description of these majestic creatures makes clear that they are not mere machines, or animals, but both highly intelligent and capable of the profoundest emotions associated with the highest kind of worship.

It is also evident that they are volitional creatures. Lucifer's sin was a willful pride. He said in his heart,

> "I *will* ascend to heaven;
> above the stars of God
>   I *will* set my throne on high;
> I *will* sit on the mount of assembly
>   in the far reaches of the north;
> I *will* ascend above the heights of the clouds;
>   I *will* make myself like the Most High" (Isaiah 14:13–14).

God himself appeals to the wills of angels. Hebrews 1:6 records God the Father's command to the angels at the birth of his son: "When he brings the firstborn into the world, he says, 'Let all God's angels worship him.'" Obedience to any command involves an act of the will.

Not only do angels have all the attributes of personality, but they are also lofty creatures, slightly higher in majesty and authority than humans. When Christ became a man, Scripture says he was made "lower than the angels" (Hebrews 2:7). So angels occupy a higher state than we do—at least for the time being. Someday redeemed humanity will judge the angels—and this may imply that we will also rule over them in heaven. Paul wrote, "Do you not know that we are to judge angels? How much more, then, matters pertaining to this life!" (1 Corinthians 6:3). Jesus promised the churches of Asia Minor, "The one who conquers, I will grant him to sit with me on my throne, as I also conquered and sat down with my Father on his throne" (Revelation 3:21). Sharing the throne of Christ seems to imply that we will have rule over the angels. If so, this is a stunning concept.

What Do Angels Do?

The life and the world of angels is as involved and as active and as complex as ours is. They dwell in another dimension, but our worlds intersect often, and at least some of their business is related to the affairs of this world. Hebrews 1:14 calls them "ministering spirits sent out to serve for the sake of those who are to inherit salvation."

Martin Luther believed that an angel is a spiritual creature without a body created by God specifically for the service of Christendom and the church. Whether that is really the *main* function of angels or not, we simply are not told, but it certainly is *one* of their duties. (The fact that they are organized in a highly structured chain of command may suggest that angelic duties are varied according to rank.)

As ministering spirits who minister to the elect, angels are no doubt active in human affairs, though usually unseen. Undoubtedly they do many things on our behalf, but nowhere does Scripture encourage us to look further into how this occurs. We are never encouraged to try to discern the unseen work of angels in our lives. We're merely reminded to exhibit a Christlike hospitality, because we never know when or in what form an angel may be our guest.

Hebrews 1:14 specifically calls the angels "ministering *spirits*," which implies that they do not have material bodies. Nonetheless, they do appear in visible form from time to time, when God chooses to let them be manifest. And whenever Scripture describes any such angelic appearance in an earthly context, the angel always appears as a man. Masculine pronouns are invariably used to refer to them. For example, in Genesis 18–19, when angels came to visit Abraham and paid a visit to Sodom, they were fully human in appearance. They sat down with Abraham. They ate with him. They walked with him. They conversed in human language. Every detail of their visible form and behavior was in appearance human.

At other times angels appear as men, but with extraordinary, even supernatural, qualities. In Matthew 28:3–4, for example, the angel who appeared at Jesus's empty tomb was no normal-looking man: "His countenance was like lightning, and his raiment white as snow: and for fear of him the keepers did shake, and became as dead men" (KJV).

Biblical appearances of angels—unlike those of popular lore—

often cause trauma and great fear. When an angel appeared to Mary, from the moment that he greeted her, "she was greatly troubled at the saying, and tried to discern what sort of greeting this might be" (Luke 1:29). When angelic messengers appeared to the shepherds who attended Jesus's birth, "they were sore afraid" (Luke 2:9, KJV). When the Roman soldiers guarding Jesus's tomb spotted the angel there, "for fear of him the guards trembled and became like dead men" (Matthew 28:4).

On those rare occasions when angels do appear visibly to people in Scripture, it is in the role of a messenger. This is one of their main roles. In fact, "messenger" is the primary meaning of the Greek word *angelos*. So the angels provide a sort of heavenly messenger service, and we get glimpses of this throughout Scripture. The angel who appeared to Mary at the annunciation identified himself by name: "I am Gabriel. I stand in the presence of God, and I was sent to speak to you and to bring you this good news" (Luke 1:19). On this particular occasion, perhaps because of the sacred importance of the message, this high-ranking angel (cf. Daniel 8:16; 9:21), who normally stood in the very presence of God, was sent to Mary to deliver the word.

Finally, as we have seen, angels are constantly ministering around the throne of God in worship. Worship is plainly one of their chief functions (Isaiah 6:3; Revelation 4:6–9; 5:9–14).

How Will We Relate to the Angels in Heaven?

Scripture indicates that in heaven we will join the angels in worshiping God around his throne. Revelation 4:4 describes the very first scene John witnessed in his vision of heaven: "Around the throne were twenty-four thrones, and seated on the thrones were twenty-four elders, clothed in white garments, with golden crowns on their heads." Those elders represent the church. The fact that permanent seats are there for them indicates that the redeemed people of God will perpetually be worshiping there alongside the angels.

John goes on to describe the incredible creatures who worship nonstop around God's throne, and adds this in verse 8: "Day and night they never cease to say, 'Holy, holy, holy, is the Lord God Almighty, who was and is and is to come!'" Never tiring of their ministry, they offer the purest, most perfect worship around the clock, exactly as Isaiah described it in his vision (cf. Isaiah 6:3):

> And whenever the living creatures give glory and honor and thanks to him who is seated on the throne, who lives forever and ever, the twenty-four elders fall down before him who is seated on the throne and worship him who lives forever and ever. They cast their crowns before the throne, saying, "Worthy are you, our Lord and God, to receive glory and honor and power, for you created all things, and by your will they existed and were created." (Revelation 4:9–11)

Revelation 5:8–12 portrays a similar scene, with multiplied thousands of voices singing of the worthiness of God and the Lamb.

That is the song of heaven. I cannot wait to hear it. I cannot wait to sing it with a glorified voice, and be part of the great chorus of the redeemed, with the entire host of heaven joining in.

Instantly, when we hear that sound, all earth's troubles will recede into utter insignificance. All our labors will be over, all our tears will be dried, and there will be nothing left but the sheer bliss of heaven and our perfect enjoyment of God—forever.

A Final Word to the Reader

We have reached the end of our biblical overview of heaven and its inhabitants. Whatever sense of the glory of heaven I have been able to convey through mere words on a page is surely paltry indeed compared to what heaven's glory will be like when we see it in all its spectacular fullness. Nonetheless, I hope your heart is stirred, as my own is, by the matchless grace of a God who would manifest his goodness to unworthy creatures like you and me—people who have sinned against him repeatedly—and bring us into his own dwelling place forever. To think that he would permit us to share in the glory of heaven is a wonder too great for the human mind to fathom. Such grace and mercy are impossible for us even to begin to appreciate. Only in the eternity of heaven will we be able to verbalize adequately the worship and thanksgiving that are due him. Even there, we will sing of it for all eternity—and never begin to exhaust the wonder and glory of it.

If this study has in any way aroused a desire within you to participate in the glory and blessedness of heaven, then my design for writing it has been met.

My prayer for you, dear reader, is that you will look beyond the fading realities of this world and see just a glimpse of the glory of heaven. And having caught that tiny ray of heaven's glory, may you be like the man who found a treasure in a field, and sold all his earthly possessions in order to buy it (Matthew 13:44). If you have never trusted Christ for salvation, may you flee to him right now for forgiveness and cleansing, and receive the pure white robe of his righteousness.

All that is glorious, all that is noble, and all that is blessed awaits us in heaven. I hope you are headed there, and that your heart yearns for reunion with Christ.

And heaven may be closer than you think. As the apostle Paul wrote,

> You know the time, that the hour has come for you to wake from sleep. For salvation is nearer to us now than when we first believed. The night is far gone; the day is at hand. So then let us cast off the works of darkness and put on the armor of light. Let us walk properly as in the daytime, not in orgies and drunkenness, not in sexual immorality and sensuality, not in quarreling and jealousy. But put on the Lord Jesus Christ, and make no provision for the flesh, to gratify its desires. (Romans 13:11–14)

Appendix 1:

Seduced by the Light

One of the earliest heaven-and-back stories to capture the attention of the reading public was Betty J. Eadie's remarkable book *Embraced by the Light*.[1] As of this writing the book is more than two decades old and well past its fortieth printing. It is still selling briskly.

Eadie recounts how she "died" in her hospital room while recovering after a hysterectomy in 1973. Her memories of what happened are extraordinarily vivid:

> My spirit was suddenly drawn out through my chest and pulled upward, as if by a giant magnet. My first impression was that I was free. There was nothing unnatural about the experience. I was above the bed, hovering near the ceiling. My sense of freedom was limitless and it seemed as if I had done this forever. I turned and saw a body lying on the bed. I was curious about who it was, and immediately I began descending toward it. Having worked as an LPN, I knew well the appearance of a dead body, and as I got closer to the face I knew at once that it was lifeless. And then I recognized that it was my own. That was *my* body on the bed. I wasn't taken aback, and I wasn't frightened; I simply felt a kind of sympathy for it. It appeared younger and prettier than I remembered, and now it was dead.[2]

Eadie goes on to describe how three robed men suddenly appeared by her side, telling her they had been with her for "eternities." She began to remember "an existence before [her] life on earth" and her

---

[1] Betty J. Eadie, *Embraced by the Light* (Detroit: Gold Leaf, 1992).
[2] Ibid., 29.

relationship with these men "before."[3] She writes, "The fact of a pre-earth life crystallized in my mind, and I saw that death was actually a 'rebirth' into a greater life of understanding and knowledge that stretched backward and forward through time."[4]

Already Eadie's near-death experience seems to have all the classic New Age overtones of reincarnation, out-of-body experiences, telepathy, and so on. She goes on to describe a ghostly visit to her own home, where she watched her children and was even able to look into their futures.

But then her story takes this extraordinary turn:

> I saw a pinpoint of light in the distance. The black mass around me began to take on more of the shape of a tunnel, and I felt myself traveling through it at an even greater speed, rushing toward the light. I was instinctively attracted to it, although again, I felt that others might not be. As I approached, I noticed the figure of a man standing in it, with the light radiating all around him. As I got closer the light became brilliant—brilliant beyond any description, far more brilliant than the sun—and I knew that no earthly eyes in their natural state could look upon this light without being destroyed.[5]

Eadie describes a dazzling, golden radiance that surrounded this being. She says he reached out to her with pure, unconditional love. "There was no questioning who he was," she writes. "I knew that he was my Savior, and friend, and God. He was Jesus Christ."[6]

From that point on, all of Eadie's heavenly exploits center on this Jesus figure and what she says he taught her. She claims her mind assumed a supernatural ability to know and understand things—almost as if she were "remembering" what she had always known:

> I understood, or rather, I *remembered*, his role as creator of the earth. His mission was to come into the world to teach love. This knowledge was more like remembering. Things were coming back to me from long before my life on earth, things that had been purposely blocked from me by a "veil" of forgetfulness at my birth.[7]

---

[3] Ibid., 31.
[4] Ibid., 31–32.
[5] Ibid., 40.
[6] Ibid., 42.
[7] Ibid., 44.

If it sounds like Eadie is claiming virtual omniscience for herself, that is precisely what she means to convey. She writes: "The word 'omniscient' had never been more meaningful to me. Knowledge permeated me. In a sense it *became* me, and I was amazed at my ability to comprehend the mysteries of the universe simply by reflecting on them."[8]

Eadie obviously believes she retained this understanding of "the mysteries of the universe" even after her return from heaven, and her book is filled with glib answers to questions she says had always perplexed her before her heavenly sojourn. She gives a little homily, for example, about why she is not concerned that there are so many different religions. She seems to want everyone to suspend discernment and cease all attempts to sort out the truth from spiritual falsehood:

> I wanted to know why there were so many churches in the world. Why didn't God give us only one church, one pure religion? The answer came to me with the purest of understanding. Each of us, I was told, is at a different level of spiritual development and understanding. Each person is therefore prepared for a different level of spiritual knowledge. All religions upon the earth are necessary because there are people who need what they teach. People in one religion may not have a complete understanding of the Lord's gospel and never will have while in that religion. But that religion is used as a stepping stone to further knowledge. Each church fulfills spiritual needs that perhaps others cannot fill. No one church can fulfill everybody's needs at every level. As an individual raises his level of understanding about God and his own eternal progress, he might feel discontented with the teachings of his present church and seek a different philosophy or religion to fill that void. When this occurs he has reached another level of understanding and will long for further truth and knowledge, and for another opportunity to grow.[9]

"Having received this knowledge," she concludes, "I knew that we have no right to criticize any church or religion in any way."[10]

Nevertheless, Eadie also emphasizes that there is a certain uniqueness about Christ: "Of all knowledge, however, there is none more

---

[8] Ibid., 45.
[9] Ibid., 45–46.
[10] Ibid.

essential than knowing Jesus Christ. I was told that he is the door through which we will *all* return. He is the only door through which we can return."[11]

Because she blends some biblical allusions and familiar Christian terminology with her universalist reincarnationist self-deificationist ideas, many Christians have wrongly assumed that Betty Eadie herself is an evangelical Christian. Rapt audiences across the nation have listened as she has retold her story, and many who call themselves Christians insist her experience should not be written off. I've heard from a surprising number of evangelicals who wonder if it is possible that Eadie's account of heaven and the afterlife might be a reliable and true account of what Christians can expect after death.

The answer, emphatically, is *no*. Many of Betty Eadie's claims contradict Scripture, as we shall shortly see. Also, although she never discloses her own religious affiliation in her book, she is a Mormon. Some of the truths she said she learned in heaven bear an uncanny resemblance to Mormon doctrines. In fact, despite her long discourse about the value of all religions, what Eadie does not say in her book— but apparently told a Utah reporter—is that during her visit to heaven she learned that the Church of Jesus Christ of Latter-Day Saints (the Mormon Church) is "the truest Church on the earth."[12] In a promotional package targeting Utah readers, Eadie's publisher (a spinoff from a Mormon publishing house) inserted special promotional flyers into the original edition of the book. Titled, "Of Special Interest to Members of the Church of Latter-Day Saints," the flyers touted Eadie as a recent convert to Mormonism.[13]

In the wake of growing book sales, however, Eadie and her publisher began to downplay her church affiliation—almost to the point of seeming to want to obscure the fact that she was a Mormon. In an interview with *The Christian Research Journal*, she repeatedly refused to admit that she is a Mormon.[14]

Eadie's doctrine is not straight-up Mormonism, however. It is a

---

[11] Ibid., 85.
[12] The Ogden, Utah, *Standard-Examiner* (March 6, 1993), cited in "News Watch," in *The Christian Research Journal* (Winter 1994): 7.
[13] Doug Groothuis, *Deceived by the Light* (Eugene, OR: Harvest, 1995), 22.
[14] *Christian Research Journal*, 7.

curious mixture of Mormonism and New Age philosophy. There have been ripples of controversy about her teachings within the Mormon church itself, and church leaders, while pleased with the public relations bonanza Eadie's book has been, stopped short of treating her as an actual prophet.

In any case, Eadie's claims as a whole are obviously heavily influenced by Mormon teaching. She is badly out of step with essential teachings of Scripture regarding theology proper (the doctrine of God), anthropology (the doctrine of man), hamartiology (the doctrine of sin), and eschatology (the doctrine of future things—especially concerning heaven and how one gets there).

Angels of Deception

Scripture plainly warns us to be on guard against emissaries of Satan who appear to be angels of light (2 Corinthians 11:13–15). The most influential false doctrines that have ever been loosed against the church have always been those that masquerade as orthodox, employing the familiar language of Scripture but skewing the truth. In other words, using the *terminology* of biblical Christianity is not the same as being biblical.

The fact that Betty Eadie is a pleasant woman who says she has had encounters with angels is certainly no guarantee that she is not deceived, or a deceiver, or both. In fact, the nature of her case gives us all the more warrant to examine her teachings with the utmost care and scrutiny. Eadie is claiming to have received a comprehensive revelation of divine truth directly from the Lord himself. Her description of her experience is more sensational and far more detailed than the apostles' account of the Transfiguration. Her portrait of heaven goes miles beyond the apostle Paul's own meager account of his being caught up into the third heaven. If true, Eadie's story supersedes every recorded revelation of heaven found in Scripture. Moreover, if Betty Eadie is right, Christian theology needs to be completely revamped. According to her system, no one else has had it right in two thousand years of Christianity.

Obviously, based on what we have already said in this book, it ought to be clear to anyone with a basic understanding of biblical truth that Eadie's claims are sheer rubbish, and dangerous to anyone who takes them seriously.

Embraced by Darkness

Some of Betty Eadie's ideas are echoes of her Mormonism; others are drawn from New Age teaching; and others are simply unbiblical inventions that either sprung from her imagination or were planted there by some demonic spirit.

The Mormon Doctrines

Mormon influences are clearly evident throughout Eadie's account of heaven. Among the chief Mormon doctrines that find their way into her tale are these:

PREEXISTENCE OF HUMAN SPIRITS. Betty Eadie claims all of us had an existence in the "pre-mortal world." This is a prominent doctrine in Mormon teaching, but it is nowhere taught in Scripture.

We noted above that Eadie claimed she could remember having had a previous relationship with her robed "monk" guides for "eternities." Elsewhere she writes,

> I *remembered* the creation of the earth. I actually experienced it as if it were being reenacted before my eyes. This was important. Jesus wanted me to internalize this knowledge. He wanted me to know how it felt when the creation occurred. And the only way to do that was for me to view it again and *feel* what I had felt before.
>
> All people as spirits in the pre-mortal world took part in the creation of the earth.[15]

What does Scripture say about this? First of all, the biblical account of creation very clearly places the creation of the first human soul *after* the rest of creation was complete. The Bible says, "The LORD God formed the man of dust from the ground and breathed into his nostrils the breath of life, and the man became a living creature" (Genesis 2:7). The word translated "creature" is *nephesh*, the primary Hebrew word for "soul." The root of the word speaks of the *breath* that is in the creature.

---

[15] Eadie, *Embraced by the Light*, 47.

It is common Old Testament shorthand for the seat of both our life and our personhood. Indeed, in the King James Version, the word is quite properly translated as "soul." Notice: it was not until God was finished with creation that Adam *became* a living soul. There is no room for any sort of preexistence of human souls in the biblical account.

In fact, one of the crucial arguments for divine sovereignty posed to Job by God himself was that when the universe was created, Job was nowhere around: "Where were you when I laid the foundation of the earth? Tell me, if you have understanding" (Job 38:4). Job could not boast of having been there. He hadn't been; he did not exist at the time—not even as a disembodied soul. Scripture nowhere suggests that our human souls existed prior to our conception—in fact, all the biblical data argues otherwise (cf. Psalm 51:5). God *alone* created the universe (Genesis 1:1; Colossians 1:16–17).

MULTIPLE GODS. Betty Eadie's account eliminates the doctrine of the Trinity. She writes, "I was still laboring under the teachings and beliefs of my childhood."[16] What were those teachings and beliefs? "My Protestant upbringing had taught me that God the Father and Jesus Christ were one being."[17] But her heavenly experience convinced Betty Eadie differently: "I understood, to my surprise, that Jesus was *a separate being from God*, with His own divine purpose."[18] This is perfectly in accord with Mormon doctrine but plainly at odds with Scripture. From cover to cover the Bible teaches the unity of the divine Godhead (Deuteronomy 6:4; 1 Corinthians 8:6; 1 Timothy 2:5; James 2:19). Jesus himself said, "I and the Father are one" (John 10:30). There is no possibility of differing purposes between the Father and the Son (John 4:34; 5:30; 8:29).

Granted, the Trinity is a difficult concept to explain or understand, but every major branch of Christianity has agreed for nearly two thousand years that while God the Father and Jesus Christ are distinct persons, they are *not* separate beings, or separate gods. This is the clear teaching of Scripture: "Hear, O Israel: The LORD our God, the LORD is one" (Deuteronomy 6:4).

---

[16] Ibid., 43.
[17] Ibid., 47.
[18] Ibid. (emphasis added).

THE DEIFICATION OF THE HUMAN SOUL. We have already noted that Betty Eadie claimed she enjoyed omniscience in heaven. This is in harmony with the Mormon notion that all believers are progressing toward godhood. Elsewhere she writes, "I understood with pure knowledge that God wants us to become as He is, and that he has invested us with god-like qualities."[19]

Scripture teaches that we will be like Christ in holiness, but not that we will share the incommunicable attributes of God, such as his omnipotence and omniscience. Even in the glory of heaven, we will remain God's creatures. We will not attain a divinity of our own, or even share his deity. "I am the LORD," he says. "That is my name; my glory I give to no other" (Isaiah 42:8).

EVE'S ACT SEEN AS NOBLE. Eadie echoes the Mormon notion that Eve's eating of the forbidden fruit was a noble act. A common Mormon view is that Eve willfully partook of the fruit as a sort of selfless sacrifice, so that she would be able to bear children and thus progress toward the state of divinity. Thus her disobedience becomes a positive act. *The Book of Mormon* says, "Adam fell that men might be; and men are, that they might have joy."[20]

Recounting what she learned when she was supposedly permitted to watch a replay of creation, Eadie writes,

> I had seen then the differences between Adam and Eve. I was shown that Adam was more satisfied with his condition in the Garden and that Eve was more restless. I was shown that she wanted to become a mother desperately enough that she was willing to risk death to obtain it. Eve did not "fall" to temptation as much as she made a conscious decision to bring about conditions necessary for her progression, and her initiative was used to finally get Adam to partake the fruit, then, they brought mankind to mortality, which gave us conditions necessary for having children—but also to die.[21]

Scripture plainly teaches, however, that Eve was deceived by Satan and that the fall was wholly an act of sin (1 Timothy 2:14; 2 Corinthians 11:3).

---

[19] Ibid., 61.
[20] The Book of Mormon, 2 Nephi 2:25.
[21] Eadie, *Embraced by the Light*, 109.

THE POSSIBILITY OF SALVATION AFTER DEATH. Mormonism is well known for the practice of baptizing people for the dead. Mormons believe that people who die without having heard the Mormon gospel will have an opportunity to hear and believe even after they die. Since baptism is viewed as essential to their salvation, the dead are baptized "by proxy"—that is, living Mormons stand in for the souls of people whom they know have died without being baptized in the Mormon church.[22]

Betty Eadie's book reflects the Mormon belief that death does not settle the question of a soul's eternal destiny. Her guides in the afterlife told her

> that it is important for us to acquire knowledge of the spirit while we are in the flesh. The more knowledge we acquire here, the further and faster we will progress there. Because of lack of knowledge or belief, some spirits are virtual prisoners on this earth. [This echoes Mormon doctrine as well.] Some who die as atheists, or those who have bonded to the world through greed, bodily appetites, or other earthly commitments find it difficult to move on, and they become earth-bound. They often lack the faith and power to reach for, or in some cases even to recognize, the energy and light that pulls us toward God. These spirits stay on earth until they learn to accept the greater power around them and to let go of the world. When I was in the black mass before moving towards the light, I felt the presence of such lingering spirits. They reside there as long as they want to in its love and warmth, accepting its healing influence, but eventually they learn to move on to accept the greater warmth and security of God.[23]

But Scripture says, "It is appointed for man to die once, and after that comes judgment" (Hebrews 9:27). Scripture repeatedly teaches that the judgment of the wicked is based on works they do while on earth (Romans 2:5–6; 2 Corinthians 11:15).

The New Age Beliefs

So there are definite overtones of Mormonism in Betty Eadie's concept of heaven. But she is no doctrinaire Mormon. There are also some ideas

---

[22] A few years ago some zealous Mormons created a furor in the Jewish community by taking published lists of Holocaust victims and "baptizing" them by proxy (*Los Angeles Times*, May 6, 1995, 1).
[23] Eadie, *Embraced by the Light*, 85.

in her book that seem more in harmony with the mysticism of the New Age movement than with the beliefs of orthodox Latter-Day Saints.

The New Age movement is a loosely related array of ideas and philosophies that have much in common with both Hinduism and ancient gnosticism. New Age religions are *pantheistic* (believing in the divinity of both Creator and creation), *mystical* (viewing truth as something one finds within oneself), and *syncretistic* (blending and merging religious ideas from any number of sources). There is also a large dose of occult superstition in most New Age thought.

Many New Age doctrines are naturally fairly compatible with Mormonism. (There are, for example, obvious elements of pantheism, mysticism, and syncretism in Mormon belief as well.) But Betty Eadie's account draws more freely from New Age thought than traditional Mormonism normally would. These are the elements of New Age thought evident in her book:

UNIVERSALISM. In Betty Eadie's heaven, everyone will ultimately attain entrance. Oddly enough, she juxtaposes her strongest statement about the exclusivity of Christ with an unqualified statement of universalist conviction. We noted earlier her acknowledgment that Jesus is the only door to salvation. Yet she immediately states that through that door *"all"* will one day enter.[24] In her description of the afterlife she never makes any reference to hell. She quite clearly does not believe anyone will spend eternity there.

This universalism is no doubt closely related to Eadie's suggestion, cited earlier, that all religions are equally necessary. In her way of thinking, it matters not what religion a person embraces while on earth, because everyone will eventually be fully enlightened in the afterlife. Thus religious error and false doctrine are seen as things that pose no real long-term danger. This kind of thinking is characteristic of New Age philosophy. In effect, it erases any important distinction between truth and error, and easily suits Satan's strategy of proliferating as many forms of false religion as possible. This he has done, because he wants something attractive to every person. He doesn't care what false religion people accept, because he is not trying to establish a false

---

[24] Ibid., 85.

system. He only wants to destroy the truth of Christianity. As long as people do not accept the gospel truth of Scripture, Satan doesn't care what anyone believes. All false religions work together against the truth. Occultism, Mormonism, New Age religion, Hinduism, and whatever else attacks biblical truth furthers the aims of Satan's kingdom.

POSITIVE AND NEGATIVE ENERGIES. Here's a sample that demonstrates how profoundly Betty Eadie has been influenced by New Age teachings:

> Within our universe are both positive and negative energies, and both types of energy are essential to creation and growth. These energies have intelligence—they do our will. They are our willing servants. God has absolute power over both energies. Positive energy is basically just what we would think it is: light, goodness, kindness, love, patience, charity, hope, and so on. And negative energy is just what we would think it is: darkness, hatred, fear (Satan's greatest tool), unkindness, intolerance, selfishness, despair, discouragement, and so on.
> Positive and negative energies work in opposition to each other. And when we internalize these energies, they become our servants. Positive attracts positive, and negative attracts negative. Light cleaves to light, and darkness loves darkness.... There is power in our thoughts. We create our own surroundings by the thoughts we think.[25]

Eadie continues like that for several pages, reciting a litany that could well stand as the basic credo of the New Age movement.

SPIRITUAL HEALING. New Age advocates speak frequently about the healing properties of the mind. Betty Eadie's writings reflect a strong belief in that tenet. If, as she believes, "we create our own surroundings by the thoughts we think," it stands to reason that we can heal ourselves by thinking positive thoughts. That is precisely what Eadie claims:

> Our thoughts have exceptional power to draw on the negative or positive energies around us. When they draw at length on the negative, the result can be a weakening of the body's defenses. This is especially true when our negative thoughts are centered on ourselves. I understood that we are at our *most* self-centered state when we are depressed. . . .

[25] Ibid., 57–58.

> All healing takes place from within. Our spirits heal our body. A doctor's sure hands may perform surgery, and medicine may provide ideal circumstances for health, but it is the spirit that effects the healing. A body without a spirit cannot be healed; it cannot live for long.[26]

Eadie states that there is spiritual power within us to enable us actually to alter our bodies' cells for healing. In fact, focusing on one's infirmities is a wrong use of negative energy and can be counterproductive:

> I saw that I had often yielded to negative "self-talk," such as, "Oh, my aches and pains," "I'm not loved," "Look at my sufferings," "I can't endure this," and more. Suddenly I saw the *me, me, me* in each of these statements. I saw the extent of my self-centeredness. And I saw that not only did I claim these negativisms by calling them mine, but I opened the door and accepted them as mine. My body then lived a sort of self-fulfilling prophecy: "Woe is me," was translated in the body as "I am sick." I had never thought of this before, but now I saw how clearly I had been a part of the problem.[27]

Of course, many others *have* thought of this before, including Mary Baker Eddy and virtually all the metaphysical science-of-mind cults that flourished a century or so ago. Such groups were the forerunners of the modern New Age movement, which holds very similar doctrines about healing and the mind.

CREATING ONE'S OWN REALITY. Another corollary of Betty Eadie's assertion that "we create our own surroundings by the thoughts we think" is the idea that truth and reality are subjective, unique to every individual. All our "surroundings"—including metaphysical realities— are merely the product of our thoughts. "If we understood the power of our thoughts," Eadie writes, "we would guard them more closely. If we understood the awesome power of our words, we would prefer silence to almost anything negative. In our thoughts and words we create our own weaknesses and our own strengths."[28] In other words, our thoughts determine what "reality" is.

The moral effects of such relativism are abominable. This means,

---

[26] Ibid., 63.
[27] Ibid., 64.
[28] Ibid., 58.

for example, that people afflicted with illnesses and disabilities are viewed as having brought these things upon themselves. Eadie writes, "To my surprise I saw that most of us had selected the illnesses we would suffer, and for some, the illness that would end our lives."[29] On a 20/20 interview with Hugh Downs, Eadie stated that the victims of the Nazi Holocaust had chosen their own fate before birth.[30] This has the effect of trivializing human suffering and absolving the Nazi butchers of their crimes.

An evangelical expert on the New Age movement, Doug Groothuis, has written, "If the Holocaust victims were not really victims at all but willing participants, then the Nazis should not have been morally condemned; they were simply enacting the wishes of their subjects. Surely, this is morally absurd."[31]

PANTHEISM. Pantheism is the notion that God and the universe are one. As noted, pantheism entails a belief in the divinity of the creature as well as the Creator. No doubt the best-known example of New Age pantheism in popular culture is actress Shirley MacLaine's claim that she is God. Such a claim is actually quite common in the world of the New Age; most New Age philosophies include the notion that God is embodied in all creation. That is why the New Age movement has such an affinity with those who want to deify nature and worship "Mother Earth."

Betty Eadie believes we are all divine. In her New Age and Mormon belief system, human spirits are literally the offspring of God and therefore essentially divine. As we have seen, she claimed omniscience for herself. Elsewhere she specifically states that human nature is "divine,"[32] and that prior to birth all human spirits possess "divine knowledge"—an omniscience that enables them to know exactly what they will face here on earth.[33]

Eadie describes one event in her heavenly travels where she noticed a rose by a river. As she looked at the rose, she says, its presence surrounded her. "I experienced it as if I *were* the flower! . . . I felt God

---

[29] Ibid., 67.
[30] Broadcast May 13, 1994.
[31] Groothuis, *Deceived by the Light*, 26–27.
[32] Eadie, *Embraced by the Light*, 50.
[33] Ibid., 48–49.

in the plant, in me, his love pouring into us. We are all one!"[34] That is sheer pantheism.

As she describes her first meeting with the Jesus figure in her vision, Betty Eadie writes, "I felt his light blending into mine, literally, and I felt my light being drawn to his. It was as if there were two lamps in a room, both shining, their light merging together. It's hard to tell where one light ends and the other begins; they just become one light. . . . I felt his enormous spirit and knew that I had always been part of him, that in reality I had never been away from him."[35]

There is a sense, of course, in which Scripture teaches that Christians are united with Christ. But not in a way that obscures the Creator-creature distinction, and certainly not in a way that harks back to some eternal relationship between the human and the divine. Betty Eadie's theology is antibiblical, anti-Christian pantheism.

DUALISM. An unbiblical dualism also pervades all New Age belief. Dualism is the notion that everything is reducible to two fundamental principles—yin and yang, good and evil, light and darkness, or whatever. To the dualist, all reality is explainable in terms of the struggle between these two fundamental principles—rather like The Force and the Dark Side of the Force. In New Age philosophy the fundamental principles can be described in terms of spirit and matter, light and darkness, knowledge and ignorance, mind and body, heaven and earth—or similar dualisms.

New Age dualisms color Betty Eadie's heaven. The juxtaposition of good-evil, spirit-body, and heaven-earth dualities is a running motif throughout her book, giving it a distinctly New Age vocabulary. Dualism lies behind her concept of positive and negative energy. Dualism is the ground for her views on how spirit and body work together in the process of healing. Dualism also frames her view of sin and evil.

Dualism is inherently incompatible with a biblical view of sin. If the dualistic worldview is correct, two fundamentally opposite forces have held one another in tension from eternity past. Evil becomes just as necessary as good. And that is the nature of things in Betty Eadie's

---

[34] Ibid., 81.
[35] Ibid., 41.

heaven. As we have seen, she believes the fall of Adam and Eve was a necessary evil. Furthermore, in Eadie's dualistic system, sin itself is not really an offense against a holy God, but rather the result of too much negative energy. Anger, hatred, envy, bitterness, and a lack of forgiveness are not so much *sins* for which we need atonement, but rather negative influences we must learn to "let go of."[36]

Eadie speaks of sin only occasionally, and as Groothuis notes, when she uses the word at all, she usually puts it in quotation marks.[37] In a classic example of her dualism, Eadie asserts that "our spirit bodies are full of light, truth, and love, [but] they must battle constantly to overcome the flesh."[38] That battle has the effect of strengthening the good in us, she says, and the resulting growth process is what will eventually free us from the influence of evil. Thus "sin" is simply a necessary force to be regulated and mastered by the normal mechanisms of spiritual growth. It is not seen as an enemy that can be ultimately destroyed and vanquished—nor is there any need for expiation through Christ's substitutionary atonement.

In fact, far from acknowledging the need for atonement, Betty Eadie declares that "sin is not our true nature. Spiritually we are at varying degrees of light—which is knowledge—and because of our divine, spiritual nature we are filled with the desire to do good."[39] That flatly contradicts Scripture, which says we are *by nature* children of wrath (Ephesians 2:3), enemies of God (Romans 5:10), incapable of being subject to God's laws (Romans 8:7). Scripture says there is none who does good—no not one (Romans 3:12).

But according to Betty Eadie, "In the spirit world they don't see sin as we do here. *All* experiences can be positive."[40]

All dualism inevitably has this tendency to obliterate the moral significance of evil. If evil is an eternal cosmic force, then it is something to be tolerated and understood and even used—not an enemy that can ever be destroyed. Perhaps this explains Betty Eadie's nonchalant approach to humanity's sin problem. For example, Eadie says that

---

[36] Ibid., 51.
[37] Groothuis, *Deceived by the Light*, 28.
[38] Eadie, *Embraced by the Light*, 50.
[39] Ibid., 49–50.
[40] Ibid., 70.

while in heaven, she underwent a review of her entire life, displayed before her "in the form of what we might consider extremely well-defined holograms."[41] As she watched the replay of her life, she began to feel ashamed:

> I saw the disappointment I had caused others, and I cringed as their feelings of disappointment filled me, compounded by my own guilt. I understood all the suffering I had caused, and I felt it. I began to tremble. I saw how much grief my bad temper had caused, and I suffered this grief. I saw my selfishness, and my heart cried for relief. How had I been so uncaring?[42]

Eadie describes what she saw as the "ripple effect" of her wrong deeds. When she had wronged people, they had in turn wronged others, and so on. As she began to understand the far-reaching effects of her wrongs, she says, her pain multiplied and became unbearable.

In the midst of this, Eadie claims, the Savior stepped forward and urged her not to feel so bad about herself. "You're being too hard on yourself," she claims Jesus told her. Then he showed her that her good deeds had an equal and opposite "ripple effect."[43] All the good deeds in effect undid the bad ones—dualism again. "My pain was replaced with joy," she writes.

That kind of thinking obliterates the need for atonement. If one can cancel out one's own sin simply by doing enough good to undo sin's effects, Christ's work on the cross becomes superfluous. This is not true Christianity. It is the result of a pagan dualism.

Someone might wonder whether Christianity itself is dualistic. After all, don't Christians understand the conflict of the ages as a battle between good and evil, or God and Satan? Is this not a proper dualism?

No, it is not. Satan is neither eternal nor equal to God. He is a created being. There is no fundamental, eternal principle besides God himself. Evil is not an abiding challenge to his goodness. It is a condition into which creation has fallen and from which creation will be redeemed. Evil is *not* an eternal force on a par with God himself. God and Satan are not equal opposites. Nor are good and evil.

---

[41] Ibid., 112.
[42] Ibid., 112.
[43] Ibid., 113.

Christians believe in one, and only one, eternal principle—God himself. He alone is sovereign over Satan and evil. Or in other words, in orthodox Christian thought, at the beginning of all reality and all existence, there is only God. "He is before all things, and in him all things hold together" (Colossians 1:17). Even the doctrine of the Trinity does not alter the essential unity of a Christian worldview. God is three persons in *one* essential being.

So the nature of Christian truth rules out dualism. And history reveals that all who have tried to mix dualism with Christianity have fallen into serious heresy. The long history of gnosticism provides ample proof of this.

GNOSTICISM. Betty Eadie's doctrine, like all New Age philosophy, is infected with gnosticism. Ancient gnosticism was always dualistic, mystical, and seriously heretical. Strains of gnosticism have survived across the ages, and gnostic thinking is really the foundation of the New Age movement. In fact, one could say that the New Age movement *is* a revival of gnosticism.

Though gnostics often use Christian language and a biblical vocabulary, gnostic ideas are hostile to true Christianity. Therefore, genuine believers must be on guard against the influx of neo-gnosticism.

As discussed earlier in this book, the key idea underlying all gnosticism—the one from which it takes its name—is the belief that some higher knowledge than the revealed truth of Scripture is available to enlightened souls. Gnostics don't always agree on *what* the "secret" to enlightenment is, but they agree that it is kept secret from all but the enlightened ones, and is found in some "key" to truth that lies, inevitably, beyond Scripture.

Gnosticism is therefore inherently mystical—teaching people to look within themselves for the secret knowledge. This knowledge can be acquired through dreams and visions, angelic messengers, direct communication from God into the mind, biofeedback, one's own emotions, an out-of-body experience—or as in Betty Eadie's case, a combination of all of these, combined with a journey of the soul to the realm beyond.

Eadie's entire claim rests on the assertion that she is now, by virtue of her supposedly postmortem experience, privy to the secrets of the universe. She claims to hold knowledge that goes beyond what Scripture reveals about heaven. Therefore she sets herself up as a higher authority on heaven than Scripture itself. This is classic gnosticism.

Other Unbiblical Ideas

Betty Eadie's book is filled with other unbiblical ideas—some lesser and some greater in importance. Here are a few of them:

THE SOVEREIGNTY OF THE HUMAN WILL. Eadie espouses a radical free-will doctrine that erases the biblical doctrine of divine sovereignty. She describes her thoughts as she looked in on her own children from the realm of the dead: "They were individual spirits, like myself, with an intelligence that was developed before their lives on earth. Each one had their own free will to live their life as they chose. I knew that this free will should not be denied them."[44] She says she realized that her children were living their lives according to an agenda that they had chosen for themselves before their births. And, according to Betty Eadie, their free-will choices could not be denied them. "There was no need for sorrow or fear."[45]

She expands on these notions later in the book, writing,

I saw that in the pre-mortal world we knew about and even chose our missions in life. . . . We were given agency to act for ourselves here. Our own actions determine the course of our lives, and we can alter or redirect our lives at any time. I understood that this was crucial; God made the promise that he wouldn't intervene in our lives *unless we asked him*. And then through his omniscient knowledge he would help us attain our righteous desires. We were grateful for this ability to express our free will and to exercise its power. This would allow each of us to obtain great joy or to choose that which would bring us sadness. The choice would be ours through our decisions.[46]

Scripture teaches no such thing. Far from exalting the freedom of the human will, Scripture describes us as hopelessly in bondage to sin

---

[44] Ibid., 34–35.
[45] Ibid., 35.
[46] Ibid., 48–49.

and wrong desires. "The mind that is set on the flesh is hostile to God, for it does not submit to God's law; indeed, it cannot" (Romans 8:7). We are subject to sin's bondage all our lives (Hebrews 2:15).

Scripture also uses the metaphor of death to describe the spiritual condition of the human heart. We are said to have been "dead in the trespasses and sins in which [we] once walked" prior to regeneration (Ephesians 2:1–2). We lived our lives enslaved to wrong desires, "in the passions of our flesh, carrying out the desires of the body and the mind, and were by nature children of wrath" (v. 3). Far from promising not to intervene unless we ask him, God's sovereign intervention is *necessary* for our salvation (vv. 4–5). Ours would be a hopeless situation indeed if God agreed to permit us to choose our own way and promised "that he wouldn't intervene in our lives unless we asked him."

Scripture plainly teaches that God's will is sovereign, not the sinner's. Our salvation and eternal well-being "depends not on human will or exertion, but on God, who has mercy" (Romans 9:16). He saves sinners in spite of their love for sin and their hatred of his righteousness. A choice was indeed made before the foundation of the world, but it was God, not us, who chose "that we should be holy and blameless before him" (Ephesians 1:4).

HUMAN SELF-SUFFICIENCY. In addition to making the sinner's will sovereign, Betty Eadie's theology insists that humans are in and of themselves sufficient to meet all their own spiritual needs.

This doctrine renders God virtually superfluous. No wonder Eadie claims God has promised to stay out of human affairs. She believes people are capable of helping themselves without divine intervention: "I saw that we *always* have the right attribute to help ourselves, though we may not have recognized it or learned how to use it. We need to look within. We need to trust our abilities; the right spiritual tool is always there for us."[47] This is a damning doctrine to proclaim to sinners who are utterly incapable of doing anything to save themselves. Jesus's message was exactly opposite: "Apart from me you can do nothing" (John 15:5).

---

[47] Ibid., 94.

SALVATION BY HUMAN WORKS. Nonetheless, the notion that sinners are both sovereign in the exercise of their will and spiritually self-sufficient naturally puts the burden of salvation on the sinner's own back and establishes a system of works. This is a common failing of all cults and false doctrines.

By Betty Eadie's way of thinking, our earthly lives are simply part of an eternal growth process. Our sins are nothing but tools for us to learn by.[48] Divine grace is an unwelcome intruder in such a system, because when God does anything *for* us, it is essentially a lost growth opportunity. (That's why she suggests God has promised not to intervene unless we ask him.) And since all our human deficiencies are simply imperfections that can be outgrown, we must pursue the process on our own. "We are to create our own lives, to exercise our gifts and experience both failure and success. We are to use our free will to expand and magnify our lives."[49]

And love is supreme.[50] "Love is really the only thing that matters."[51] It's all "so simple. *If we're kind, we'll have joy.*"[52]

AN UNDUE EMPHASIS ON ANGELS. Although Betty Eadie claims God doesn't want to intervene in human affairs, angels evidently have no compunctions about doing so. Eadie claims angels orchestrate the workings of providence.[53] They answer people's prayers.[54] Guardian angels hover around us all the time and are available to us virtually on command.[55] She says angels frequently come to us from the realm beyond, to prompt us to be faithful to the commitments we made before our birth.[56]

Scripture, of course, teaches none of this.

CHUTZPA. Like every other recent returnee from heaven, Betty Eadie came back with a very high opinion of herself.

Indeed, she seems to have gone there with a sizable ego in the first

---

[48] Ibid., 115–116.
[49] Ibid., 59.
[50] Ibid.
[51] Ibid., 114.
[52] Ibid.
[53] Ibid., 115.
[54] Ibid., 90, 103.
[55] Ibid., 115, 121.
[56] Ibid., 101.

place. Far from falling on her face in holy fear (as Ezekiel did when he glimpsed God), Eadie describes how *she* spelled out the terms under which she would agree to return to earth—and, she says, "They agreed to *my* terms."[57] Instead of trembling at her own uncleanness (as Isaiah did) in the presence of God (Isaiah 6:5), Eadie claims she couldn't tell where her own light left off and Jesus's light began to shine.[58] Instead of seeing Jesus Christ (the way the apostle John saw him) as "the Alpha and the Omega, the first and the last, the beginning and the end" (Revelation 22:13), Betty Eadie says she remembered how she had personally been with him as an observer at creation.

Such a vision of "heaven" plainly has nothing to do with the heaven Scripture tells us about.

MISCELLANEOUS UNBIBLICAL CLAIMS. Betty Eadie's book is filled with many other teachings that find no support whatsoever in Scripture, such as her claim that infant souls "can choose to enter their mother's body at any stage of her pregnancy."[59] She also suggests that prayers on behalf of departed people can be helpful to them in the spirit world.[60] And she completely omits any reference to the role of the Holy Spirit. She evidently does not believe in his personality.

Enchanted with Error

If it seems I have belabored the errors in Betty Eadie's account of heaven, it is because these are very serious errors, yet it appears that millions have been influenced by them. People are inexplicably enchanted with tales from the afterlife. And *Embraced by the Light* was the first and remains one of the best-known and most popular of such accounts.

Believe it or not, there are many more dangerous books in this genre, with even more ominous doctrinal overtones than Betty Eadie's. One such example is a book titled *Saved by the Light*,[61] by Dannion Brinkley, which (like virtually all of the other books we have discussed) had a stint on the *New York Times* best-seller list.

---

[57] Ibid., 119 (emphasis added).
[58] Ibid., 41.
[59] Ibid., 95.
[60] Ibid., 84.
[61] Dannion Brinkley, *Saved by the Light: The True Story of a Man Who Died Twice and the Profound Revelations He Received* (New York: Villard, 1994).

Brinkley's journey into the afterlife occurred after he was struck by lightning. There are many close similarities between his account and Eadie's, but one major difference is that Dannion Brinkley is overtly hostile to Christianity—biblical Christianity in particular. He suggests that Christianity is responsible for making people think that they are "not capable of being what it is that we truly are."[62]

Brinkley believes he was sent back from the afterlife to convey a message to the world. The message is this: The way mankind will go is not carved in stone. We have an opportunity to change things. In Brinkley's words, a heavenly being told him—

> that I was to come back—just in case people didn't change, since the world as we know it was going to change and pass away; that religion would crumble and institutions would crumble, and governments would collapse because of the lies—and that what I had to do was prepare a system that people could come to that didn't have dogma, didn't have religion attached to it, and that they could go through an eight-step program to really find a way to renew themselves and their spirit in a world that was no longer secure, a world that you could not trust.[63]

Dannion Brinkley has found that "system without dogma" in the New Age movement, and now he is an evangelist for every New Age aberration. Asked how to reconcile his experience with Betty Eadie's, he said,

> People relate a little differently because of the cultural heritage or the religious heritage. Like the being of light I saw, Betty Eadie saw Jesus. Some see Mohammed, some see Krishna. Everybody has a name for it. *Nonetheless, it is still the same experience.* I have found in talking to Raymond [Moody] and talking to people myself, the near death experience is so uniform, so specific, that no matter what the culture, it's there, it exists—regardless of whatever particular dogma is attached to it . . . . When you reach that spiritual level of consciousness, you see whatever your life's course has taught you.[64]

That is a virtual admission, from one of the leading advocates of near-death experiences, that such experiences can teach us nothing objec-

[62] "A Conversation with Dannion Brinkley," *The Monthly Aspectarian*, September 1995.
[63] Ibid.
[64] Ibid.

tive about life after death. They are inevitably shaped and interpreted by the person's existing worldview. They are no more reliable than dream analysis for giving us any reliable understanding of the unseen world, and people are playing with fire if they draw their opinions about life after death (or any other spiritual matters) from the tales such mystics tell.

Appendix 2:

The Boy Who Came Back from Heaven

Kevin Malarkey's book about his young son's near-death experience bears a strong resemblance to Todd Burpo's. In all fairness, it is a better-written, more compelling story, but ultimately it is no less biblically and theologically bankrupt. Both Burpo and Malarkey trivialize heaven. Both imply that human experience can shed more light on heaven than God's Word does. Both ask readers to suspend discernment and accept figments of human fancy as fact. And both are dangerously misleading.

The Boy Who Came Back from Heaven is Malarkey's account of his family's experiences after a horrific automobile accident in November 2004 in which his eldest son, Alex (at age six), was nearly decapitated. The book's cover lists Kevin and Alex as joint authors, but the copyright notice is in Kevin's name alone, and it is clearly Kevin who tells the story. Also on the book's cover, in large type, are the words "a true story." But as we shall see, there is considerable evidence that Kevin Malarkey has embellished, exaggerated, and even fabricated the supposed visions and experiences he attributes to Alex.

Kevin's description of how Alex was paralyzed is poignantly heart-rending. He and Alex were on the way home from church. They had recently moved into a new home and were visiting a church in their new neighborhood that morning. Kevin's wife, Beth, had given birth to the family's fourth child only days earlier and was just home from the hospital with the newborn, so little Alex and his dad were alone in the car.

On the way home Kevin came to an unfamiliar intersection in a remote area. He did not realize it, but this intersection did not offer a complete view of the crossroad. There was a large dip in the road a few yards beyond the intersection. If an approaching car happened to be at the low point of that dip, the car would be completely obscured from view for a second. If a driver at the intersection glanced down the road at precisely that moment and did not take a lingering look, he might think the road was clear of all traffic.

Partially distracted by a phone call and totally fooled by the optical illusion, Kevin accidentally pulled out in front of an oncoming vehicle and was hit broadside. Alex suffered the kind of neck trauma people rarely survive. In Kevin's words, "He had suffered an internal decapitation—his skull was detached from his spinal column. Skin, muscle, and ligaments were holding his head on his body, but his spinal cord tendon sheath was severed."[1]

Against doctors' expectations, Alex survived. But he suffered the loss of all sensation and motor ability below the point of his injury. The trauma to his spinal cord was so severe that Alex was left unable to swallow, requiring a feeding tube for nourishment. He was unable even to breathe on his own—dependent on a ventilator attached to a tracheotomy tube at the neck.

Alex's initial recovery was of course a long ordeal, most of which he spent in a coma. But he gradually awoke and learned to communicate again. A major milestone in his long rehabilitation came about four years after the accident, when surgeons implanted a device that artificially stimulates his own diaphragm to make breathing possible. Thus he was finally liberated from the ventilator, but he is still bound to a wheelchair.

By itself, the story of Alex's survival and his adaptation to life as a quadriplegic would be an amazing story of courage and faith. But Kevin Malarkey has overlaid his son's testimony with so much that is unbiblical that the book considered as a whole is dangerously misleading. Alex himself posted a similar assessment of his father's narrative at a webpage publicizing the book, but the comment was quickly

---

[1] Kevin Malarkey and Alex Malarkey, *The Boy Who Came Back from Heaven: A Remarkable Account of Miracles, Angels, and Life beyond This World* (Carol Stream, IL: Tyndale, 2010), 33.

deleted.[2] Beth Malarkey reposted Alex's comment at her own blog, saying, "Alex voiced accurately what the book was about but he was silenced." Like Alex, she emphatically disavows many of the claims that are made in her husband's book, adding this: "Buyer beware. There is only one absolutely infallible and 'true' book: God's Word! It does not need fancied up or packaged for sale. It is incredible as it stands!"[3]

Admiring readers of the book were unfazed. One of them replied to Alex's comment as if it must have been written by an impostor: "Alex would *not* say that his book is false." Then the person added an addendum addressed to "the *real* Alex: your story is one of the most truthful, honest encounters I've ever read. God shines through your story and YOU so I know it is REAL and true."

On a purely human level, it is easy to see why impressionable readers who lack clear biblical understanding might be fooled. *The Boy Who Came Back from Heaven* packs a potent emotional punch. It starts with an engrossing account of how Alex sustained his injuries. It is impossible to read this part of the book without empathizing with both Alex and Kevin Malarkey. The narrative churns with pathos as Kevin recounts how a beautiful, sunny day of joy, rejoicing, and sweet fellowship between a father and his young son turned without warning into an unspeakable horror that left a family's lives forever changed.

But as soon as Kevin moves from his own testimony into an account of what he claims Alex saw and heard, the book immediately begins to veer into the realm of gnostic mysticism and word-faith doctrine. It turns out to be a dangerous blend of fantasy, superstition, aberrant doctrines, and Bible references, composed with lots of evangelical-sounding language and peppered with patently false ideas about heaven, angels, and the afterlife.

A sidebar section titled "I Went to Heaven" purports to quote Alex,[4] saying he remembers seeing angels carry his father outside the car. "Then," he says, "I looked to the front passenger seat, and the devil

---

[2] http://amomonamission.blogspot.com/2012/11/following-is-post-that-my-son-alex.html
[3] Ibid.
[4] In an e-mail to my editor, Beth Malarkey writes, "Know that Alex never concluded he was in heaven. He was a small boy who experienced something extraordinary. The adults made it into what would sell to the masses." She gave permission for her e-mail to be quoted here.

was looking into my eyes."[5] Supposedly the devil told him, "Yeah, that's right, your daddy is dead, and it is your fault."

The "Alex" voice in Kevin's narrative turns quickly from this satanic apparition to visions of heaven. Without even pausing to begin a new paragraph, the narrative continues: "I went to Heaven shortly after the car hit us, but I am not sure of the exact moment I actually left my body. I do know that when I was in Heaven, everything was perfect."[6] Kevin says Alex traversed the same long tunnel many people describe in their near-death experiences, but for him it was brightly lit instead of dark. He says the music in the tunnel was not to Alex's liking—"really bad music played on instruments with really long strings."[7]

Kevin Malarkey claims Alex told him that by the time he arrived in heaven, "Daddy was in Heaven too. The angels stayed with me so Daddy could be alone with God. Daddy had bad injuries like mine, but God was healing him in Heaven."[8] Kevin had lost consciousness for only a brief time and was not seriously injured. He says he has no memory of any angels, nor does he recall being transported to the heavenly realm, but he nevertheless seems to want readers to accept the notion that Alex saw him there.

Alex was flown by helicopter to a hospital equipped to deal with serious trauma, while Kevin, naturally frustrated to be separated from his critically injured child, was directed to a local emergency room for treatment.

The "Positive Confession" Heresy

One of the paramedics on Alex's medevac flight, Dave Knopp, was a strong believer in the prosperity-gospel doctrine of *positive confession*. Many charismatic televangelists teach this doctrine along with their promises of healing and financial prosperity. It is based on the false idea that our words have a kind of magical or spiritual power to create reality. Faith, according to this doctrine, is exercised by making an audible claim for whatever blessing or windfall or answer to prayer one desires. The catch is that if you accidentally say anything nega-

---

[5] Malarkey and Malarkey, *Boy Who Came Back from Heaven*, 14.
[6] Ibid.
[7] Ibid., 16.
[8] Ibid.

tive—especially if you express some degree of fear or doubt—the deal is off and God will not answer your prayer. This turns prayer into an exercise in magic—a superstitious contest in which the supplicant just has to say the right kind of abracadabra. When the healings and miracles don't come, the healer or miracle worker can say it was the fault of the person seeking the miracle. He or she didn't make a positive enough confession.

During Alex Malarkey's flight to the hospital, Dave Knopp says he laid hands on Alex and claimed a healing. "[I] prayed that he would be healed in the name of Jesus. Then I simply thanked the Lord for healing Alex."[9]

Later, at the hospital, Knopp encountered Beth Malarkey and informed her that he had claimed a healing for her son. But he strongly cautioned her that the words *she* spoke could make the whole difference between Alex's healing and his death:

> "Listen to me," Dave continued, intently looking into Beth's eyes. "You're going to go in the trauma room and you're going to hear some horrible things. In fact, they're going to tell you your son's going to die. But I laid hands on your son and prayed for him in the name of Jesus. I'm telling you, he's not going to die. . . . But if you go in there and agree with what they're saying and start speaking that, he will die. You'll negate what's been started by my praying for him. But if every time you get scared or hear a bad report, you thank the Lord for His healing, He will do His part. Have you got it?"
>
> "Yes," Beth said, nodding her head earnestly. "I got it."
>
> "Okay, then. I want you to repeat back to me what I just said you need to do."
>
> Beth dutifully repeated back his instructions.
>
> "Okay," said Dave with approval. "God bless you."[10]

The book includes a sidebar with Dave Knopp's own account of what he was thinking. The superstitious character of his "faith" is easily seen:

> I cautioned her that if she gave in to fear and began to say he was going to die, he would. I spent several minutes reminding her that God honors His Word and that Alex was being healed as we spoke. As

---

[9] Ibid., 12.
[10] Ibid., 26.

I walked away, that boldness left and I thought to myself, What did I do? I'm in trouble now. However, I didn't speak anything contrary to Alex's being healed; I just continued to thank the Lord.[11]

The positive confession theme permeates this book. Kevin says Beth Malarkey, "informed by Dave in the parking lot," scolded emergency-room doctors who tried to tell her how serious her son's injuries were. "Alex is going to be fine," she said, fearful of making any kind of negative confession. "His health will be fully restored, and his story is going to have a national impact, bringing hope to thousands of people."[12]

Kevin Malarkey says he thought his wife was "totally losing it" but that she was emphatic, and the doctor listened patiently, sympathetically. "Beth was just getting started. 'I know you don't believe me, but he is going to get better, and I mean completely healthy.'"[13]

Kevin stresses (repeatedly) that he too is now convinced God will still one day heal Alex completely. He goes to great lengths to make that confession as positively and as frequently as possible. This is a running theme throughout the book.

A friend claiming he has a message from God tells Kevin, "It suddenly came to me that Alex is going to be fully healed."[14] Kevin connects that with Dave Knopp's positive confession and his own wife's confident assertions. "I wanted to believe," he writes. "I wanted it all to be true."[15]

Then one day, he says, "a thought burst into my consciousness, as clear as if Pastor Brown had spoken it from the pulpit: *Alex is going to be healed.*"[16] Kevin was in church, listening to the preacher, when the impression finally struck him. "One minute I was closely following the pastor's words, and the next I was hearing: *He will be fully healed.* I shrugged it off and went back to listening to the pastor, but it kept coming: *He will be fully healed.* The message was so persistent, I knew it wasn't coming from me."[17] From that point on, the book is filled with repeated declarations about Alex's impending healing.

---

[11] Ibid., 27.
[12] Ibid., 32–33.
[13] Ibid., 34.
[14] Ibid., 61.
[15] Ibid., 61.
[16] Ibid., 148.
[17] Ibid., 149.

This is not some kind of supernatural faith bred by positive confession. It is merely superstitious fear. That fact is evident throughout the book as well. For example, when Kevin talks about retrofitting their home for wheelchair access, he says they were "a little uncomfortable with giving in to a permanently installed ramp—it felt like surrender, a resignation that God would never heal Alex. We said okay to the ramp, *but we called it a 'bike ramp.'* After all, there was no doubt that our kids would use it that way."[18]

Near the end of the book, Kevin Malarkey does give some sound advice: "If I may offer a humble word of exhortation, the enemy is a deceiver who masquerades as an angel of light. We all need to be on guard against counterfeit truth. Anything that doesn't square with Scripture is counterfeit."[19]

But he himself fails to apply that principle when it counts most. He begins the book by acknowledging that he has no sound theological explanation for certain aspects of the tale he is about to unfold. "I have no clue what to make of Alex's supernatural life—I have no theological box to put some of this stuff in." He clearly wants readers to accept his interpretation of these events anyway. So he says, "I humbly offer a challenge: Suspend your judgment for just a few chapters."[20]

So much for being on guard against counterfeit truth and examining the Scriptures carefully to see if these things are so (cf. Acts 17:11).

The problem is magnified when it becomes clear that positive-confession doctrine is one of Kevin Malarkey's basic presuppositions. This is an idea that emphatically does *not* square with Scripture. Scripture says some prayer requests go unfulfilled no matter how positively or persistently someone might confess them (James 4:3). That is particularly true of prayers for health, wealth, and material prosperity—the very kinds of requests most positive-confession teachers tend to encourage the most. But "this is the confidence that we have toward him, that *if we ask anything according to his will he hears us*" (1 John 5:14).

God has *not* promised full physical healing for every believer in this life. We still suffer the debilitating effects of the curse. We are susceptible to every kind of physical ailment up to and including death.

---

[18] Ibid., 157 (emphasis added).
[19] Ibid., 189.
[20] Ibid., x.

That is why "not only the creation, but we ourselves, who have the firstfruits of the Spirit, groan inwardly as we wait eagerly for adoption as sons, the redemption of our bodies" (Romans 8:23). God is gracious and often restores our strength or grants us temporal healing from many of our earthly afflictions, but the full redemption of our bodies will not occur until the resurrection.

Meanwhile, a strong impression, a voice in one's head, or even a supposed vision of heaven is not a reliable revelation from God on which to base a confession of faith or claim a miracle. If someone truly believes that truth claims must "square with Scripture" before we can embrace them as sound and reliable, that person will not try to build doctrine on mental impressions or make "positive confessions" without biblical warrant.

An Unbiblical Perspective of Heaven

Finally, if we compare the descriptions of heaven in Kevin Malarkey's book with Scripture, we find they don't meet the standard that Kevin himself cites as the test of accuracy. For example, Kevin claims Alex told him, "There is a hole in outer Heaven. That hole goes to hell."[21]

Kevin attributes several whimsical and typically childish remarks about heaven to Alex: Angels are "completely white and have wings." And some of them are merely two feet tall.[22] "There are lots of buildings in Heaven, but I only really notice the Temple. God never leaves the throne in the Temple. There is a scroll in a glass container. It describes the end times. No one can read this scroll but Jesus."[23] "The devil's mouth is funny looking, with only a few moldy teeth. And I've never noticed any ears. His body has a human form, with two bony arms and two bony legs. He has no flesh on his body, only some moldy stuff. His robes are torn and dirty."[24] Asked if he has ever seen the devil take on any other form, Alex supposedly replied, "No. He is always the same freaky devil."[25] One would of course expect a child to have a childlike concept of heaven. It is nevertheless dangerous and deceptive

---

[21] Ibid., 49.
[22] Ibid., 86.
[23] Ibid., 88.
[24] Ibid., 171.
[25] Ibid.

to peddle such ideas as trustworthy postscripts to the biblical teaching about heaven and expect adult readers to take the story seriously. Alex was exactly right when he said his father's book is "deceptive."

In short, Kevin Malarkey's version of heaven utterly lacks biblical plausibility. The stories he tells contrast sharply with the combined accounts of Isaiah, Ezekiel, and John and present an entirely different picture.

But Kevin Malarkey seems totally untroubled by the discrepancy. According to him, Alex may have seen more of heaven than all the biblical writers combined. He claims that (unlike most who visit heaven in near-death experiences) Alex makes occasional return trips there. Sometimes he can't go, because there's "too much warfare going on."[26] But according to Kevin, heaven sometimes comes to Alex. In Kevin's words,

> Up to the time he was about eight—the period of Alex's most serious physical struggle—there was a particular group of angels that would surround his bed in our master bedroom. Alex knew them all by name, and he would carry on conversations with them. John, Vent, and Ryan were names he mentioned. A typical reaction, of course, is to observe that a little boy on a ventilator, who has a baby brother named Ryan, is going to give those names to his imaginary friends. We know that children create imaginary friends to help them cope with new and difficult situations. Passing tedious hours in a wheelchair without the use of anything below his neck would surely inspire a child's imagination as a coping mechanism. Couldn't this explain these bizarre angel adventures, as well as the suspiciously familiar names? I wrestled with these doubts for a long time.[27]

A Faulty Idea of Faith

Just how long Kevin wrestled with his "doubts" isn't clear. But doubt ultimately gave way to reckless credulity. Kevin claims Alex told him, "Just try to be transparent in your spirit. Then you'll see the angel."[28] Kevin felt frustrated by the challenge—"spiritually uncoordinated. My son couldn't function in the physical world, but I was handicapped in

---

[26] Ibid., 172.
[27] Ibid., 166–167.
[28] Ibid., 184.

the spiritual world. Who had the greater disability?"[29] Kevin says, "I really was trying, because I believed Alex."

Finally, while walking outdoors and pondering his inability to "see" invisible angels, Kevin found himself speaking aloud. "Suddenly I said, 'I have anointed you with a message of hope.'

"*Where did that come from?* A sudden chill ran over my body as I glanced around. There was nothing out of the ordinary to see, but Someone had just spoken to me in my spirit."[30] Kevin continues:

> Like a radio signal tuning in to the right frequency, it came first in fits and starts. My heart raced within my chest. The Lord was directly communicating His will for me. I took off running up the driveway and burst through the door. I was all thumbs riffling through the counter and desk, looking for anything to begin writing: *I have anointed you with a message of hope* . . .[31]

Kevin records a lengthy message in poetic form that he believes came directly from God, commissioning him to "Use Alex to show who I am."[32] He is convinced that Alex's story will have an impact that rivals the fame of Billy Graham—because a man with a supposed word of prophecy told him so. ("Alex is going to emerge from his coma, and his ministry will be to show people what God is like. But just like Dr. Graham, your son will have an impact across the world.")[33]

In short, *The Boy Who Came Back From Heaven* is a study in how human passion unchecked by discernment can give way to blind gullibility. It also illustrates the danger of setting a child's (or anyone's) imagination free in the spiritual realm without proper biblical boundaries. And it shows how subtly and how easily our fallen hearts can breed superstition, pride, and self-deception.

---

[29] Ibid.
[30] Ibid., 186.
[31] Ibid.
[32] Ibid., 187.
[33] Ibid., 62.

Appendix 3:

To Heaven and Back

Mary Neal's "extraordinary account of her death, heaven, angels, and life again"[1] conveys a completely different perspective of heaven. Dr. Neal is a spine surgeon who nearly lost her life in a kayaking accident in Chile. Trapped in a waterfall for close to fifteen minutes, she lost consciousness and says her soul left her body and went on a journey that took her "to heaven and back."[2]

According to her evangelical publisher, Dr. Neal "is actively involved in a Reformed church."[3] Her testimony, however, is so skewed doctrinally that she might as well be a universalist or a Buddhist. Her book, though published by an evangelical company, has far more in common with Betty Eadie's view than with any of the other stories currently being marketed by and for evangelical Christians. It's a slightly different blend of Mormon, New Age, and Christian doctrines.

She describes, for example, a conversation she had with a heavenly being ("I don't really know what he was: angel, messenger, Christ, or teacher. I do know that he was of God, in God, and from God.")[4] She writes that as their dialogue progressed—

I received the following wisdom.
We are each given the opportunity and privilege to come to earth for different reasons. Sometimes we come in order that we may personally develop and strengthen the fruits of our spirit: those of love,

---

[1] That is the book's subtitle.
[2] Mary C. Neal, *To Heaven and Back: A Doctor's Extraordinary Account of Her Death, Heaven, Angels, and Life Again* (Colorado Springs: Waterbrook, 2012).
[3] Cited in Randy Alcorn, "Dialogue with Publisher about Mary Neal's To Heaven and Back," blogpost August 10, 2012, at http://www.epm.org/blog/2012/Aug/10/dialogue-publisher-heaven-and-back.
[4] Neal, *To Heaven and Back*, 97–98.

kindness, patience, joy, peace, goodness, faithfulness, gentleness, and self-control. Sometimes we come to help someone else develop the fruits of the spirit. We all come to earth to become more Christ-like, as noted in Romans 8.

In preparation for our journey to earth, we are able to make a basic outline for our life. This is not to imply that we, the humans, are entirely in charge of our life's design. It is more like God creates it, then we review it and discuss it with our "personal planning" angel. Within the algorithm are written branch points in our lives at which times we may exit, returning to God, or we may be redirected to a different task and goal.[5]

The notion that human souls do not originate at conception but exist in a conscious state in heaven prior to being born is not a Christian doctrine. As we saw when we examined Mary Eadie's story, Mormonism teaches that. The Bible does not. It is nevertheless a belief Mary Neal holds and works into her story repeatedly.

For example, describing how her eighteen-month-old son clung to her when she returned home after her accident, she says, "I believe he still remembered God's world, which seemed to give him an understanding of the spiritual aspect of my experience and what I was going through."[6]

About thirty pages later, she adds,

> I need to categorically state, once again, that I believe very young children clearly remember where they came from and are still quite connected to God's world. I believe they easily recall the images, knowledge, and the love of the world they inhabited before their birth. I believe children may still be able to see angels.[7]

Neal also believes in the possibility of postmortem salvation. She describes a hall in heaven where she was taken on her arrival there:

> I felt my soul being pulled toward the entry and, as I approached, I physically absorbed its radiance and felt the pure, complete, and utterly unconditional absolute love that emanated from the hall. It was the most beautiful and alluring thing I had ever seen or experienced.

---

[5] Ibid., 98.
[6] Ibid., 114.
[7] Ibid., 147.

I knew with a profound certainty that it represented the last branch point of life, the gate through which each human being must pass. It was clear that this hall is the place where each of us is given the opportunity to review our lives and our choices, and where we are each given a final opportunity to choose God or to turn away—for eternity.[8]

Mary Neal says she was turned away from the hall and told it wasn't her time to enter there. At that point she says her soul was returned to the riverbank where she had nearly drowned, and she reentered her body. But she had established contact with heaven, she says, and that connection stayed active. Neal says that while recovering from her injuries, she was repeatedly visited by an angelic being who would take her to a sun-drenched field for long talks, where he would instruct her about various mysteries of life. Though she doesn't really make much of the fact, she believes the angel was Jesus.[9]

Of all the books on near-death experiences published by evangelical publishers, Neal's book is the least theologically informed. Furthermore, of all these authors, she is the least aware of her own theological limitations. "I am not superstitious," she writes, "but events frequently occur in threes."[10] She is in fact *highly* superstitious, believing not only that she could detect the true identity of an angel who was posing as an owl, but also that she could discern a message the owl communicated to her telepathically. ("The bird clearly had something to say and, when I finally paid attention, I felt the owl urging me to go with my mother to North Carolina.")[11]

Dr. Neal speaks with stunning conceit, intuiting mystical knowledge she has no legitimate way of knowing, frequently declaring her "profound certainty" of patently unbiblical notions. She doesn't stop with the preexistence of souls and the possibility of postmortem salvation; she also holds a view of human free will and free choice that allows for the possibility that God might regularly need to change his plans based on choices we make. She apparently believes God does not actually know the future with complete certainty.

---

[8] Ibid., 73.
[9] She reveals her belief about the angel's identity in a question-and-answer section later added at the end of the book's electronic edition.
[10] Neal, *To Heaven and Back*, 152.
[11] Ibid., 131.

All these aberrant views feed the superstition that permeates and warps Neal's worldview. For example, because she believes children have memories of a previous spiritual existence (and that they carry knowledge from that realm into this life), Neal was convinced for years that her son Willie would die before his eighteenth birthday. That belief was based on a remark Willie himself made to her when he was "perhaps four or five."[12] She says that as she was chatting with him before bed, she said something to him about "when you are eighteen. . . ."

Little Willie interrupted at that point: "I'm never going to be eighteen. That's the plan. You know that."

Dr. Neal seems oblivious to the melodrama in her reaction to such an offhand "revelation" from the lips of a preschooler: "This exchange was like a knife to my heart. I never forgot it and did not dismiss it. I cherished each subsequent day I had with this son, wondering which one would be his last. . . . As the date of Willie's eighteenth birthday neared, I became filled with anticipatory grief."[13]

Willie did not die before reaching eighteen, however, and Neal concluded that God's plan for him had somehow changed. "I had a dream in which a boy, who I did not know, told me that he had 'traded places with Willie.'"[14] When Willie survived to celebrate turning eighteen, Dr. Neal said she concluded that he had "reached a branch point in his life that led either to the death he had predicted so many years earlier or to his continued life. . . . I felt like the plan for Willie had changed. Because I was alive, Willie stayed alive."[15]

Tragically, however, on the day Dr. Neal completed what she believed would be the final draft of her book, Willie was hit by a car while roller-skiing on a Maine road, and he died at age 20.

Thus her already-convoluted belief system was thrown into further disarray. Visiting the site of the accident that took Willie's life, she was certain Willie himself had determined his destiny—even to the point of choosing where he would die: "I had the sense that he had tried to make it as nice a spot for us as was possible—accessible, identifiable, and beautiful."[16]

---

[12] Ibid., 149.
[13] Ibid., 150.
[14] Ibid., 151.
[15] Ibid., 154.
[16] Ibid., 178.

The brisk sales of Neal's book are frankly hard to account for. The point of view it represents is so thoroughly unbiblical and the ideas she floats are so far-fetched that it is hard to imagine evangelicals (who seem to be the primary audience the book aims to reach) will be much influenced by it. Noting that Neal's book had "made its debut on the *New York Times* list of bestsellers," Tim Challies nevertheless declined to review it on his blog. He wrote,

> I gave it a skim—I just couldn't bear to read it all the way—and found that it is much the same as the others. In fact, it may be worse than the others in that it contains even less Christian theology, less gospel and far more New Age, sub-Christian nonsense. That a publisher of Christian books would even consider taking this to print is appalling.
>
> I am not going to review To Heaven and Back. It's pure junk, fiction in the guise of biography, paganism in the guise of Christianity. But I do want to address a question that often arises around this book and others in the genre: How do I respond to them? How do I respond to those who say they have been to heaven? When a Christian, or a person who claims to be a Christian, tells me that he has been to heaven, am I obliged to believe him or at least to give him the benefit of the doubt?
>
> No, I am under no such obligation. I do not believe that Don Piper or Colton Burpo or Mary Neal or Bill Wiese visited the afterlife. They can tell me all the stories they want, and they can tell those stories in a sincere tone, but I do not believe them (even when they send me very angry and condescending emails that accuse me of character assassination). I am not necessarily saying that these people are liars—just that I am under no obligation to believe another person's experience.[17]

He's absolutely right, and the fact that so many evangelicals seem drawn to books like that makes an unmistakable statement about the appalling spiritual state of the church at the moment.

We need to have a better understanding of the glory of heaven. We must learn to set our affections on heavenly things, as we are commanded in Scripture. As Christians, we know that "our citizenship is in heaven" (Philippians 3:20). Our hearts should be there as well—set on the real heaven as Scripture describes it, not on someone's mystical, made-up notion of paradise.

---

[17] Tim Challies, "Heaven Tourism," blogpost June 18, 2012, http://www.challies.com/articles/heaven-tourism.

One last thought: When Jesus taught us to "lay up for [ourselves] treasures in heaven, where neither moth nor rust destroys and where thieves do not break in and steal. For where your treasure is, there your heart will be also" (Matthew 6:20), why do you think he gave that command?

Surely his point was not that he wants our *treasures*. What he wants is our *hearts*. He was affirming the great principle of true faith, that we should "[look] forward to the city that has foundations, whose designer and builder is God" (Hebrews 11:10). He was urging us to fix our hearts on heaven, to long for the glory of heaven, and above all, to "seek the things that are above, where Christ is, seated at the right hand of God" (Colossians 3:1).

Heaven is *his* realm. He has gone there to prepare a place for us. That truth is what makes heaven so precious for the Christian. Our eternity there will be an eternity in the presence of Christ, sharing warm fellowship with him personally, and living forever in the light of his countenance. That is heaven's chief appeal for any Christian whose priorities are straight. Christ himself *is* the glory of heaven:

> And the city has no need of sun or moon to shine on it, for the glory of God gives it light, and its lamp is the Lamb. (Revelation 21:23)

General Index

23 Minutes in Hell (Wiese), 24

Abraham, 80, 103, 116, 139, 150, 170; "Abraham's side," 86, 92, 93
Adam, 22, 145, 182
Adams, John Quincy, 70
afterlife, the, medical research concerning, 25–26
angels, 58, 148, 157–161; angelic worship of God, 168–169; biblical appearances of, 170–171; creation of, 162–166; demons disguised as (angels of deception), 160, 179–180; description of in Scripture, 161–162; fall of, 166–167; number of, 165–166; popular books concerning, 157–158; quotations from publishers concerning popular angel guidebooks, 158–160; relating to angels in heaven, 171–172; TV shows concerning, 157; what angels are like, 167–169; what angels do, 170–171
Armageddon, 105
arrabōn (Greek: down payment; installment on debt), 72–73

Barham, Jay, 27
Baxter, Richard, on a heavenly mind, 80–81
believers, perfecting of, 130–135; and becoming a redeemed soul, 135–140; and conversion, 131–132; and glorification, 136; and the inside-out transformation of believers, 134; and the problem of our physical bodies/flesh, 132–133; and the reflection of Christ in us, 134–135; role of justification in, 131; role of sanctification in, 131
Boy Who Came Back from Heaven, The (K. Malarkey), 199, 208; basic storyline of, 199–201; emotional impact of, 201; "I Went to Heaven" section of, 201–202; and the "positive confession" heresy, 202–206; unbiblical perspective of heaven in, 206–207

Brinkley, Dannion, 195–196; hostility of toward biblical Christianity, 196
Burpo, Colton, 14, 24, 41–42, 44n16, 54; description of the Holy Spirit by, 43–44; description of Jesus in heaven by, 45; meeting of with dead family members, 44; meeting of with John the Baptist, 42–43
Burpo, Sonja, 41, 42, 43
Burpo, Todd, 14, 40–42; evangelical nature of, 40–41. See also *Heaven Is For Real* (T. Burpo and Vincent)

Challies, Tim, 24, 46, 213
cherubim, 58
Christian worldview, 68–70
Christianity, 25, 49, 65, 142, 179, 181, 190, 191, 213; hostility toward, 196. See also Christian worldview
Christians, 160, 178; attachment of to the things of earth rather than heaven, 63–66; and belief in heaven, 16; charismatic influence on, 39–40; "defeated Christians," 111; in heaven, 137; inheritance of, 112–115; and materialism, 63–64. See also believers, perfecting of
Christlikeness, 131, 145
Crosby, Fanny, 155

Daniel, 53
David, 154–155
death, and entering heaven, biblical views of, 91–94. See also death, and entering heaven, speculative views of
death, and entering heaven, speculative views of, 85–86; Hades, 86; purgatory, 87–90, 91, 94; soul sleep, 86–87
dualism, 188–191

Eadie, Betty, 31–32; danger of her ideas/writings, 179–180; high opinion of herself, 194–195; "omniscience" of, 176–177; on sin, 189–190; on the uniqueness of

Christ, 177; on world religions, 177. *See also* Eadie, Betty, Mormon and New Age beliefs of; Eadie, Betty, unbiblical ideas of; *Embraced by the Light* (Eadie)

Eadie, Betty, Mormon and New Age beliefs of, 178–179, 183–184; belief in creating our own reality, 186–187; belief in positive and negative energies, 185; deification of the human soul, 182; dualism, 188–191; Eve's act seen as noble, 182; gnosticism, 191–192; multiple gods, 181; pantheism, 187–188; possibility of salvation after death, 183; preexistence of human spirits, 180–181; spiritual healing, 185–186; universalism, 184–185

Eadie, Betty, unbiblical ideas of, 192; human self-sufficiency, 193; salvation by human works, 194; sovereignty of the human will, 192–193; undue emphasis on angels, 194

earth/creation: dissolution of, 105–108; remaking of by God, 103–105

Elijah, 38, 93, 149

Elvis after Life: Unusual Psychic Experiences Surrounding the Death of a Superstar (Moody), 30

Embraced by the Light (Eadie), 31, 32; basic storyline of, 175–176; numerous errors of, 195–197; success of, 178

endēmeo (Greek: to be at home), 73

Eutychus, 38

evangelicals, 34, 39, 40, 178, 213; addiction of to fads, 160

Eve, 22, 182

Ezekiel, 39, 53, 195; Ezekiel's wheel, 94–97; on the glory of God, 55–56

faith, 27, 47, 69, 73, 87, 112, 130, 138, 139, 142, 205; authentic/true faith, 16, 48, 54, 214; justification by, 89, 90; Scripture as the sole rule of, 49

false religion, corruption of, 24

Fourth Symphony (Mahler), 83

Franklin, DeVon, 15

Glasscock, Ed, 161–162

glorification, 136; of the body, 71

gnosis (Greek: knowledge), 29

gnosticism, 28–29, 37, 191–192

God, 161, 214; and the creation of the world and humans, 22–23, 143; decline in the belief in, 13–14, 14n5; delay of his judgment, 106–107; fellowship with, 151–155; glorifying of, 121–122, 138–139; glory of, 53–54, 55–56, 98, 100; as the God of heaven, 97; grace of, 52, 102, 106–107, 131, 172, 194; heaven as the dwelling

place of, 74–77; Jewish conception of, 76–77; judgment of, 140–141, 167, 183; justice of, 110–111; love of, 102; mercy of, 102, 107, 111, 172, 193; plan of, 72; praise of, 59–61; promise of to the redeemed, 111–112; remaking of heaven and earth by, 103–105; righteousness of, 66, 193; will of, 193; wisdom and power of, 23

guilt, 22–24, 52, 54, 90, 122, 138

heaven, 214; attainment of perfect knowledge in, 139; belief in by Americans (Gallup poll, 2007), 13; as a euphemism for God himself, 76–77; as an expression of divine glory, 117; fellowship in, 149–150; fellowship with God in, 151–155; glory of, 51–56, 117, 122–123, 172, 173; as God's dwelling place, 74–77; "heaven tourism," 24–25; hostility toward the concept of, 16–18; perfect comfort in, 139; perfect joy in, 139–140; perfect love in, 139; perfect pleasure of, 138–139; perfect relationships in, 146–151; perfection of, 129–130; perfection of in spite of the existence of hell, 110–111; physical dimension of, 71–72; praise of Christ in, 60; praise of God in, 59–61; question of whether there is a temple in, 100–102; reality of in New Testament accounts, 37–40; as the realm of God's kingdom, 77–80; remaking of by God, 103–105; reunification with family and friends in, 150; spiritual joy in, 84–85; unbelievers' portrayal of, 83–84; what it is, 73–77. *See also* heaven, books/stories/accounts of ("heaven travelogues"); heaven, biblical glimpses of; heaven, preciousness of; heaven, things missing from; new heaven and new earth, the; New Jerusalem, the

heaven, books/stories/accounts of ("heaven travelogues"), 32–35; disagreements within concerning descriptions of heaven, 34; familiar reoccurring features of, 40; fixation with worldly things in, 33–34; macabre phenomena and "revelations" in, 33; marketing of as nonfiction, 35

heaven, biblical glimpses of, 94; Ezekiel's wheel, 94–97; John's apocalypse, 97–100

heaven, preciousness of, 66–68; brothers and sisters in Christ are there, 66; our citizenship is there, 67; our Father is there, 66; our inheritance is heaven, 66–67; our names are recorded there, 66

heaven, things missing from, 121; lack of anything being accursed, 126–127; lack of a light source, 122–124; lack

of marriage, 147–149; lack of personal
needs, 125–126; lack of security system,
124–125; lack of a temple, 121–122
Heaven Is For Real (T. Burpo and Vincent),
14–15, 40, 41; biblical references in, 40,
41; danger in the message of, 48–49; facile method of proof-texting in, 46–47; as
a faulty view of faith, 46–48; privileging
of personal experience over Scripture in,
47–48; success of, 15, 15n9, 40; unhesitating credulity as the tone of the book,
41–42;
heavens: atmospheric heavens, 73–74; planetary heavens, 74
hell, 34, 37, 49, 84, 105, 110–111, 118, 123,
139, 140, 184, 206; belief in by Americans (Gallup poll, 2007), 14
Hodge, A. A., 150–151
holiness, 79, 82, 87, 100, 108, 131, 135–136,
155, 182; of God's throne, 164; and sanctification, 136
Holy Spirit, 54, 57, 79, 82, 96, 99, 130, 154,
195; as a guarantee for believers, 72–73
humans: as fallen beings, 22–24; rejection
of the knowledge of God by, 23–24; as
spiritual creatures made in God's image,
21–22

inheritance, of believers, 112–115
Isaac, 150, 195
Isaiah, 39, 53, 59; description of angels, 169;
promise of, 104–105

Jacob, 103, 149, 150
Jerusalem. *See* New Jerusalem, the
Jesus Christ, 45–46, 78–80, 130, 131, 152,
163, 165, 214; as the "Alpha and Omega,"
195; crucifixion of, 93–94; fellowship
with, 127; glory of, 135; perfect righteousness of, 89–90, 136; reflection
of in ourselves, 134–135; resurrection
of, 71, 72, 140, 141, 145; sufferings of,
90–91; teaching of on marriage, 147–148;
transfiguration of, 93, 124, 149. *See also*
Sermon on the Mount
John, 39, 53, 77, 82, 104–105, 115, 125; and
the concept of the "overcomer," 112; description of angels, 171–172; description
of the Passover, 93–94. *See also* Revelation, book of
justification, 114, 131, 136, 138; by faith,
87, 89–90, 91; Roman Catholic view of,
90–91
Knopp, Dave, 202–204
Kübler-Ross, Elisabeth, 25, 27; and New
Age occultism, 27–28; questioning of the
reality of death by, 28

Lazarus of Bethany, 38, 86, 132
Lazarus, parable of the rich man and,
92–93
Lenin, Vladimir, 17
Lewis, C. S., 136
Life after Life (Moody), 26; sequels to, 26
Luther, Martin, 170

MacLaine, Shirley, 187
Mahler, Gustav, 83
Malarkey, Alex, 199–201; description of
angels, 206; description of the devil, 206;
on his father's book as "deceptive," 207;
multiple visits of to heaven, 55
Malarkey, Beth, 201n4, 203
Malarkey, Kevin, 55, 199–201, 202, 205;
faulty idea of faith, 207–208; unbiblical
perspective of heaven, 206–207. *See also*
Boy Who Came Back from Heaven, The (K.
Malarkey)
marriage, 146–147
Marx, Karl, 17
Mary, 148; appearance of the angel to, 171
materialism, 27, 63, 67; as a hallmark of
postmodern culture, 18
Moody, Raymond A., 25–26, 27, 196; building of a *psychomanteum* by, 30; conversation with his dead grandmother, 30–31,
31n16; as a medium, 30–31; obsession of
with necromancy, 30; rejection of the
Bible's teachings on death and the soul,
29–30
Mormonism, 32, 178–179, 180–183
Morse, Melvin, 31–32; arrest of, 31n19
mortality, sentimentalizing of, 26–28
Moses, 53, 54, 93, 99, 124, 134, 147,
149–150, 153
Mount Zion, 66, 116, 123, 166
"My Savior First of All" (Crosby), 155

Neal, Mary C., 15; belief in postmortem
salvation, 210–211; conceit of, 211;
conversation of with a heavenly being,
209–210; death of her son, 212; greeting
of in heaven, 54–55
necromancy, 30, 37
New Age movement, 27, 31, 32, 37. *See also*
Eadie, Betty, Mormon and New Age beliefs of; Kübler-Ross, Elisabeth, and New
Age occultism
new heaven and new earth, the, 108–115:
all things made new, 108–110
New Jerusalem, the, 77, 115, 123, 125;
building materials of, 120; as the crown
jewel of heaven, 116–117; glorious walls
and gates of, 117–118; light of, 123–124;
preparation of as a bride, 115–116; super-

stitious worldview of, 212; symmetrical measurements of, 118–120

Nietzsche, Friedrich, 17

nihilism, 70

occultism, 27, 29, 30, 37

On Death and Dying (Kübler-Ross), 25

ouranos (Greek: heaven), 73

"overcomers," 111, 112, 113, 125

pantheism, 187–188

Paul, 85, 86, 102, 129, 131, 152, 163, 179; on angels as "cosmic powers," 164; on Christians in heaven, 137; as an example of proper perspective between heaven and earth during his persecution, 68–69; expectation of for heaven, 71–72; experience of heaven, 38–39; on the heirs of Christ, 114–115; on the Holy Spirit, 72–73; on the inside-out transformation of believers, 134; on justification by faith, 89; on marriage and family, 146–147; on our physical bodies/flesh, 132–133; on the resurrection of the body, 141–142, 143–145

Peter, on the dissolution of the old world and Christ's return, 105–108

Pharisees, 65, 79, 87, 93, 147

Philip, 154

philosophy, 17

Piper, Don, 24

"positive confession" heresy, 202–206

purgatory, 87–90, 91, 94, 136

rationalism, 17

redemption: of creation, 59; of the human race, 59

resurrection, of the body, 86–87, 140, 150; importance of to the Christian message, 142; necessity of, 140–142; Paul's description of, 143–145; the resurrected body as Christlike, 145; the resurrected body as imperishable, 144

Revelation, book of, 56–61, 97–100; attention of placed on the throne of God, 57–58, 97–98, 99–100; description of angels in, 58; the expression "seven spirits" in, 99; as the most prophetic vision we have in Scripture, 57; name of (translation of the Greek *apokalypsis* [apocalypse]), 56

righteousness, 75, 84, 103, 108, 130–131, 133, 134, 135–136, 145, 154, 173; and entrance to heaven, 87–89; of God, 66,
193; of Jesus Christ, 89–90, 136; personal righteousness, 90

Sadduceeism, intellectual, 17–18

Sadducees, 147–148, 150

salvation, 60, 66, 85, 88, 102, 112, 130, 134, 170, 173, 184, 193, 194; biblical definition of, 151; possibility of salvation after death, 183, 210

sanctification, 131, 136

Satan, 79, 105, 125, 160, 166–167, 168, 179, 182, 185, 190–191

Saved by the Light (Brinkley), 195–196

science, 17

Scripture, as the only reliable source of information concerning heaven, 18–19

Seiss, J. A., 123–124

seraphim, 58

Sermon on the Mount, 75

shamayim (Hebrew: heaven), 73

sin, 22–24, 54, 102, 133–134, 135, 189–190; captivity to, 137; covering of by the blood of Christ, 91; freedom from the guilt of, 138; past sins, 137–138

sinners, destruction of, 110–111

Smith, Wilbur, 16–17, 86

sola scriptura (Latin: Scripture alone), 49–50

Solomon, 74

"sons of the kingdom," 114n6

soul sleep, 86–87

spiritism, 31

Spurgeon, Charles, 18

Tada, Joni Eareckson, 71, 72

theology, 17, 161, 179, 213

To Heaven and Back (Neal), 15, 209; success of, 213

"tree of life," 125

uniformitarianism, 105

universalism, 184–185

unrighteousness, 137–138

Vincent, Lynn, 14

Whitehead, Alfred North, 17

Wiese, Bill, 24

works, testing of, 113–114

world religions, and the concept of paradise, 22

worldliness, 18, 63, 67, 80

worship, 75, 110–111, 121–122, 126, 163, 168–169, 171–172

Scripture Index

Genesis
1	74
1:1	181
1:7	106
1:14–17	74
1:26	21
2:7	140, 180
2:9	125
2:10	125
3:7–11	22
3:24	164
5:1	21
7:11–12	74
9:12–16	107
18–19	170
23:20	103
25:8	149
35:29	149
49:29	149

Exodus
3:6	150
19:16	98
24	99–100
24:9–10	100
25:31–37	99
28:17, 20	98
33:18	153, 154
33:20	53, 153
34:29–33	134
34:30	54
37:7	164

Leviticus
20:27	37

Numbers
20:24	149
29:29	162

Deuteronomy
6:4	181
8:10–12	37
13:1–5	34

17:3	165
25	147
26:15	74
29:29	39

Judges
2:10	149

2 Samuel
12	149
12:23	149
22:11	164

1 Kings
6:20	119
8:27	74
17:17–24	38
22:19	165

2 Kings
2:1, 11	93

Nehemiah
9:6	162, 163

Job
1:6	162
2:1	162
14:1	85
38	165
38:4	181
38:7	162, 165, 168

Psalms
8:5	162
16	92
16:10–11	92
16:11	84, 138
17:15	154
18:10	164
23	93
23:6	119, 122
27:4	122
33:13–14	75
42:1–2	154

46:4–5	125
51:5	181
68:5	110
73:25–26	122
80:1	58
89:6	162
99:1	58
102:25–26	104
116:15	151
139:1–3	139
139:8	74
145:9	107
147:8	74
148:2–5	163
148:5	163

Proverbs
30:4	52

Ecclesiastes
3:11	16, 21
7:1	85

Isaiah
6	58
6:1–2	58
6:1–3	168–169
6:2	59
6:2–6	164
6:3	59, 171, 172
6:5	53, 195
11:2	99
14:12–15	166
14:13–14	169
24:23	123
30:26	123
35:10	84, 130
42:8	182
57:1–2	85
57:15	75, 78
60:19	53, 117
61:10	91, 131
63:15	75
65:17	104, 110
65:17–19	104
66:22	104
66:23–24	111

Jeremiah
17:9	22
29:8–9	34

Ezekiel
1	34, 94–96
1:5–6	58
1:6	59
1:8	59
1:10	59
1:14	55
1:15–18	58
1:16	55
1:17	55
1:22	100
1:24	56
1:28	53, 56
10	58
10:1–22	164
28:12	167–168
28:12–16	166
36:26	130

Daniel
8:16	164, 171
9:21	164, 171
10:8–9	53
10:10–11	53
10:13	162
10:13, 21	164
10:15	53
10:16–17	53
12:3	145

Habakkuk
1:13	153

Matthew
3:2, 10–12	106
4:17	78
5:8	54, 154
5:12	67
5:16	75
5:20	87
5:30	140
5:34	75
5:45	75
5:48	87
6:1	75
6:9	66, 75
6:19	65
6:19–20	82
6:19–21	67
6:20	214
6:33	66
7:11	75
7:13–14	119
7:15–16	34
7:21	75
8:11	149
8:12	111, 114n6
10:32–33	75
11:11	113, 114
11:28	138
12:50	75–76
13:11	77
13:44	173
16:14	76
16:17	76

16:19	76
17	93
17:3	93, 149
17:4	155
18:10	52
19:17	88
19:17–21	88
19:20	88
19:23	88
19:25	89
19:26	89
22	147
22:24	147
22:25–28	148
22:29–30	148
22:30	165
22:32	150
23:5	65
23:22	77
24:4–5	34
24:14	79
25	140
25:21–24	113
25:23	140
27:52	87
28:3–4	170
28:4	171
28:5	168

Mark

4:19	82
7:21–23	129
10:30	79
12:30	19
15:32	94
16:12	141

Luke

1:19	171
1:19, 26	164
1:29	171
2:9	171
2:13	165
8:10	77
9:31	93
10:20	66
12:19–20	70
12:20	65
13:24	79
15:9	168
15:10	168
15:18	77
16	92
16:22	92
16:22–23	86
16:25	139
16:26	34
17:20–21	79

17:21	79
18:14	89
18:18	79
18:22	65
18:24	80
18:26	80
19:16–19	113
22:17–18	149
23	93–94
23:42–43	94
24:13–18	141
24:26	141
24:39	141
24:42–43	141
24:51	141
26:53	165

John

1:1	164
1:12	82, 113
1:14	154
1:18	16, 153, 154
3:13	16, 52
4:23	168
4:34	181
5:24	131
5:28–29	140
5:30	181
5:34	79
6:33	76
6:37	138
6:38	76
6:41	76
6:50–51, 58	76
7:38	132
8:29	181
10:10	132
10:30	181
11:11	86
11:17	38
12:24	143
13	92
13:1	139
13:23	92
13:25	92
13:36	152
14:1–3	152
14:2	119, 153
14:3	102, 116
14:8	154
14:16–17	99
15:5	193
17:20	152
17:21	152
17:24	152
17:24	85
20:15	148

20:19	141
20:27	141
21:20, 24	93

Acts
1:9	141
17:11	46, 205
20:9–12	38

Romans
1:18	23
1:20	21
1:21–25	23
2:5	56
2:5–6	183
3:12	189
4	89
4:5	89, 131
5:1	89, 131
5:10	189
6:18	131
6:22	133
6:23	132
7:15–21	132–133
7:21	133
7:22	133, 134
7:23	133
7:24	129, 132
8:1	89, 131, 141
8:7	189, 193
8:13	133
8:15	150
8:15–17	114
8:17	113, 114
8:18	69, 134
8:19–22	108
8:22	69, 129
8:23	71, 132, 141, 206
8:24	139
8:28–30	130
8:29	130
8:30	131
9:16	193
10:17	48
12:12	71
13:11–14	173
14:10	30

1 Corinthians
2:9	126
2:10	126
2:16	82
3	91
3:12	91
3:13–15	91
3:14	114
3:15	114
4:6	37, 39

4:16	140
6:3	169
6:9–11	138
7:29–31	146
7:32–34	147
8:6	181
10:31	121
12:4	99
12:11	99
12:13	99
13:6	168
13:12	110, 127, 135, 139, 152, 155
13:13	139
15	142
15:16–17	142
15:26	109
15:35	143
15:35–36	142
15:36–37	143
15:39	143
15:40–41	144
15:42–44	144
15:45–48	145
15:51–52	142
15:53	85
15:53–54	72

2 Corinthians
3	134
3:7	134
3:13	134
3:18	134
4:6	134
4:8–10	68
4:16–17	68
4:18	16
4:18––5:1	69
5	72
5:1	141
5:1–4	72
5:2	69, 71, 141
5:4	85
5:5	72
5:6–8	73
5:8	85, 87, 92, 137
5:17	79, 108, 131, 132
5:21	89
11:3	182
11:13–15	160, 179
11:15	160, 183
12	74
12:2	73
12:2–3	38, 57
12:3	94
12:4	39
12:7	38

Galatians
3:29   115
4:6–7   115
4:26   82
5:22–23   79

Ephesians
1:3   78, 131
1:4   130, 193
1:14   72
1:21   164
2   102
2:1   102
2:1–2   193
2:3   102, 189, 193
2:4–5   193
2:6   131
2:7   102
2:5–6   78
2:18   99
2:19   81
3:10   162
4:4   99
6:12   164

Philippians
1:6   130
1:21   85
1:23   85, 137
3:20   16, 67, 78, 82, 213
3:20–21   81
3:21   71, 72, 145

Colossians
1:16   163, 164
1:16–17   181
1:17   164, 191
1:27   135
2:9–10   131
2:15   164
2:22   65
3:1   65, 214
3:1–2   16
3:2   19, 68, 82
3:17   121

1 Thessalonians
4   141
4:13–17   142
4:14   86
4:17   102, 127, 150
5:21   46

1 Timothy
2:5   181
2:14   182
6:15–16   165
6:16   53, 153

2 Timothy
3:17   19

Hebrews
1:4   163
1:6   163, 169
1:10–12   104
1:14   170
2:7   169
2:15   193
4:13   23
6:4   126
7:25   66
9:24   66
9:27   29, 183
10:26–27   91
11   16, 103
11:9–10   103
11:10   64, 116, 214
11:13   16, 67
11:14   16
11:16   16, 54
12:14   135
12:22   166
12:22–23   116
12:22–24   66
12:23   135, 137
13:2   161
13:5   127

James
1:17   102
1:18   79
2:19   181
3:9   21
3:16   68
4:4   67

1 Peter
1:3–7   69
1:4   67
1:5   112
1:12   168
3:7   147

2 Peter
1:3   131
1:16, 18   48
1:19   48
1:21   39
2:1   34
3:3–4   105
3:5   106
3:5–6   106
3:6–7   107
3:8–9   107
3:10   74, 107
3:11–12   108
3:13   103, 108

1 John
1:3	150
1:5	123
2:13–14	112
2:15–17	67–68
2:16	82
2:17	82
2:19	112
3:2	54, 116, 130, 135, 141
4:1	34
4:4	112
4:12	153
5:4–5	112
5:14	205

Revelation
1:1	56
1:4	99
1:10	57
1:16	145
1:17	53
2	104–105
2–3	99
2:7	125
2:7, 11, 17, 26	112
3:1	99
3:5, 12, 21	112
3:12	77, 100–101, 101–102
3:21	169
4	34, 57, 59–60, 97
4:1–2	57, 97
4:2	57
4:3	97
4:4	100, 171
4:5	98, 99
4:6	99, 100
4:6–7	58
4:6–9	171
4:7	59
4:8	59, 171
4:9–11	172
4:10	60, 114
4:11	60
5	60
5:6	99
5:8	60–61
5:8–10	60
5:8–12	172
5:9–14	171
5:11	61, 165
5:12	60
5:13–14	60
5:14	61
6:11	135

7:9	119
7:14	135
7:15	101, 121, 153
11:13	97
11:19	101
12:3–4	167
12:7	164
14:1–4	87
14:13	85, 87
16:11	97
19	105
19:10	163
20:7	105
20:11–15	105
20:14–15	117
20:15	118
21	105, 123
21:1	105, 108
21:2	115
21:3	153
21:3–7	109
21:4–5	84
21:5	111
21:6	111
21:7	111, 115
21:8	118
21:10	77
21:10–27	116
21:11	117
21:12	117
21:15–16	118
21:17	119
21:18	120
21:19–20	120
21:21	120
21:22	101, 121
21:22–23	101
21:23	53, 117, 122, 153, 214
21:24	123, 124
21:25	124
21:26	124
21:27	124, 137
22:1	109
22:1–2	125
22:2	109, 125, 126
22:3–4	155
22:3–5	126
22:4	127
22:5	53
22:8–9	163
22:13	195
22:14–15	118, 137
22:15	124
22:17	138